J.K. LASSER'S

PICK STOCKS LIKE WARREN BUFFETT

Look for these and other titles from J.K. Lasser™—Practical Guides for All Your Financial Needs

J.K. Lasser's Pick Winning Stocks by Edward F. Mrkvicka, Jr.
J.K. Lasser's Invest Online by Laura Maery Gold and Dan Post
J.K. Lasser's Year-Round Tax Strategies by David S. DeJong and Ann Gray Jakabcin
J.K. Lasser's Taxes Made Easy for Your Home-Based Business by Gary W. Carter
J.K. Lasser's Pick Winning Mutual Funds by Jerry Tweddell with Jack Pierce
J.K. Lasser's Your Winning Retirement Plan by Henry K. Hebeler
J.K. Lasser's Winning with Your 401(k) by Grace Weinstein
J.K. Lasser's Winning with Your 403(b) by Pam Horowitz
J.K. Lasser's Strategic Investing After 40 by Julie Jason
J.K. Lasser's Winning Financial Strategies for Women by Rhonda Ecker and Denise Gustin-Piazza
J.K. Lasser's Pick Stocks Like Warren Buffett by Warren Boroson

J.K. LASSER'S™

PICK STOCKS LIKE WARREN BUFFETT

Warren Boroson

John Wiley & Sons, Inc.

New York • Chichester • Weinheim • Brisbane • Singapore • Toronto

This book is printed on acid-free paper. ♾

Published by John Wiley & Sons, Inc.
Published simultaneously in Canada.

Library of Congress Cataloging in Publication Data:

0-471-39774-1

Printed in the United States of America

10 9 8 7 6 5 4 3 2 1

Contents

Introduction: What Investors Can Learn from Warren Buffett

Berkshire Hathaway's stock has risen nearly 27 percent a year for the past 36 years. For its consistency and profitability, this company, managed by Warren E. Buffett of Omaha, has been amazing.

If you asked Buffett how you, as an individual investor, could go about imitating his spectacularly successful investment strategy, his answer would be: buy shares of Berkshire Hathaway. He happens to be an unusually sensible person, and that is clearly the best answer.

But if you buy or intend to buy other stocks on your own, either one-at-a-time or through a managed mutual fund, there is much that you can learn by studying Buffett's tactics.

Why not just do the obvious and put all your money into Berkshire Hathaway stock? One reason: It's mainly an insurance holding company—Buffett is an authority on insurance. Because of this, the stock has virtually no exposure to many areas of the stock market, such as technology and health care. A second reason: Berkshire has become so enormous that its future performance is handicapped, much like the odds-on favorite in a horse race being forced to carry extra weights.

In short, you might do better on your own. First, because you have a smaller, more nimble portfolio. And, second, because you might shoot out the lights by overweighting stocks in whatever field you're particularly knowledgeable about—health care, technology, banking, whatever. Buffett refers to this as staying within your "circle of competence." (There's nothing wrong, of course, with your also buying Berkshire stock. I have. The Sequoia Fund, run by friends of Buffett's, has one-third of its assets in Berkshire.)

While the average investor can learn a thing or two from the master, he or she simply cannot duplicate Buffett's future or past investment performance. One obvious reason: Buffett has the money to buy entire companies outright, not just a small piece of a company. He also buys preferred stocks, engages in arbitrage (when two companies are merging, Buffett may buy the shares of one, sell the shares of the other), and buys bonds and precious metals. He's also on the board of directors of a few companies Berkshire has invested in. Perhaps the most difficult thing for individuals to duplicate is Buffett's small army of sophisticated investors around the country who fall all over themselves to provide him with "scuttlebutt" about any company he's thinking of buying. Also, Buffett has the word out to family-owned businesses: "I'll buy your company and let you keep running it" (another thing individuals can't duplicate).

Let's not forget, too, that Buffett also happens to be extraordinarily bright, a whiz at math, and to have spent his life almost monomaniacally studying businesses and balance sheets. What's more, he has learned from some of the most original and audacious investment minds of our time, most notably Benjamin Graham.

Still, while it's true that trying to emulate Pete Sampras or the Williams sisters does not guarantee that you will wind up in Wimbledon, you could very likely benefit from any of the pointers they might give—or from studying what it is they do to win tennis matches.

Buffett has often said that it's easy to emulate what he does, and that what he does is very straightforward. He buys wonderful businesses run by capable, shareholder-friendly people, especially when these businesses are in temporary trouble and the price is right. And then he just hangs on.

There is, in fact, a whole library of books out there about Buffett and his investment strategies. There are Berkshire web sites, Internet discussion groups, and annual meetings that are beginning to resemble revival meetings. There is also a Buffett "workbook" that helps people invest like Warren Buffett. It even includes quizzes.

This book isn't written for the Chartered Financial Analyst or the sophisticated investor (readers familiar with Graham and Dodd's *Security Analysis*). It is for ordinary investors who know that they could do a lot better if they knew a little more. And the truth is, much of Buffett's investment strategy is perfectly suited for the everyday investor. His advice, which he has been generous in sharing, is simple and almost surefire.

Buffett buys only what he considers to be almost sure things—stocks of companies so powerful, so unassailable, that they will still dominate their industries ten years hence. He confines his choices to stocks in industries that he is thoroughly familiar with. He will seek out every last bit of information he can get, whether it's a company's return on equity or the fact that the CEO is a miser who takes after Ebenezer Scrooge himself. He scrutinizes his occasional mistakes, quickly undoes them, and tries to learn lessons from the experience. While he is loyal to the management and employees of companies he buys, he is first and foremost loyal to his investors. To Warren Buffett, the foulest four-letter word is: r-i-s-k.

Beyond that, he avoids making the mistakes ordinary investors make: buying the most glamorous stocks when they're at the peak of their popularity; selling whatever temporarily falls out of favor and thus following the crowd (in or out the door); attempting to demonstrate versatility by buying all manner of stocks in different industries; being seduced by exciting stories with no solid numbers to back them up; and tenaciously holding onto his losers while shortsightedly nailing down the profits on his winners by selling.

In short, as Buffett has modestly confessed, the essential reason for his success is that he has invested very sensibly and very rationally.

Another way of putting it: Buffet invests as if his life depended on it.

A word of warning: Not all of Buffett's strategies should necessarily be imitated by the general investing public, in particular Buffett's penchant for buying only a relatively few stocks. A concentrated portfolio, in lesser hands, can be a time bomb.

There are some things that geniuses can (and should) do that lesser mortals should be wary of; there's a law for the lion and a law for the lamb. Ted Williams, the great baseball slugger, never tried to bunt his way onto first base, even during the days of the "Williams Shift," when players on the opposing team moved far over to the right side of the field to catch balls that Williams normally whacked down that way. He wasn't being paid to bunt toward third base and wind up with a mere single, much the way Warren Buffett isn't expected to do just okay. But you and I, not being quite in the same class as those two, should be perfectly content with getting on base consistently using such unimpressive techniques as bunt singles.

No doubt, overdiversification—owning a truckload of different securities—is something that gifted investors should steer clear of. But underdiversification, owning just a few securities, is something that ungifted investors (in whose ranks I happily serve) should also avoid like the plague.

In 1996 there appeared a short, charming book with a cute title: *Invest Like Warren Buffett, Live Like Jimmy Buffett: A Money Manual for Those Who Haven't Won the Lottery* (Secaucus, NJ: Carol Publishing Group, 1996). The author is a Certified Financial Planner, Luki Vail.

The text talks about the blessings of an investor's owning a diversified portfolio, not a concentrated portfolio. Writes the author, "Diversification of your investment dollars along with appropriate time strategies are your best tactics to protect you against such things as stock market crashes." ("Time strategies" means suiting your portfolio to your needs. If you think you'll need your money in fewer than five years, go easy on stocks.)

Why buy mutual funds? "Here is your chance to own stocks in 50 to 75 companies."

"Generally, stay away from individual stocks until you have about $250,000 to invest; then you can have a well-diversified portfolio, like your own personal mutual fund. That way when a stock takes a nose dive on you, it will only have a small position in a very large portfolio, and you will take only a small loss, which could possibly be offset by the gain of some other stock."

In brief, she is recommending that readers of her book not swing for the seats but bunt for singles. That's no doubt sensible counsel for her readers, but it is not the Warren Buffett way.

I might offer a compromise suggestion: The ordinary investor, the lesser investor, might have a core portfolio of large-company index funds composing 50 percent or more of the entire stock portfolio. (Buffett has recommended that tactic for most investors.) And outside the core portfolio, the lesser investor might swing for the seats by imitating the strategy of the man generally acknowledged to be the greatest investor of our time.

Warren Boroson
Glen Rock, N.J.

CHAPTER 1

It's Easy to Invest like Warren Buffett

Buying shares of Berkshire Hathaway is the easiest way to invest like Warren Buffett. While the A shares cost around $70,000 apiece as of this writing, the B shares sell for only around $2,300 each—roughly $^1/_{30}$ of the A shares. The B shares do have their disadvantages. For example, holders have less in the way of voting rights and aren't entitled to indicate where Berkshire charitable contributions go. (Berkshire is unusual in allowing shareholders to recommend how Berkshire's charity money should be allocated.) And while you can convert A shares into B, it doesn't work the other way around.

Which to buy? Berkshire is nothing if not shareholder friendly, and Buffett has given this advice: Buy the A shares, if you can afford them, unless the B shares are trading cheaply. "In my opinion, *most* of the time the demand for B will be such that it will trade at about $^1/_{30}$ of the price of the A. However, from time to time, a different supply–demand situation will prevail and the B will sell at some discount. In my opinion, again, when the B is at a discount of more than, say, 2 percent, it offers a better buy than A. When the two of them are at parity, however, anyone wishing to buy 30 or more B should consider buying A instead."

An investor might dollar-cost-average into Berkshire's B shares using a discount broker. So, for example, in order to build a $13,200 position, he or she might buy two shares six times a year. Or, if the buyer is less patient, two shares for three straight months.

It is also a good idea to check whether two leading newsletters, The Value Line Investment Survey and Standard & Poor's "The Outlook," give the stock a decent rating at the time of purchase, and perhaps either wait a bit or buy energetically depending on their views. (Hardly any other analysts cover Berkshire.) As of this writing, Value Line rated Berkshire, at $70,000 a share, average; "The Outlook"—whose Berkshire analyst, David Braverman, is probably the very best—above average.

Another guide: Consider whether the stock is closer to its yearly high or low. Buying Berkshire low is certainly appropriate for someone intending to be a follower of Warren Buffett's value-oriented investment strategy.

Buying Individual Stocks

Another practical possibility for Buffett followers is to buy the publicly traded stocks that Berkshire owns—like Coca-Cola, Gillette, H&R Block, and General Dynamics. (Berkshire is also the sole owner of various companies, like See's Candy and GEICO, the insurance company, but these companies are not publicly traded.) Because of Buffett's history of purchasing reasonably priced stocks, these stocks should still be worth buying.

A danger, of course, is that Berkshire may have begun unloading those stocks, the way it began quietly bailing out of Disney in 2000, as you are just beginning to purchase them. Another danger is that your portfolio will be askew: You will have more exposure to certain stocks and industries than Berkshire itself has. As a result, your portfolio might be a riskier version of Berkshire.

You can balance out your Buffett-like portfolio with stocks from the holdings of mutual funds that invest roughly the way Buffett does, such as Sequoia, Tweedy, Browne Global Value and American Value, Legg Mason Focus Trust (omitting from the last any technology stocks, which Buffett tends to avoid), Third Avenue Value, Clipper, Longleaf Partners, Torray, and Vontobel U.S. Value. You can examine a list of these funds' recent holdings either by going to their web sites or by consulting Morningstar Mutual Funds, a newsletter to which most large libraries subscribe. The list of holdings will be somewhat outdated, but, again, most of these value stocks should remain reasonably priced.

You might also balance your portfolio by concentrating on stocks in industries outside the ones you already have covered in your Buffett-like portfolio, along with foreign stocks, which Buffett also tends to avoid. For suggestions of foreign stocks to buy, check those in the portfolio of Tweedy, Browne Global Value.

For U.S. stocks, I would single out health-care stocks because Berkshire has tended to ignore this entire industry, perhaps because the stocks have almost always been high-priced or because they are outside Buffett's "circle of competence."

You can also balance out your Buffett-like portfolio with stocks chosen from the list compiled at Quicken.com by Robert Hagstrom. He derives this list using his criteria for picking Buffett-type stocks, Hagstrom being an authority on Buffett's strategy. (See Chapter 20.)

For more on Sequoia, see Chapter 21; for Legg Mason Value Trust, Chapter 22; for Tweedy, Browne, Chapter 24; for Third Avenue Value, Chapter 25; for Torray, Chapter 27; for Vontobel, Chapter 28; and for Clipper, Chapter 29.

Buying Buffett-like Mutual Funds

Instead of buying individual stocks, you could buy one or more Buffett-like mutual funds—in effect, having someone else buy Buffett-type stocks for you. Even granting that Buffett is in a class by himself, cheap imitations—cheap in the sense of your being able to buy many shares for a low minimum—aren't to be sneezed at. These funds, in some cases, do not deliberately emulate Buffett's strategy. For example, Third Avenue Value, under Martin J. Whitman, doesn't. Others, to a certain extent, do—notably, Sequoia, Tweedy, Browne

Getting Into Closed Funds

With a fund closed to new investors, you can ask a current shareholder to sign over just one share to you and use that one share to obtain more shares on your own. Unfortunately, owners of Sequoia shares have, in my experience, never evinced any interest in selling shares.

American Value, Legg Mason Focus Trust, Torray, Longleaf Partners, and Vontobel U.S. Value.

Which fund most resembles Berkshire? No doubt Sequoia, which was started by a Columbia Business School friend of Buffett's and which invests a big chunk of its assets in Berkshire. (Unfortunately, Sequoia is closed to new investors.) Table 1.1 shows Sequoia's recent holdings.

Sequoia suffered a dismal 1999, along with Berkshire itself and with many other value funds. But its long-term record is splendid. Over the past 10 years it has outperformed the S&P 500 by 2.31 percentage points, returning 17.56 percent a year.

Which of the other funds most resembles Sequoia? Buffett has reportedly said that the Clipper Fund is close to his investing style.

A lesser-known fund that has much in common with Berkshire is Vontobel U.S. Value, run by Edwin Walczak. He readily acknowledges Buffett's influence; his portfolio recently had a 5 percent exposure to Berkshire, its fifth largest position. Other stocks in Walczak's portfolio that have overlapped with Berkshire: Mercury General, Gannett, McDonald's, Gillette, Wells Fargo. The fund is classified by Morningstar as mid-cap value.

One possible way to search for other funds that imitate Buffett's

TABLE 1.1 Sequoia's Holdings (3/31/00)

STOCK	% OF ASSETS
Berkshire Hathaway A	31.43
U.S. Treasury note 6.125%	14.98
Freddie Mac	13.09
First Third Bancorp	10.23
Progressive	7.88
U.S. Treasury note 5.5%	6.51
Harley-Davidson	4.00
U.S. Bancorp	2.47
Household International	1.79
National Commerce Bancorp	0.58
Mercantile Bankshares	0.27

Data Source: Morningstar

strategy is to compare their R-squareds, numbers indicating how closely a fund follows an index.

You might search for a fund with an R-squared close to Sequoia's. (If A is equal to B and B is equal to C, then A is equal to C.) The Vanguard Index 500, which mirrors the Standard & Poor's 500 Stock Index, has an R-squared of 100. The higher the R-squared, the more closely a fund mirrors an index. (Table 1.2 lists the R-squareds of some Buffett-like funds.)

TABLE 1.2 R-Squareds of Buffett-like Funds

FUND	R-SQUARED
Sequoia	37
Tweedy, Browne American Value	70
Legg Mason Focus Trust	79
Torray	71
Third Avenue Value	52
Clipper	63
Longleaf Partners	49
Vontobel U.S. Value	27

Data Source: Morningstar

Understanding R-Squared

R-squared measures how much of a mutual fund's performance is explained by its similarity to an entire market. If a fund owns large-company stocks, both growth and value, and they are well diversified by industry, it should have a high R-squared compared to the Standard & Poor's 500 Stock Index. Fidelity Disciplined Equity has an R-squared of 93. A fund that deliberately attempts to duplicate the Standard & Poor's 500 might have an R-squared of 99. (The Vanguard Index 500 Fund, which mirrors the S&P 500, actually has an R squared of 100.) A fund that is nowhere near as well diversified by industry, or that buys small-company stocks or foreign stocks, might have a very low R-squared (compared to the S&P 500, but not compared to other indexes). The Fasciano Fund, which specializes in small companies, has an R-squared of 64. Vanguard Emerging Markets Stock Index has an R-squared of 54 compared with the S&P 500, but 78 when compared to a foreign-stock index.

Apparently R-squared is simply not a useful guide to identifying Buffett-like mutual funds, perhaps because the concentrated nature of some Buffett-like funds loosens their ties to the S&P 500.

Now let's look at the same funds, zeroing in on (1) concentration, (2) low turnover, (3) low price-earnings ratios, and (4) low price-book ratios. (See Table 1.3.) Even with these criteria, it's hard to tell which fund is most similar to Sequoia.

Value funds differ from one another because their criteria for assessing what a company is worth may be different. Many managers, like Buffett, use the current value of future cash flow; others may check the prices paid for similar companies recently taken over. Some managers are "deep value"; others, further along the continuum toward growth. Value versus growth investing will be covered in Chapter 6.

In any case, Buffett-like stocks or mutual funds might constitute only a portion of your portfolio. Value funds do tend to underperform during long stretches of time, and you might do well to own some good growth stocks and growth mutual funds, along with Buffett-like stocks, just to keep your portfolio more stable over the years.

TABLE 1.3 Statistics of Buffett-like Funds

FUND	CONCENTRATED?	TURNOVER	AVERAGE P/E RATIO	AVERAGE P/B RATIO
Sequoia	Yes	12	24.6*	4.9
Tweedy, Browne American Value	No	19	20.6	4.1
Legg Mason Focus Trust	Yes	14	33	9.6
Torray	No	33	25.1	4.5
Third Avenue Value	No	5	25.8	2.9
Clipper	Yes	63	18.4	4.7
Longleaf Partners	Yes	50	19.3	3.2
Vontobel U.S. Value	Yes	67	19.3	3.6

*Based on 50% or less of stocks.
Data Source: Morningstar

A Sensible Solution

All in all, a sensible solution for a Warren Wannabe is to own:

- Some shares of Berkshire Hathaway
- Some of the individual stocks that Berkshire owns, or other Buffett-like stocks
- A mutual fund or two that seem Buffett-oriented

CHAPTER 2

The Achievement of Warren Buffett

Warren Buffett is widely acknowledged to be the best investor of our time. When John C. Bogle, founder of the Vanguard Group, named three investors who seem to have been able to beat the market because of their special gifts, they were Buffett, Peter Lynch (formerly of Fidelity Magellan), and John Neff (formerly of Vanguard Windsor).

In the 36 years that Buffett has been the chairman of Berkshire, its per-share book value has climbed more than 23 percent a year. (The change in value is the best way to evaluate an insurance company's performance.) In 32 of those 36 years, Berkshire has beaten the S&P, sometimes by astonishing amounts. (See Table 2.1.) The stock has risen from $12 a share to $71,000 at the end of 2000, an annual growth rate of 27 percent.

Soros' Dilemma

When Ron Baron, the fund manager, worked for Soros, Soros told him he wasn't interested in stock tips. He had too much money to invest. He needed *themes*.

TABLE 2.1 Berkshire Hathaway vs. the S&P 500

YEAR	ANNUAL PERCENTAGE IN PER SHARE BOOK VALUE OF BERKSHIRE	CHANGE IN S&P 500 WITH DIVIDENDS INCLUDED	RELATIVE RESULTS
1965	23.8	10.0	13.8
1966	20.3	(11.7)	32.0
1967	11.0	30.9	(19.9)
1968	19.0	11.0	8.0
1969	16.2	(8.4)	24.6
1970	12.0	3.9	8.1
1971	16.4	14.6	1.8
1972	21.7	18.9	2.8
1973	4.7	(14.8)	19.5
1974	5.5	(26.4)	31.9
1975	21.9	37.2	(15.3)
1976	59.3	23.6	35.7
1977	31.9	(7.4)	39.3
1978	24.0	6.4	17.6
1979	35.7	18.2	17.5
1980	19.3	32.3	(13.0)
1981	31.4	(5.0)	36.4
1982	40.0	21.4	18.6
1983	32.3	22.4	9.9
1984	13.6	6.1	7.5
1985	48.2	31.6	16.6
1986	26.1	18.6	7.5
1987	19.5	5.1	14.4
1988	20.1	16.6	3.5
1989	44.4	31.7	12.7
1990	7.4	(3.1)	10.5
1991	39.6	30.5	9.1
1992	20.3	7.6	12.7
1993	14.3	10.1	4.2
1994	13.9	.3	12.6
1995	43.1	37.6	5.5
1996	31.8	23.0	8.8
1997	34.1	33.4	0.7
1998	48.3	28.6	19.7
1999	0.5	21.0	(20.5)
2000	6.5	(9.1)	15.6

Source: Berkshire Hathaway

Perhaps other investors have made more money. Author John Train, in his latest book, *Money Masters of Our Time*, contends that George Soros, the hedge fund manager, has been more successful.

But Soros' strategy is rather inimitable (not many of us could have made billions by shorting the British pound), and his writings are somewhat inaccessible to the ordinary investor.

In contrast, Buffett has put together an extraordinary record by doing (in many cases) what the average investor could have done—buying shares of GEICO, Coca-Cola, Gillette, and other publicly traded companies. Also, his pronouncements have not been mysteries wrapped in enigmas. Time and again he has explained what he does and what he doesn't, and why. He has generally urged investors to follow his straight-from-the-shoulder, easy to follow precepts that essentially boil down to this: Buy wonderful companies when their stocks are a little cheap, then hold them forever.

Buffett's writings are—for the most part—easy to understand, leavened with a lively wit and funny stories, and convey the sense that he is having a wonderfully good time. And, while he has not made himself as available to the press as some of us would like (he courteously declined an interview for this book), he has not been as standoffish as many others.

Buffett—both his persona and his real personality—seems to appeal to and intrigue a great many people. There is his faux naif, "aw shucks" persona: The fourth-or-so richest person in America (according to Forbes) wears rumpled suits, dines on hamburgers and cherry Cokes at fast-food restaurants, lives in a big old house in Omaha, has rarely ventured beyond Omaha, and has made a fortune in the stock market doing simple, obvious things that anyone else could do. He seems like the kid who catches a record-sized bass using a wooden stick as a fishing pole and a rusty old hook. Huck Finn

Getting to Warren

About 15 years ago, as a matter of fact, I came close to interviewing Buffett. I was writing an article for *Sylvia Porter's Personal Finance Magazine* on what successful investors would tell young people—high school students, say—about investing. Buffett's secretary, a friendly voice on the phone, asked me to call the next day and she would have an answer. I did. She told me, with unfeigned admiration in her voice, "You came *very* close!"

conquers Gotham. Some of this is true, or was true. Some of it is not. Don't forget that he also went to Columbia Business School; studied under one of the audacious and original investment minds of our time, Ben Graham (who gave him, reportedly, the only A+ he ever handed out); and in his investments, uses arbitrage, preferred stock, and other somewhat off-the-beaten-path strategies. Huckleberry Finn he's not.

Buffett also has a reputation for decency and honesty, and this is clearly deserved. When Salomon Brothers got into a pickle, Buffett was the logical man to straighten things out. When a local baseball team needed financial help, Buffett proved their benefactor.

He is careful about his reputation, time and again making sure that shareholders know that he's not engaging in any hanky-panky. If you order T-shirts that say Berkshire Hathaway on them, you are assured that the money won't be taken out of your credit-card account until the shirts are on the way. You're also told it may take a month for the shirts to arrive; they arrive in a few days.

Buffett is unshakably loyal to his friends. He never loses an opportunity to express his admiration for Ben Graham, coming to New York City to attend Columbia University festivities celebrating Graham, and sometimes just dropping in to astonish students at the business school.

Buffett is especially loyal to his shareholders, many of whom are old-time friends. For around five hours once a year, he and Charlie Munger answer shareholders' questions. (Other companies, to avoid shareholders, have been known to schedule their annual meetings in faraway places in the dead of night.) As Buffett's friend, the *Fortune* writer Carol J. Loomis, has written, ". . . this is a company that thinks first and foremost about its shareholders. . . ."

Not surprisingly, Berkshire is No. 7 on *Fortune*'s list of most admired companies in America.

Warren Wannabes

Buffett has an army of Warren Wannabes, from money managers who try to imitate his strategies down to the letter (Edwin Walczak, who manages Vontobel U.S. Value and calls himself a Buffett Moonie) as well as individual investors strongly influenced by his views.

Peggy Ruhlin, a Certified Financial Planner in Columbus, Ohio, has never met Buffett and been to only one annual meeting. "Unless you're a complete fanatic, one is enough," she reports. "Still, it's a once-in-a-lifetime experience. Before the meeting people are lined up an hour or two ahead outside the meeting room, and when the doors open they run in as fast as they can, jumping over rows, standing on chairs, just to be up close. Many wear the Nebraska colors, red and white." (She attended her only meeting before the Yellow Hatters, a fan club, became so vociferous.)

Buffett has been so spectacularly successful an investor, Ruhlin believes, because "he buys only what he knows. And he buys well-managed companies, takes a hands-off attitude, and leaves everything in place. He really is an outside investor."

In buying part and not complete ownership of companies, like Coca-Cola and Gillette, she believes, his purchases "have not always been so stellar. Some have been good, some have been bad."

She herself follows the value investing philosophy. "I've read Graham and Dodd [*Security Analysis* by the two Columbia professors, Benjamin Graham and David Dodd], and it's been hard to be a value investor these past few years. Some of my clients aren't 100 percent value. Some of them are 50 percent in growth. But almost all of my clients own Berkshire Hathaway, the A shares or the B shares. At our office, we even have a Warren Buffett Room.

"As a person, he's easy to like. He's so self-deprecating. He's a regular person, and he has good Midwestern values, which I relate to."

Someone else who has attended an annual meeting is David Braverman, the Standard & Poor's analyst, who went with his 16-year-old daughter, Stacey, who owns one B share. She ran into Buffett at a jewelry store, and because he likes young people, he went over to her and whispered into her ear: "I want to give you a hot stock tip: Buy the next Internet stock IPO at its opening on Monday."

At the meeting itself, Stacey asked a question—then publicly thanked Buffett for recommending his favorite Internet stock. The audience roared.

Buffettology or Mythology?

People with an ax to grind may be dubious of Buffett's accomplishments, and one ax they typically are seeking to have ground is their adherence to the Efficient Market Hypothesis, the notion that stocks are always reasonably priced because all information about all companies is immediately dispersed to the general populace, and the general populace is composed of equally intelligent, rational individuals. One person who harbors doubts about Buffett's abilities is

Larry E. Swedroe, an advocate of index funds and the author of *What Wall Street Doesn't Want You to Know* (New York: St. Martin's Press, 2001).

He professes himself to be an "agnostic" regarding Buffett.

Certainly Buffett's long-term record is impressive, Swedroe admits, and it may have three causes:

1. He may be a genius.
2. He may have been just lucky.
3. He may have benefited specially from his being an active participant in companies he buys into, such as Coca-Cola and Gillette. "He often takes an influential management role, including a seat on the board of directors, in a company in which he invests." So it may be his contribution to the companies in which he invests that explains his record.

(One might add: Another explanation someone might advance is that Berkshire has used the float from its insurance company premiums to compound its returns—at little or no cost. This, observes analyst Braverman, is akin to Buffett's having used leverage, or borrowing money.)

Swedroe continues: From 1990 to February 29, 2000, Berkshire gained 407 percent. But that was only 0.2 percent per year more than the S&P 500. Swedroe then does some data mining, and, he admits, searches specifically for periods of time when Berkshire Hathaway under-performed. From June 19, 1998, its all-time high, to February 29, 2000, Berkshire fell 46 percent. The S&P 500 rose 24 percent, not including dividends. From 1996 through 1999, Berkshire rose by 75 percent. But the S&P 500 climbed by 155 percent.

The lesson from Buffett's record, Swedroe concludes, is that "choosing active managers, even perhaps the greatest one of all, is no guarantee of better results." Whereas diversifying among index funds, he argues, is.

The obvious answer to Swedroe is that the 1990s were a great time for the S&P 500 Index because technology stocks ruled the roost, especially in the last few years of the decade, and the S&P 500 was dominated by its tech stocks. For Berkshire to have beaten the index by even a small amount over that period of time is impressive, considering Buffett's aversion to technology stocks. And the fact that Berkshire endured some mediocre years and some poor years is not surprising; the S&P 500 has suffered dry spells as well. In any case, value stocks are notorious for trailing behind the general market during long time periods, which might explain why value investors wind up being so generously rewarded.

Why It's So Hard to Beat an Index Fund

Beating the stock market, as represented by an index fund, is ferociously difficult, which is why Buffett's record is so unusual. Here are a few reasons why a large-company index fund, like one modeled on the S&P 500, is so formidable an opponent:

- The Standard & Poor's 500 is well diversified by industry.
- It is well diversified by stocks. (The Vanguard 500 Index has around 506 stocks, the extra ones being for both A and B shares, like those of Berkshire Hathaway, which—for some strange reason— are not in the S&P 500.)
- An index fund based on the S&P 500 will normally have low expenses. There are few changes in its composition, so trading costs are minimal; there aren't high salaries for a manager or for various analysts.
- Most index funds are capitalization weighted; the bigger companies (measured by price times shares outstanding) have more effect on the index than the smaller ones. So, in a sense, an index fund practices momentum investing; stocks that do well begin to occupy a greater and greater role in the index, and stocks that do poorly begin to occupy a lesser and lesser role. This explains why value investing and index-fund investing may alternate periods of glory. If they buy stocks in the S&P 500 Index, value investors tend to buy the companies that have been shrinking.
- The indexes are not so passively managed as some people think. The better companies are chosen for the index in the first place; when a stock must be replaced, it is replaced by a stellar company; when a company already in the index has been doing abysmally, like Westinghouse or Woolworth, it may also be replaced by a thriving company. (Granted, the committee that decides which securities should remain in an index and which should be booted out is not infallible; in 1939, IBM was kicked out of the Dow Jones Industrial Average.)
- An index fund won't have a manager to blame if the fund does poorly; shareholders may be more likely to continue holding on because, clearly, there's no one to heap abuse on for any mistake. Shareholders may be more likely to desert an actively managed fund—and when they do flee, the manager may be forced to sell stocks at what may be the wrong time. Or the

manager may be discharged, and his or her successor may drastically revamp the portfolio—just when the first manager's strategy is finally kicking in. I once told John Bogle that one benefit of an index fund is that the guy who's not managing it today will be the same guy who's not managing it 20 years from now. He smiled.

CHAPTER 3

Buffett: A Life in the Stock Market

In some ways Warren Buffett resembles another plainspoken, outspoken, ordinary-but-not-so-ordinary Midwesterner: President Harry Truman. This is so even though Truman, after having been burned in a zinc mining adventure, mostly confined his investing to Treasuries.

Many of the terms used to describe Truman describe Buffett equally as well. Historian David McCullogh called Truman a man "full of the zest of life." Others talked about his "fundamental small-town genuineness," and his "appealing mixture of modesty and confidence."

Against Ostentation

Truman thought little of the palace at Versailles, feeling that the money to build it had been "squeezed" from the people. In a similar vein, Buffett was contemptuous of William Randolph Hearst's self-indulgent San Francisco castle, San Simeon, with its art treasures from all over the world. He felt that it had taken "massive amounts of labor and material away from other societal purposes."

Much like Buffett, Truman was known for his integrity and character, and for being scrupulously ethical. These traits seem to have served Buffett and Truman equally well.

Warren Edward Buffett was born in Omaha on August 30, 1930, the son of Howard Buffett, a stockbroker and later a Republican congressman. He was the second of three children, and the only son.

From his father Buffett learned the basic moral values, possibly along with a deep respect for people who have money—his father's clients. From his mother, who was difficult and disapproving, he may have developed a strong need to prove his worth, perhaps by accumulating a large fortune.

In his youth Buffett displayed his intellectual gifts by memorizing the populations of scores of U.S. cities. He displayed his commercial instincts by selling chewing gum to passersby, setting up a lemonade stand, selling cans of soda pop, even selling a tip sheet at the track. He played Monopoly for hours.

When he was 11, he began working in his father's brokerage firm, marking prices on a blackboard. He bought his first stock when he was 11: three shares of Cities Service Preferred, at $38 a share. The price fell to $27, then bopped up to $40, at which point he sold. His profit was $6, minus commissions. The stock soon rose to $200 a share; perhaps Buffett had learned a lesson in being patient.

When his father was elected to Congress, he took his family to Fredericksburg in Virginia. Warren, who all his life has been upset at the prospect of change, was wretched. He was allowed to return to Omaha and live with his grandfather, Ernest. Later, he worked in his grandfather's grocery store.

Buffett returned to Washington, D.C., as a teenager. He began delivering the *Washington Post* and other newspapers, and in 1945, at 14, took his savings from his paper routes and bought 40 acres of Nebraska farmland for $1,200 and leased them to a farmer. He also made money by searching for lost golf balls on a golf course, and by renting old, repaired pinball machines to barber shops.

In high school, he was something of a nerd; he wore the same

His Picture in the Paper

At seven, Buffett was hospitalized. In bed, he played with numbers, explaining to his nurse, "I don't have much money now, but someday I will and I'll have my picture in the paper."

sneakers all the time, even in the dead of winter. But he had developed such a reputation for stock-market wisdom that even his teachers would ask him for advice. He graduated high school 14th in his class of 374, and the yearbook described him this way: "Likes math . . . a future stockbroker."

He went on to the Wharton School of Finance, where, Warren reported, he knew more than his professors. And, indeed, he was a standout student. After a year, he transferred to the University of Nebraska in Lincoln.

He himself dabbled in charting and technical analysis, but then, while a senior at the University of Nebraska, read Benjamin Graham's *The Intelligent Investor*, advocating that investors buy good, cheap companies and hang on—and the veils promptly fell from his eyes.

At 19 Buffett applied to and was turned down by the Harvard Business School, surely a blunder as egregious as the Boston Red Sox's selling Babe Ruth to the Yankees. He then moved to New York to study with Ben Graham at the Columbia Business School. He was a splendid student.

After getting his M.B.A., Buffett applied for a job with Graham's firm, offering to work for no pay, but was turned down. Buffett wasn't resentful: He joked that Graham had "made his customary calculation of value to price and said no."

At the same time that Howard Buffett lost his seat in Congress, Warren received a phone call from Ben Graham. He offered Buffett a job as an analyst with Graham–Newman in the Chanin Building on 43rd Street. There Buffett shared a room with Walter Schloss (Chapter 26), and later with Tom Knapp, who started the Tweedy, Browne funds (Chapter 24).

Although he admired Graham, Buffett complained that he "had this kind of shell around him." Graham also didn't really say yes to Buffett's proposed stock picks—or anyone else's. He also discouraged Buffett from visiting companies and talking to management. Either a stock fit Graham's mathematical matrix or it didn't.

Buffett began courting Susan Thompson, and when she didn't return his affection, befriended her father. Susan was dating Milton Brown, a Jew, and Susan's parents—her father was a Protestant minister—were disapproving. Buffett told Susan's father that he was Jewish enough for Susan and Christian enough for him. ("Jewish enough for Susan" probably meant: He was unconventional and iconoclastic.) Eventually Susan gave in to her father, and began dating Buffett; they married in 1952.

In 1956 Graham retired to California, and Buffett—now worth $140,000 thanks to shrewd investing—returned to Omaha.

There, Buffett began working in his father's business. The first stock he sold: GEICO. Then he started his own investment partnership. He persuaded a group of investors to hand over $25,000 each; Buffett contributed $100, and he was on his way. His goal: to beat the Dow Jones Industrial Average by an average of 10 percent a year.

When he ended the partnership in 1969, because he couldn't find cheap stocks to buy, his investments had compounded at 29.5 percent a year versus the Dow's mere 7.4 percent a year. Ending the partnership was a good call. The Dow plunged in 1973 and 1974.

Buffett suggested that his ex-partners invest money with his friend Bill Ruane in a new mutual fund called Sequoia. (See Chapter 21.)

In 1962, Buffett had begun buying cheap shares of a textile mill in New Bedford, Massachusetts, called Berkshire Hathaway. He began buying it at less than $8 a share, then took it over completely in 1964, when its book value was $19.46.

He had promised to hold onto the textile mill, but eventually had to give it up because the business was eroding thanks to foreign competition.

He then went into insurance, a wise decision because insurance

A Telling Anecdote

The Omaha Club, a downtown dining club for businessmen, did not admit Jews, and at least one Jewish businessman told Buffett that he was upset. When Buffett mentioned this to the club's board, he was told, "They have their own club." Buffett argued that some Jewish families had been in Omaha for a hundred years, they had contributed to the community, and yet they could not join a club that a Christian newcomer could join immediately. "That is hardly fair." ("Fair," along with "certainty," is one of Buffett's favorite words.)

Buffett then applied for membership in the all-Jewish Highland Country Club. Astonishingly, some of its members didn't want to accept him, claiming that Gentiles would wind up taking over the club. (These members, obviously, had goyishe kopfs.) On October 1, 1969, Buffett was admitted. The Omaha Club promptly began admitting Jews.

With characteristic modesty and good humor, Buffett explained that he had wanted to join the Highland Club only because the food was better.

companies give their owners free money from customers to invest for a time (until claims must be paid)—and Buffett knew how to invest spare money.

When the markets crashed in 1973–1974, Buffett went in with a wheelbarrow and scooped up bargains.

His wife, Susan, apparently didn't enjoy the good, quiet life in Omaha as much as Buffett did, and moved to San Francisco, helping him find another housemate, Astrid Menks, a Latvian-born waitress at a local café. Mrs. Buffett nonetheless joins him on most of his public appearances, gets along famously with Ms. Menks, and will inherit all his stock should he predecease her.

They have three children: Howard, Susan, and Peter.

Buffett still lives on Farnam Street in the same big, gray house he purchased 40 years ago for $31,500. He drives his own car, does his own taxes.

The Buffett Foundation, which he set up in the mid-1960s, helps family-planning clinics.

His most notable purchases include the Washington Post, GEICO, Coca-Cola, Gillette, American Express, and General Re. He prefers buying companies outright to buying partial shares, and he now owns a well-diversified portfolio of companies. (See Appendix 2.)

In the early 1990s, perhaps mistakenly, Buffett and Munger got involved in the Salomon scandal over its hogging of Treasury bonds, and Buffett took over as chairman. He tried to curtail the greediness of Salomon bond traders, and certainly managed to rescue the company from bankruptcy, but in retrospect it seems to have been a no-win situation—a dragon that Buffett might have been better off avoiding rather than trying to slay.

His annual reports are reader friendly, literate, learned, and sometimes funny (although he mistakenly believes that St. Augustine's plea, "Give me chastity, but not now," is apocryphal).

Berkshire does things differently. Both Buffett and Munger receive only $100,000 a year in salaries. The shares were split into A and B varieties in 1996 only to fend off sharpies, who were about to sell small units of Berkshire for less than the $48,000 a share it was then selling for. (Buffett never split the stock, despite its lofty price, because he believes that low prices lead to a high turnover, attract investors who are short-term oriented, and cause stock prices to diverge from their intrinsic value.)

The fun-filled annual meetings, Woodstock for Capitalists, lure thousands of contented shareholders, and every year more and more people flock there to enjoy the Warren and Charlie Show. Celebrities turn up, too, including Michael Eisner of Disney.

Apparently the man designated to succeed Buffett when he leaves is Louis Simpson, GEICO's chairman. (See Chapter 23.)

In 2001 Buffett went on what was, for him, a buying spree, purchasing shares of such companies as H&R Block, GPU, and Johns Manville, the company riddled with asbestos problems. He joined with other very wealthy people in publicly opposing legislation to eliminate the estate tax, arguing that it is simply unfair for one child to be born with far more financial resources than another. And he began issuing warnings that the stock market was overvalued. He is only 70 years old as of this writing, and one can confidently expect that he will be entertaining and enlightening us many more times during this decade, and yes, even getting his picture in the papers.

CHAPTER 4

The Influence of Benjamin Graham

U.S. Steel sold for $262 on September 3, 1929. On July 8, 1932, it sold for $22.

General Motors fetched $73 on September 3, 1929. On July 8, 1932, it was down to $8.

Montgomery Ward was $138 in 1929. In 1932, it was $4.

AT&T was $304 in 1929. In 1932 it was $72.

Those were the better stocks. Some of the very worst stocks were called investment trusts. These were actually what we now call closed-end mutual funds. The problem with many of these trusts was that they were leveraged up the Wazoo. Even more troublesome, they had substantial holdings in other highly leveraged trusts. In 1929 they were fireworks waiting for a spark.

One well-known fund, United Founders, sold for $70 in 1929. In 1932 it sold for 50 cents. American Founders was $117 in 1929. In 1932, also 50 cents.

Goldman Sachs Trading Corporation once sold for as much as $222.50 a share. At that point its premium to its underlying assets was 100 percent. In 1932 Walter E. Sachs was hauled before a senate committee. What, a senator asked, was the price of Goldman

Sachs Trading Corporation stock now? Answer: approximately $1.75.

People tend to simplify and overdramatize. The Crash of 1929 was exaggerated. The stock market's decline through the entire year of 1929 was only 17 percent—not enough to qualify as a bear market, which calls for a 20 percent decline. In fact, 1930 was worse. Even worse was to come. All in all, the stock market fell around 80 percent from 1929 through 1932. By contrast, during the horrendous bear market of 1973–1974, stocks lost only 45 percent of their value.

After the Crash of 1929, many sophisticated and experienced investors, accustomed to buying when stocks retreated, bought on the dip. After all, Herbert Hoover announced at the end of 1929 that "The worst is behind us." And Calvin Coolidge, the departing president, insisted that "Stocks are cheap at current prices." (Coolidge, famous for his taciturnity, clearly talked too much.) These cagey investors had their heads handed to them. Among them were Joseph P. Kennedy, the first chairman of the Securities and Exchange Commission (and father of President John F. Kennedy), along with a brilliant young money manager named Benjamin Graham. Graham was wiped out.

The crashes of 1929–1932 etched themselves into Graham's mind. Stocks and the stock market were dangerous and treacherous. To protect himself, he was forever seeking a "margin of safety." (Warren Buffett was to call those words "the three most important words in investing.") Graham may also have been the first person to claim that the first rule of investing is: Don't lose money. The second rule is: Don't forget the first rule. Buffett, who called Graham the smartest man he had ever met, was in later years to say the exact same thing.

History

Benjamin Graham was born Benjamin Grossbaum, and his family came from England to New York City in 1895, when he was one year old. His father, who ran a chinaware firm, died when Benjamin was nine. His widow put her savings into the stock market and lost it all in the panic of 1907, leaving the family in sorry financial shape.

Graham went to Boys High in Brooklyn, a renowned high school, then to Columbia College. He was a genuine polymath. Graduating

Phi Beta Kappa, he was offered teaching posts in three Columbia departments: English, philosophy, and mathematics. Instead he headed for Wall Street, working as a messenger for an old-line firm. Eventually he began analyzing companies and by age 25 became partner in the firm of Newburger, Henderson & Loeb, earning $600,000 a year.

In 1926 Graham formed a mutual fund, which he managed in return for a share of the profits. He was soon joined by a partner, Jerome Newman. The fund declined 70 percent from 1929 to 1932, and Graham was thinking of surrendering. Newman put up $75,000 to enable the firm to survive. The firm eventually regained its footing and went on to prosper, although it never became especially large. Among the people who once worked for Graham and Newman was a young Columbia Business School graduate named Warren Buffett.

From 1928 to 1956 Graham had taught a popular evening course at Columbia Business School. In 1934, at a time when people didn't even want to hear the word "stocks," Graham and Professor David Dodd published their revolutionary book, *Security Analysis*, a text for serious students. *Security Analysis* carries on its frontispiece a quote from Horace: "The last shall be first and the first shall be last." (Graham was a Latin scholar.)

In brief, Graham recommended buying cheap stocks, their cheapness being apparent in (1) their price being less than two-thirds of their net asset value, and (2) their stock having low price-to-earnings ratios.

To Buffett, Graham's philosophy consisted of three principles:

1. Look at stocks as real businesses, not as gambling chips to be wagered.
2. Buy stocks cheaply—obtain a "margin of safety."

Tough Sledding

When I asked Peter Lynch if he had read *Security Analysis*, he made a face and said, "Too dry." Readers might be interested in another book of Graham's, *The Intelligent Investor,* which features an introduction and appendix by Warren Buffett. It is more reader friendly.

3. Be a true investor. "If you have that attitude, you start out ahead of 99 percent of all the people who are operating in the stock market—it's an enormous advantage."

An Aversion to Risk

Graham was risk averse to a fault. It was hard for his employees to persuade him to purchase a stock if it seemed to entail a slightly-more-than-usual risk, something out of the ordinary.

When one employee, Walter Schloss, talked up a company called Haloid, Graham told him that it wasn't cheap enough. Haloid became the Xerox Corporation.

David Dreman, a famous value investor of more recent times, has argued that Graham's investment approach was so timid that it would have kept investors out of much of the bull market of 1947 as well as the awesome bull market that began in 1982.

When Buffett graduated from Columbia Business School, Graham—and Buffett's own stockbroker father—told him to keep away from Wall Street, at least until the next crash was over.

Mr. Market

Graham's central thesis may have been his observation that investors become too optimistic and too pessimistic, and that smart investors should buy when investors are so gloomy they will accept almost any price to get rid of their stinkers, and sell when investors are so euphoric they will pay ridiculously high prices for sure winners. As he put it, one should buy "when the current situation is unfavorable, the near-term prospects are poor, and the low price fully reflects the current pessimism."

A famous metaphor he invented: You are in business with a sweet but slightly loony gentleman named Mr. Market, who happens to go to emotional extremes. Either he's euphoric or he's depressed. And every business day Mr. Market is willing to buy our stocks or sell us his. You can just ignore his offers. Or, when he wants to buy your stocks at absurdly high prices, sell, and when he wants to sell you his stocks at absurdly low prices, buy. In fact, when Mr. Market has a great many cheap stocks to sell you, it's probably time to stock up in general. When Mr. Market has very few stocks to sell, it's probably time to sell. Graham's greatness, says author John Train, "may well have consisted in knowing how to say no. . . . He felt no need to invest at all unless everything was in his favor." That, of course, was a rule that Buffett has followed carefully. (See Chapter 8.)

Another famous metaphor of his: Some good stocks are like cigar butts. These are stocks abandoned by investors that, like

Graham's 10 Signs of a Bargain Stock

A company would have to meet seven of the following ten criteria (as laid out in *Security Analysis*) before Graham would consider it a cheap stock:

1. **An earnings-to-price yield (the opposite of the price-earnings ratio) that is twice the current yield of an AAA (top-rated) bond. If bonds are yielding 5 percent, the earnings yield of a stock should be 10 percent. In other words, you could get 5 percent fairly safely; to take on the risk of a stock, you want twice the possible reward.**
2. **A p-e ratio that is historically low for that stock. Specifically, it should be two-fifths of the average p-e ratio the shares had over the past five years.**
3. **A dividend yield of two-thirds of the AAA bond yield. (Obviously, stocks that don't pay dividends wouldn't qualify under this rule.)**
4. **A stock price that is two-thirds of the tangible book value per share.**
5. **A stock price that is two-thirds of the net current asset value or the net quick-liquidation value.**
6. **Total debt lower than tangible book value.**
7. **A current ratio of two or more.**
8. **Total debt that's not more than net quick-liquidation value.**
9. **Earnings that have doubled within the past ten years.**
10. **Earnings that have declined no more than 5 percent in two of the past ten years.**

The individual investor, Graham counseled, should adapt these rules to his or her own situation.

- **If an investor needs income, he or she should pay special attention to rules 1 through 7—especially, of course, to rule 3, the one requiring high dividends.**
- **An investor who wants safety along with growth might pay special attention to rules 1 through 5, along with 9 and 10.**
- **An investor emphasizing growth can ignore dividends, but should pay special attention to rules 9 and 10, underweighting 4, 5, and 6.**

cigar butts, had a few good puffs remaining in them. (One senses that the ghost of the Depression is walking; picking up discarded cigar butts and smoking them is what desperately poor men did during the 1930s.)

Pay scant attention to stock market quotations, Graham advised. Don't become concerned by big price declines nor excited by sizable advances.

On the other hand, Graham also recommended that investors' portfolios be diversified—just in case a bargain-basement stock turned out to deserve its low price. For a defensive investor, 10 to 30 stocks were enough, Graham believed. (Buffett has argued for even fewer.)

In his writings Graham stressed the cardinal difference between investing and speculating. An investor tries to buy and hold "suitable securities at suitable prices." A speculator tries to anticipate and profit from market fluctuations. A true investment, he believed, is the result of (1) a thorough analysis of the company, which leads to a promise of (2) safety of principal, and (3) a satisfactory return.

Graham as a Writer

Graham's writing style was clear, muscular, lively. Buffett's writing style is similar.

> "To achieve *satisfactory* investment results is easier than most people realize; to achieve *superior* results is harder than it looks."
>
> "If you want to speculate do so with your eyes open, knowing that you will probably lose money in the end; be sure to limit the amount at risk and to separate it completely from your investment program."
>
> "Never buy a stock immediately after a substantial rise or sell one after a substantial drop." Wait until the dust settles.
>
> ". . . a sufficiently low price can turn a security of mediocre quality into a sound investment opportunity—provided that the buyer is informed and experienced and that he practices adequate diversification."
>
> ". . . the risk of paying too high a price for good-quality stocks—while a real one—is not the chief hazard confronting the average investor in securities. Observation over many years has taught us that the chief losses to investors come from the purchase of *low-quality* securities at times of favorable business conditions." In a bull market, you can mistake a dog for a thoroughbred.

Another famous comment of his: In the short run, the market is a voting machine. In the long run, it's a scale. In other words, emo-

GEICO

One of Graham's most interesting investments came in 1948, when Graham and Newman used $720,000, which was 25 percent of their firm's total assets, to buy a half interest in the Government Employees Insurance Company, which sold auto insurance to government employees directly, by mail. Because GEICO had no salespeople to pay, it could offer low rates. And government employees tend to be especially safe drivers. Eventually the $720,000 investment was to become worth a cool $500 million.

But by 1977 GEICO was in serious trouble and had lost 95 percent of its value at its peak. GEICO was to play a key role in Buffett's investment career.

tions determine where the market is now; in the long run, reality counts.

> "The farther one gets from Wall Street, the more skepticism one will find, we believe, as to the pretensions of stock-market forecasting, or timing."

He was not in favor of buying good companies and holding them indefinitely. Most businesses, he wrote, change over the years, for the better or (perhaps more often) for the worse. "The investor need not watch his companies' performance like a hawk; but he should give it a good, hard look from time to time."

On the subject of asset allocation, Graham revealed his sense of humor. He was in favor of an investor's determining what percentage of stocks and bonds should be in his or her portfolio. "The chief advantage, perhaps, is that such a formula will give him something to do. As the market advances he will from time to time make sales out of his stockholdings, putting the proceeds into bonds; as it declines he will reverse the procedure. These activities will provide some outlet for his otherwise too-pent-up energies." Those energies may have otherwise impelled him to go with the crowd and buy recent winners.

Also: ". . . any approach to moneymaking in the stock market which can be easily described and followed by a lot of people is by its terms too simple and too easy to last."

And: "A substantial rise in the market is at once a legitimate reason for satisfaction and a cause for prudent concern."

Many of his observations were provident. He was dubious of new issues, initial public offerings, because they tend to be brought to market when the pot is bubbling over.

The Later Years

Graham married three times. He liked women, Buffett observed, and women liked him. Even though physically he resembled Edward G. Robinson, the heavy-set actor, Graham "had style." In his later years Graham moved from New York to La Jolla, California, taught at the University of California at Los Angeles, and later still settled in the south of France, where he died in 1976.

In his late 70s, he told a friend that he hoped to do "something foolish, something creative and something generous every day." (Buffett joked that Graham got the foolish thing done before breakfast.)

His friends recognized him as a man of great kindness, but reserved. He lived modestly. Once he and his student, Buffett, were going out to lunch at a deli, and Graham told him, "Money won't make any difference to you and me, Warren. We'll be the same. Our wives will just live better."

He was generous with his time and with his money. On his birthday, he would give his *employees* presents. When Buffett had a son, Graham gave Buffett a movie camera and a projector. Buffett named the son Howard Graham, after his father, and his teacher.

Buffett on Graham

Buffett wrote of Graham's *Security Analysis*, "I read the first edition of this book early in 1950, when I was about nineteen. I thought then that it was by far the best book about investing ever written. I still think it is. . . .

"To me, Ben Graham was far more than an author or a teacher. More than any other man except my father, he influenced my life."

After Graham's death, Buffett wrote this tribute to him: "A remarkable aspect of Ben's dominance of his professional field was that he achieved it without that narrowness of mental activity that concentrates all effort on a single end. It was, rather, the incidental byproduct of an intellect whose breadth almost exceeded definition. Certainly I have never met anyone with a mind of similar scope. Virtually total recall, unending fascination with new knowledge, and an ability to recast it in a form applicable to seemingly unrelated problems made exposure to his thinking in any field a delight."

Buffett then referred to Graham's hope to do something foolish, creative, and generous every day of his life:

"But his third imperative—generosity—was where he succeeded

beyond all others. I knew Ben as my teacher, my employer, and my friend. In each relationship—just as with all his students, employees and friends—there was an absolutely open-ended, no-scores-kept generosity of ideas, time, and spirit. If clarity of thinking was required, there was no better place to go. And if encouragement or counsel was needed, Ben was there.

"Walter Lippman spoke of men who plant trees that other men will sit under. Ben Graham was such a man."

CHAPTER 5

The Influence of Philip Fisher

Whereas Benjamin Graham emphasized buying securities cheaply and selling them when they become reasonably priced, Philip A. Fisher emphasizes buying fine companies, "bonanza" companies, and just holding onto them. Despite their seeming differences, both men favor conservative investments—held for the long term.

Graham was number oriented: quantitative. Fisher is more of an artist: qualitative. Before buying a stock, he evaluates the excellence of a company's product or service, the quality of management, the future possibilities for the company, and the power of the competition.

Buffett seems to be ambidextrous, a disciple of both philosophies, an investor both qualitative and quantitative.

Not That Fisher

Fisher is not to be confused with Yale professor Irving Fisher, remembered best for having said in 1929, just before the crash, that stocks had seemingly reached a permanently high plateau.

Philip Fisher is a money manager and a practical, original, insightful thinker. Buffett admired his book, *Common Stocks and Uncommon Profits* (1958), and later visited with him. "When I met him, I was as much impressed by the man as by his ideas," Buffett wrote. "A thorough understanding of the business, obtained by using his techniques . . . enables one to make intelligent investment commitments."

Reading Fisher, one is struck by how much in his debt Buffett is. In fact, while Buffett has said that he is 15 percent Fisher and 85 percent Graham, the split seems closer to 50 percent–50 percent.

Philip Fisher began his career as a securities analyst in 1928, after graduating from Stanford Business School. He founded Fisher & Company in San Francisco in January 1931, seemingly not an auspicious time. But it turned out to be exactly right. After suffering two terrible years in the stock market, investors were disgusted with their current brokers and willing to listen, "even to someone both young and advocating a radically different approach to the handling of their investments as I," he wrote in *Developing an Investment Philosophy*. Besides, business was so slow, executives had plenty of time to kill. "In more normal times," he remembers, "I would never have gotten past their secretaries."

One man, on being informed by his secretary that a fellow named Fisher wanted to chat with him, decided that "Listening to this guy will at least occupy my time." He became a long-time client. Later, he told Fisher, "If you had come to see me a year or so later [when the economy had begun reviving], you would never have gotten into my office."

In 1932, after working many hours, Fisher wound up with a net profit of $35.88. The next year, business picked up considerably: The net profit surpassed $348. "This was possibly about what I would have made as a newsboy selling papers on the street."

But by 1935 his business was humming along, and eventually he developed a small band of loyal and well-to-do clients.

A Growth Investor

By accompanying one of his business school professors on visits to companies, Fisher had learned a good deal about the nitty-gritty of businesses. He is also blessed, like Buffett and Charles Munger, with a mind that sees the big picture, unencumbered by preconceptions and trivialities. His book, *Common Stocks and Uncommon Profits and Other Writings by Philip A. Fisher*, is still impressive for both its practicality and its subtlety.

Fisher is squarely in the growth camp, and writes disdainfully of value investors and their preoccupation with numbers. He grudgingly admits that the "type of accounting-statistical activity which the general public seems to visualize as the heart of successful investing will, if enough effort be given it, turn up some apparent bargains. Some of these may be real bargains. In the case of others, there may be such acute business troubles lying ahead, yet not discernible from a purely statistical study, that instead of being bargains they are actually selling at prices which in a few years will have proven to be very high." In other words, some ugly ducklings grow up into even uglier ducks.

In the nineteenth century, according to Fisher, value investing was the fashion. People would buy stocks during busts and sell them for higher prices during booms. Still, he is sure that growth investing, buying healthy, glamorous stocks, has always been the wiser course. "Even in those earlier times," he writes, "finding the really outstanding companies and staying with them through all of the fluctuations of a gyrating market proved far more profitable to far more people than did the more colorful practice of trying to buy them cheap and sell them dear."

Fisher defines outstanding companies as those "that over the years can grow in sales and profits far more than industry as a whole." His version of growth investing targets mainly big companies, not small companies, and it calls for a buy-and-hold strategy. While most growth investors trade frequently, those whose battlefields are large-company stocks, like Fisher, generally hate parting with their holdings.

In judging companies, Fisher is more the artist as opposed to the scientist. That means checking out the management, learning about company morale, studying the product or service, evaluating the sales organization and the research department—that sort of thing.

Early in his *Common Stocks* book, in fact, is a chapter entitled Scuttlebutt. You can learn a lot about a company, Fisher argues, through the business grapevine, talking to competitors, to knowledgeable people in general, in order to judge a particular company's research, its sales organization, its executives, and so forth. "Go to five companies in an industry, ask each of them intelligent questions about the points of strength and weakness of the other four, and nine times out of ten a surprisingly detailed and accurate picture of all will emerge." You can also learn much from vendors and customers, executives of trade associations, and research scientists. Also interview former employees, recognizing that some may have

A Bonanza Company

- **It has capable management, people determined that the company will grow larger and able to carry out their plans.**
- **The company's product or service has a strong potential for robust, long-term sales growth.**
- **The firm has an edge over its competitors and any newcomers.**

special grievances against the company. Finally, interview the company's own officers.

What if the information you obtain through the grapevine is conflicting? Then you're not dealing with a truly outstanding company. If it's a bonanza company, the information will be decidedly favorable.

Forget about companies that promise profits but only temporarily—because of a one-time event, such as a shortage of this metal or that product. And be dubious of new companies.

Not that Fisher doesn't have a foot in the other camp. Buy bonanza companies when the entire market is down—or when the stock is down because of bad news. Don't ignore the numbers. Check the financial statements, see how much money is spent on research, look into abnormal costs, study a breakdown of sales by product lines.

Once you have identified what appears to be a bonanza company, Fisher proposed, subject the company to a 15-point test, some focusing on the company itself, some on the management.

Fisher's 15 Questions

1. **Does the company's product or service promise a big increase in sales for several years?** He cautions against firms that show big jumps due to anomalous events, like a temporary shortage. Still, judge a company's sales over several years because even sales at outstanding companies may be somewhat sporadic. Check on management regularly, to make sure it's still top-notch.
2. **Is management determined to find new, popular products to turn to when current products cool off?** Check what the company is doing in the way of research to come up with the newer and better.

3. **How good is the company's research department in relation to its size?**
4. **Does the company have a good sales organization?** Production, sales, and research are three key ingredients for success.
5. **Does the company have an impressive profit margin?** Avoid secondary companies. Go for the big players. The only reason to invest in a company with a low profit margin is if there's powerful evidence that a revolution is in the offing.
6. **What steps is the company taking to maintain or improve profit margins?**
7. **Does the company have excellent labor and personnel relations?** A high turnover is an unnecessary expense. Companies with no union, or a company union, probably have good policies—otherwise, they would have been unionized. Lots of strikes, and prolonged strikes, are obviously symptoms of sickness. But don't rest easy if a company has never had a strike. It might be "too much like a henpecked husband" (too agreeable). Be dubious about a company that pays below-average wages. It may be heading for trouble.
8. **Does the company have a top-notch executive climate?** Salaries should be competitive. While some backbiting is to be expected, anyone who's not a team player shouldn't be tolerated.
9. **Does management have depth?** Sooner or later, a company will grow to a point where it needs more managers, ones with different backgrounds and skills. A good sign: Top management welcomes new ideas, even criticism, from below.

Quotable

One of my favorite passages from Fisher's book is: Beware of companies, too, where management is cold blooded. "Underneath all the fine-sounding generalities," he writes, "some managements have little feeling for, or interest in, their ordinary workers. . . . Workers are readily hired or dismissed in large masses, dependent on slight changes in the company's sales outlook or profit picture. No feeling of responsibility exists for the hardships this can cause for the families affected." No wonder Buffett admired him when he met him in person!

10. **How good is a company's cost analysis and accounting?** Management must know where costs can be cut and where they probably can't be cut. Most companies manufacture a large variety of products, and management should know the precise cost of one product in relation to others. One reason: Cheap-to-produce products may deserve special sales efforts.

11. **Are there any subtle clues as to how good a company is?** If a company rents real estate, for example, you might check how economical its leases are. If a company periodically needs money, a spiffy credit rating is important. Here, scuttlebutt is an especially good source of information.

12. **Does the company have short-range and long-range plans regarding profits?** A company that's too short-term oriented may make tough, sharp deals with its suppliers, thus not building up goodwill for later on, when supplies may be scarce and the company needs a big favor. Same goes for treatment of customers. Being especially nice to customers—replacing a supposedly defective product, no questions asked—may hurt in the short run, but help later on.

13. **Might greater growth in the future lead to the issuance of more shares, diluting the stock and hurting shareholders?** A sign that management has poor financial judgment.

14. **Does management freely own up to its errors?** Even fine companies run into unexpected problems, such as a declining demand for their products. If management clams up, it may not have a rescue plan. Or it may be panicking. Worse, it may be contemptuous of its shareholders. Whatever the reason, forget about "any company that withholds or tries to hide bad news."

15. **Does management have integrity?** Does management require vendors to use brokerage firms owned by the managers themselves, or their friends or relatives? Does management abuse stock options? Put its relatives on the payroll at specially high salaries? If there's ever a serious question whether the management is mindful enough about its shareholders, back off.

What and When to Buy

Investors should put most of their money into fairly big growth stocks, Fisher maintains. How much is "most"? It could be 60 percent or even 100 percent, depending on the investor.

In general, don't wait to buy. Buy an outstanding company now. What if economists fret that a recession is coming, citing all sorts of worrisome numbers? Economic forecasting, Fisher argues, is so unreliable, you're better off just ignoring it. He compares it to chemistry in the days of alchemy.

Obviously, if you buy a growth company when it's somewhat cheap, you'll wind up doing better. So "some consideration should be given to timing." For example, management might have made a mistake in judging the market for a new product, causing earnings and share price to fall off the table. Or a brief strike has hit the company. During this time, management was buying shares like mad, but the stock price kept retreating. Another good time to buy.

Clearly, an investor must make sure that management really is capable—and that a company's troubles are short lived, not permanent.

What if yours is a modest portfolio and you are nervous about stashing your savings into the stock market in one fell swoop? What if a business bust came along? Fisher advocates dollar-cost averaging—investing regularly over a period of time. Beginning investors, after having made a start buying big growth companies, "should stagger the timing of further buying. They should plan to allow several years before the final part of their available funds will have been invested."

Fisher advocates patience. "It is often easier to tell what will happen to the price of a stock than how much time will elapse before it happens." In other words, stay the course. You may just be a quicker thinker than other investors, and you'll just have to wait until they catch up to you. Occasionally, he warns, it may take as long as five years for excellent investments to reward you for your perseverance.

When to Sell

In a classic statement, Fisher wrote: "If the job has been done correctly when a common stock is purchased, the time to sell it is—almost never."

Only three reasons exist for selling the stock of a company previously judged outstanding:

1. **The original purchase was a mistake.** Trouble is, we may not be ready to come clean. "None of us like to admit to himself that he has been wrong." He goes on: "More money has probably been lost by investors holding a stock they really did not want until they could 'at least come out even' than for any other single reason." (Fisher was thus anticipating one of the theorems of the behavioral economists, that of loss aversion.)
2. **The company has changed.** Maybe the quality of management has deteriorated. "Smugness, complacency, or inertia replace the former drive and ingenuity." Forget about the nasty capital-gains taxes you might pay. Sell. Then again, maybe the company has simply aged, and so have its products and services. The growth is no longer there. The company no longer passes most of the 15 points. Again, sell. But now you can take your time.

   A good test: Will the stock climb during the next business boom as much as it has in the past? If not, the stock should probably be sold.
3. **There's a better buy out there.** But this seldom happens.

Other reasons to hold onto a stock: The capital-gains tax. And the fact that a stock that's sold now just might soar during the next bull market. And how is the investor to know when to buy back in?

What if a stock is reported to be "overpriced"? Again, this is mainly a matter of conjecture. Who knows what the earnings will be two years from now?

What if a stock has made a big run-up—isn't it time to sell now? Hasn't it used up most or all of its potential? Fisher's answer: Outstanding companies "just don't function this way." They tend to go up and up and up. And you want to be there when that happens.

Things That Investors Should Not Do

- **Don't buy into initial public offerings (IPOs).** There is a greater chance for error when you invest in a company without a track record. Besides, the hotshots who are launching the company are terrific salespeople, or inventors, but otherwise may be nerds lacking other skills, such as a knowledge of marketing. So even if an IPO is seductive, let others invest. There are plenty of wonderful opportunities among established companies:

- **Don't ignore a stock just because it's not listed on the New York Stock Exchange.** (These days, with so many fine tech stocks trading on Nasdaq, that advice is easy to heed.)
- **Don't buy a stock for trivial, secondary reasons, such as that its annual report is attractive.** The annual report may just reflect the skill of the company's public relations department—and not indicate whether the management team is capable and can work together harmoniously, or whether the product or service has a rosy future. With common stocks, "few of us are rich enough to afford impulse buying."
- **Don't assume that a stock with a high price-earnings ratio won't ever trade any higher.** If the company continues to thrive, why shouldn't its p-e ratio go higher still? Some stocks that seem high priced may be the biggest bargains. (When Jeremy Siegel of the Wharton School studied the "nifty fifty" stocks of the 1970s, he found that a few stocks with astronomically high ratios deserved them. Years later, it was clear that McDonald's, with a p-e ratio of 60 back then, deserved one of more than 90.)
- **Don't nickel and dime things.** Don't bother about small amounts of money. If you want to buy a good company with a bright future, and it's $25.50, why insist on paying just $25.40 and possibly losing out on a fortune?
- **Don't pay excessive attention to what doesn't matter that much.** For example, past earnings and past prices—or anything past. Zero in on what's going on now and what may happen in the future. (Not that you should completely ignore past earnings and price ranges.)

  "The fact that a stock has or has not risen in the last several years is of no significance in determining whether it should be bought now."
- **When considering a growth stock, think about when to buy as well as the price.** Let's say that a stock is selling at $32. You think it might fall to $20—because $20 is what it's really worth right now. Or if everything turns out for the best, the stock might climb to $75 in five years. Should you buy it now? Or wait to see if it falls to $20?

  The conventional wisdom would answer: Dollar-cost average. Nibble at it for a while.

  But Fisher's is an original mind. His curious solution: Buy the stock at a specific time in the future. Maybe five months from now, a month before a pilot plant is scheduled to go online. In short, wait until more evidence comes in.

- **Don't follow the crowd.** The conventional wisdom is often wrong. One day, the entire investment world thinks that the pharmaceutical industry is near death. A little later, the entire investment world thinks the pharmaceutical industry is a cure-all. Fisher remembers when Wall Street was sure that a depression would occur after World War II. It turned out to be a "mass delusion."

  Recognizing that the majority opinion can be just plain wrong can "bring rich rewards in the field of common stocks." It's hard psychologically to buck the crowd, of course. But it will help if you recognize that the financial community is usually slow in acknowledging that something has changed drastically. (Almost all of us, in fact, feel the pain of "cognitive dissonance" when we must change our views because of powerful evidence to the contrary.)

- **Don't overstress diversification.** It's true that every investor will make mistakes, and if you have a reasonably diversified portfolio, an occasional mistake won't prove crippling. But investors should not try to own the most but the best.

  Diversification is such an honorable word that investors aren't aware enough of the evils of being overdiversified. You may wind up with so many securities that you cannot monitor them adequately. Owning companies you aren't familiar enough with may be even more reckless than not having a well-diversified portfolio. How many stocks did Fisher think was too many? If you have only $250,000 to $500,000, he thought that as many as 25 was "appalling."

Fisher's Advice for the Small Investor

- **Confine your investments to blue chips, like IBM and DuPont.** In this case, five stocks should be enough. Put 20 percent of your money into each one. What if 10 years go by, and one of the stocks constitutes 40 percent of the portfolio—the others not having fared quite so spectacularly? If you're still happy with your original choices, let things ride. Forget about rebalancing everything back to 20 percent.

  Make sure there is little overlap among these five investments—that their products and services don't compete. Don't buy Coke and Pepsi, or two banks, or two biotech companies.

Still, if you have a good reason to concentrate in one area, go for it. It might prove a very profitable bet.

- **If you confine yourself to smaller companies, halfway between the blue chips mentioned above and young, risky growth companies with good management teams, you might have 10 investments—each with 10 percent of your assets.** In putting together this portfolio of mid-caps, you might underweight the riskier investments, giving them an 8 percent cut of your portfolio rather than 10 percent, and presumably overweighting those stocks that seem less speculative.
- **Then there are the truly speculative companies, those that promise the world and where you might wind up with sixpence.** Here, Fisher's advice is: Don't put any money in them that you cannot afford to lose. And if you're a larger investor, be sure that your original investment is no more than 5 percent of your total portfolio.

How to Find Growth Stocks

Identifying growth stocks that you should buy and perhaps hold onto forever and ever is, in Fisher's opinion, a multi-part process.

1. **Winnow down the names of promising stocks.** The best source: professional investors who have proved their worth. They provide around 80 percent of his best tips. In second place: friendly business executives or scientists. Rarely do good tips come from brokerage bulletins or from financial or trade magazines. (These days you can't walk down the street without tripping over a few stock tips. Most of them, so to speak, have been around the block a few times. Still, in my own opinion, recent tips in the media from top people, whose reputations are on the line, may be worth paying attention to. Some professional investors even rush out to buy Barron's on Saturday mornings every week, when it first comes out.)
2. **Next, study the financials.** Look at sales by product line, the competition, insider ownership, profit margins, extent of research activity, abnormal costs in previous years. Talk to key customers, competitors, suppliers, former employees, scientists in similar industries.
3. **Finally, approach the management.** And be sure that you're prepared. Fisher doesn't talk with management until he has at

least 50 percent of the knowledge he needs to make an investment. A side benefit: The more you impress management with your knowledge and insight, the more cooperative management may be with you.

How many firms does Fisher visit for every stock he buys? An acquaintance of Fisher's estimated one in 250. Another gentleman proposed one in 25. The true ratio: one to every two or 2.5. That's because of all the research he does. If the question had been, how many companies does he look at, one in 40 or 50 might be correct. If the question had been, how many companies has he considered before buying one, the answer might have been around one in 250.

CHAPTER 6

How Value and Growth Investing Differ

People tend to think of "value" and "growth" investing as being at different ends of a continuum, with "blend" in the middle.

Value stocks have low price-earnings ratios and low price-to-book ratios. They're cheap, or seem to be cheap. Growth stocks have high price-earnings ratios, high price-to-book ratios. They're not cheap, and don't seem to be cheap. If certain value stocks are cigar butts, as Graham called them, growth stocks are a big box of fresh Cuban cigars.

Blend stocks are in the middle, of course. Blend mutual funds may concentrate on blend stocks, or have a virtually equal quantity of both value and growth stocks—like an index fund of the Standard & Poor's 500 Stock Index.

But maybe these two investment strategies actually come from the same roots.

As Chris Browne of Tweedy, Browne has pointed out, an investor can buy property on the Upper West Side of Manhattan cheaply—or buy property on Park Avenue cheaply. It's just that the Upper West Side was more reasonably priced in the first place. Still, in both cases you're buying property that's undervalued. Buying and holding Park Avenue property makes *this* kind of growth investing similar to value investing. GARP, it's called, for "growth at a reasonable price."

As Buffett has observed, value and growth investing are connected at the hip.

Quite Different

The fact that growth and value are intimately connected doesn't mean that they are identical, or even blood brothers. Extreme growth and extreme value remain very different. Extreme growth is something that Buffett never buys. And if you are to invest like Buffett, you should have a clear idea of what value investing is and what it isn't.

Buffett did buy extreme value at one point in his career, and then—when the amount of money he had to invest was significantly larger than the amount of extreme value stocks to buy—he shifted toward GARP stocks, stocks of glamorous companies that, if they weren't exactly cheap, weren't exorbitantly expensive either.

Let's review some of the basic differences between growth and value stocks.

Growth stocks are those of companies doing very nicely, thank you. Their earnings are up, their sales are up, their prices are up. Up are also such measures of their popularity as their price-earnings ratios (price divided by last year's earnings, typically) and the price-book ratio (price divided by assets per share outstanding).

You can find growth stocks in the daily list of companies setting new highs for the year. Or inside the portfolios of noted growth investors, like many of the people who run Janus funds or the Alger funds (where many Janus people trained).

Value stocks are typically those of companies down on their luck, unloved and unwanted. Maybe they were once riding high, but now they're wallowing in the muck. Their price to earnings ratios are low and their price to book ratios are low. Value investors may look for good buys among stocks dropping to new lows for the year or inside the portfolios of noted value investors, like some of the people described in later chapters of this book.

Value stocks are not stocks of high-priced companies that have fallen a bit from their highs. A growth stock must fall down an elevator shaft to become a value stock. A stock that hit $120 last week, that earns $3 a year, has a p-e ratio of 40 ($120/$3.00). It may be $108 now, after having fallen 10 percent. But its p-e ratio would still be a lofty 36. Even if it dropped another 20 percent, to $96, its p-e ratio would be 32. The stock would have to drop 50 percent before its p-e

Growth, Value, and Baseball

Baseball yields a metaphor that can explain the difference between stocks.

A growth stock is a .300-hitter, a Derek Jeter. If you want to buy him for your team, you will pay dearly. But if he hits .300 or more, he will have been worth it.

A value stock is someone who batted .300 . . . two years ago. Last year he hurt his wrist and hit .212. Now he comes cheap. But if his arm heals and he hits .300 again, you'll have what Peter Lynch has called a ten-bagger. (That may help explain why, over the years, value stocks have fared better than growth stocks. Value investors are being compensated for their courage in buying out-of-favor stocks.)

ratio became a more reasonable 20 times earnings. Or its earnings would have to rise from $3 a share to $6 a share.

Growth Versus Value Funds

Some key differences between average large-company growth and large-company value funds are highlighted in Table 6.1.

Value funds tend to own companies with higher debt levels . . . to buy and sell less frequently (lower turnover) . . . to pay higher dividends . . . to have lower volatility . . . to suffer more modest losses . . . and to own smaller company stocks.

Surprisingly, the expense ratios of the two kinds of funds are similar. Because value funds trade less often, one might have expected their expenses to be lower. The number of stocks in the average portfolio was also similar, although one might have expected value funds to have fewer—because, presumably, their managers know their stocks better. The same situation holds true for small-value funds and small-growth funds.

To underscore the radical differences between value and growth, let's look at a real, no-nonsense value find: Clipper. It's a fund whose strategy resembles Buffett's: assembling a concentrated portfolio of cheap but good companies. Data are from January 6, 2001, Morningstar Mutual Funds.

At the same time, we shall examine a real, no-nonsense growth fund: Fidelity Aggressive Growth. It's a fund whose strategy is the opposite of Buffett's, assembling a varied portfolio of expensive

TABLE 6.1 Typical Large-Value Funds versus Typical Large-Growth Funds

MEASUREMENT	LARGE VALUE FUND	LARGE GROWTH FUND
Debt v. total capitalization	34.5%	26%
Turnover	71%	120%
Yield	0.8	0.1
Beta	0.81	1.14
Standard deviation	18.37	30.21
Biggest quarterly loss (since 1996)	–12.20% (3Q, 1998)	–16.50% (4Q, 2000)
Size of typical company held	34.3—giant 38.6—large 24.3—medium median market capitalization: $35,449 million	46.0—giant 37.6—large 14.3—medium median market capitalization: $69,308 million
Five biggest holdings	Citigroup ExxonMobil IBM SBC Comm. Verizon Comm.	Cisco Systems EMC Pfizer Sun Microsystems General Electric

Data Source: Morningstar

but fast-growing companies. Data are from May 31, 2000. (See Table 6.2)

Typical Mistakes

A good way to keep the differences between growth and value in mind is to focus on the worst mistakes these different kinds of investors make.

Value investors buy too soon. A stock goes down, investors buy in—then discover there's a basement below the basement. (It's called a dungeon.)

Value investors also sell too soon. A cheap stock soars—and no longer qualifies as a value stock, so value investors will sell. Sometimes the stock keeps going up. "I've left a lot of money on the table," confessed Marty Whitman, a famous value player.

TABLE 6.2 At the Extremes

DATA	S&P 500	CLIPPER FUND	FIDELITY AGGRESSIVE GROWTH
Price to earnings ratio	33.45	18.4	41.6
Price to book ratio	8.70	4.70	9.30
Three-year earnings growth rate	17.16%	11.1%	26.5%
Price to cash flow ratio	25	11.50	31.30
Turnover		63%	186%
Yield	1.1%	2.5%	0%
Beta	1	0.37	1.53
Standard Deviation	19.8	14.92	50.83
Biggest quarterly loss (since 1996)		–4.31% (3Q 1999)	–10.31% (2Q 2000)
Biggest overweightings		Financials and Staples	Technology and Services
Size of stocks		7.3% —Giant	27.4% —Giant
		49.3% —Large	42.5% —Large
		37.7% —Medium	23.7% —Medium

Data Source: Morningstar

Easy Analysis

An easy way to tell which is ahead at any particular time, value or growth, is to compare Vanguard Value Index's return with that of Vanguard Growth Index, mutual funds that follow the two different strategies. Vanguard now has small-cap value and small-cap growth, mid-cap value and mid-cap growth index funds, too, though they are newer.

When do value stocks do well and when do growth stocks? One theory is that when people are optimistic, they buy growth; when they are worried, they buy value. Another theory is that no one really knows when one or the other will start doing better.

Growth investors buy too late. A stock's price soars—and the growth player arrives just as the party is beginning to break up.

Growth investors also sell too late. A hot stock misses its earnings estimate by a few pennies, and it's boiled in oil, burned at the stake, drawn and quartered.

Funds to Consider

Obviously, Buffett would not buy true growth stocks when they are at their peak of popularity and very likely overpriced. But he would buy fine companies when they are selling at reasonable prices—and hold on and on.

Could any growth funds fit under the Buffett umbrella? Very few have low turnovers. Even the Torray Fund, which does, is categorized by Morningstar as a value fund because of its low numbers.

But a few growth funds are exceptions, a leading one being White Oak Growth, managed by James D. Oelschlager. True, the stocks in the fund have high numbers (price to earnings ratio, price to book, price to cash flow, earnings growth); and there's plenty of technology spread across the fund. Still, the fund gloms onto glamorous names and trades very seldom. Its turnover: 6 percent in 1999, 6 percent in 1998, 8 percent in 1997, 8 percent in 1996. The fund is also concentrated: 23 stocks with $5.5 billion in assets. The prospectus reports that the fund "selects securities that it believes have strong earnings potential and reasonable market valuations relative to the market in general and to other companies in the same industry." Finally, the fund has a superlative record: Over the past five years, it has beaten the S&P 500 Index by more than 10 percentage points a year.

In 2001, alas, the fund hit an air pocket and fell to earth.

Another growth fund that seems to reflect the Fisher–Munger side of Buffett: SteinRoe Young Investor. The fund's turnover in recent years has been around 45 percent; its valuation numbers are high but below average for a growth fund. And some glamorous

White Oak Fund

Minimum investment: $2,000
Phone number: (800) 462-5386
Web Address: www.oakassociates.com

SteinRoe Young Investor

Minimum investment: $2,500
Phone number: (800) 338-2550
Web address: www.steinroe.com

names pop up in the portfolio, intended to appeal to teenagers: Wells Fargo and Disney, for instance.

These low-turnover growth funds assuredly don't qualify as Buffett-type funds. But if someone already has exposure to Buffett-type stocks, a fund like White Oak might be appropriate for diversification. In 1999, when Berkshire itself did poorly, White Oak rose 50.14 percent.

CHAPTER 7

Buffett's 12 Investing Principles

Ask different people to identify what's at the heart of Warren Buffett's investment strategy, and you may get different answers: He buys only a few especially good securities or companies; he buys and holds; he buys companies with a "margin of safety"—cheaply; he buys companies that promise to grow and grow until kingdom come; he buys companies that sit on top of a mountain and cannot be dislodged; or, he buys companies whose managers sit on the right hand of God.

All of these are true enough.

But a more unifying view of Buffett's strategy is that, at bottom, he is not a gambler. He invests in what he considers almost sure things.

To reduce risk to the minimum, Buffett has followed a variety of sensible strategies, and all of them can be copied, more or less, by investors in general. They are listed below. We will explore them in the chapters to come.

1. **Don't gamble.**
2. **Buy securities as cheaply as you can. Set up a "margin of safety."**
3. **Buy what you know. Remain within your "circle of competence."**

4. **Do your homework. Try to learn everything important about a company. That will help give you confidence.**
5. **Be a contrarian—when it's called for.**
6. **Buy wonderful companies, "inevitables."**
7. **Invest in companies run by people you admire.**
8. **Buy to hold and buy and hold. Don't be a gunslinger.**
9. **Be businesslike. Don't let sentiment cloud your judgment.**
10. **Learn from your mistakes.**
11. **Avoid the common mistakes that others make.**
12. **Don't overdiversify. Use a rifle, not a shotgun.**

CHAPTER 8

Don't Gamble

At the heart of Warren Buffett's investment philosophy is simply this: He has a powerful aversion to gambling. He is unusually risk averse. If we human beings have a gene for gambling—a gene that prompts us to want to relentlessly risk our wealth on a throw of the dice or the draw of a card—Buffett either never had it or he has repressed it.

Yet a drive to gamble is something that supposedly unites wealthy people. In his entertaining book *How to Be a Billionaire*, Martin S. Fridson argues that the very wealthy got that way by taking "monumental risks." True, "Not every self-made billionaire has been a financial daredevil, but all have dared to reject the safe-but-sure path."

Examples that Fridson gives:

Developer Dennis Washington repeatedly pledged his home as security with the bonding company underwriting his projects.

Steve Ballmer, sales chief of Microsoft, bought $46 million worth of Microsoft stock after it received an unfavorable ruling in litigation with Apple Computer.

Kirk Kerkorian was known as a high roller at Las Vegas craps tables.

Fridson adduces other evidence: Billionaires, he claims, tend to be interested in card games, especially poker. Names he mentions: H.L. Hunt, John Kluge, William Gates, Carl Icahn, Kirk Kerkorian. Then he adds: "Warren Buffett's fraternity brothers at the Wharton School of the University of Pennsylvania remember him chiefly for playing bridge."

Buffett certainly enjoys playing bridge. He plays online; he plays in tournaments. But as far as I know, he has never played bridge for big money—or poker for that matter. And as card games go, bridge may depend the least upon chance.

Fridson has a point. Wealthy businesspeople may have a knack for judging the odds accurately, enabling them to win all sorts of contests beyond gambling contests.

But Buffett is no gambler. A gambler takes adventurous risks. A dictionary definition of gambling: "To stake money or any other thing of value on an uncertain event." Remember that word "uncertain." If someone bets on the odds-on favorite, is that really gambling? Is it gambling to do what John Templeton did in the 1930s, before the outbreak of World War II—buy one share of every stock on the New York Stock Exchange?

Buffett puts his money only on what he considers almost sure things. "The financial calculus that Charlie and I employ," he has said, "would never permit our trading a good night's sleep for a shot at a few extra percentage points of return. I've never believed in risking what my family and friends have and need in order to pursue what they don't have and don't need."

Writes Chris Browne of Tweedy, Browne, "The key is certainty. Mr. Buffett wants to invest in businesses that he is certain will have significant competitive advantages 10, 20, 30 years from now. This is a very high threshold, and eliminates most companies from consideration. By knowing what he cannot do, that is, knowing that he cannot predict earning power in 10, 20, or 30 years for most businesses, Mr. Buffett wastes no analytical time and effort studying the 'unknowables' and focuses on businesses he considers knowable."

An investor, Browne points out, can understand Nestle's Cocoa or Listerine, and make a good guess about their earning power. But who can estimate the future earning power of Laura Ashley's dresses or Ralph Lauren's fashion items or Martha Stewart's products?

True, Buffett does make big bets. But one can argue that a big bet on an almost sure thing does not qualify as gambling. Would it be gambling to bet that the first President of the United Sates was George Washington? Or that an ice cube will melt if tossed into a fire?

His being risk averse makes Buffett very different from many other investors—professionals and nonprofessionals, the successful and the unsuccessful. Think of Peter Lynch buying a stock, so that its being in his portfolio would prompt him to take an intense interest in that stock. Or keeping the faith in Chrysler; buying all those troubled savings-and-loan stocks in the early 1990s. (I once asked him if he could name all the stocks in his portfolio. Of course not, he answered; 150 of his stocks begin with the word "First.") Think of George Soros, shorting the British pound; losing a fortune during the crash of 1987. Garrett Van Wagoner, whose funds had dizzying turnovers of 778 percent and of 668 percent in a single year. Or think of all the investors in recent years who bought Internet stocks, just because they had been going up and up.

Make Money with Less Risk

The lesson for investors in general is that it's possible to make a lot of money in the stock market without being a daredevil—if you buy cheap, if you've done your research, if you acknowledge your limitations, if sometimes you're a contrarian.

While many investors are indeed risk averse, fearful even of investing in stocks and not CDs, many of them are also addicted to risk. They want excitement. They want to see their securities leap up, or down, because it makes their adrenalin flow, their breath come fast.

A pediatrician I know, Earle Zazove of Chicago, gave up the practice of medicine because, he confessed, he could diagnose what was wrong with all the kids in line to see him just by looking across his waiting room. So, because he was interested in investing and because many of his friends wanted him to manage their money, he gave up the practice of medicine to become a money manager.

What startled him as he settled into his new career was that so many of his clients wanted excitement more than they wanted profits. They wanted to become rich quickly—or even *poor* quickly. For them, investing was almost the same as gambling.

Some individuals, in fact, disdain mutual funds in favor of individual stocks because most mutual funds are so stable, so dull. And I confess that I'm not especially interested in buying index funds. I want to *beat* the market, not *be* the market. Buying an index fund, as someone has said, is like kissing your sister (or brother).

To invest like Warren Buffett, in short, may mean that you forgo excitement and thrills. You buy good companies temporarily out of favor—and you just hang on. You don't dart in and out, like day traders; you don't buy companies that have just a few choice breaths of life left in them; you don't buy hot stocks, intending to sell them just before they start cooling off. You buy stodgy and safe almost sure things.

Buffett has compared buying stocks to a batter swinging at pitches in baseball: If you don't swing at a pitch that's in the strike zone, you may be called out. But in the investment world, if you pass by an almost sure thing, there are no adverse consequences. So, why not wait? And wait?

Here is how Buffett has put it:

> "In his book *The Science of Hitting*, Ted [Williams] explains that he carved the strike zone into 77 cells, each the size of a baseball. Swinging at balls in his 'best' cell, he knew, would allow him to bat .400; reaching for balls in his 'worst' spot, the low outside corner of the strike zone, would reduce him to .230. In other words, waiting for the fat pitch would mean a trip to the Hall of Fame; swinging indiscriminately would mean a ticket to the minors.
>
> "If they are in the strike zone at all, the business 'pitches' we now see are just catching the lower outside corner. If we swing, we will be locked into low returns. But if we let all of today's balls go by, there can be no assurance that the next ones will be more to our liking. Perhaps the attractive prices of the past were the aberrations, not the full prices of today. Unlike Ted, we can't be called out if we resist three pitches that are barely in the strike zone. . . ."

Risk Aversion

Buffett's disdain for risk can be seen in other aspects of his investment strategy.

He stays within his "circle of confidence." He doesn't normally sell short; he has mostly avoided foreign stocks; he has avoided technology.

There is a telling anecdote about Buffett.

Every other year, he and some old friends go to Pebble Beach to play golf. In the 1980s, Jack Byrne, who had taken over GEICO, proposed a side bet among the players. If someone put up $11, then made a hole-in-one during that weekend, Byrne would pay that person $10,000. Everyone else put up the $11.

Buffett thought it over and decided that the odds weren't favorable enough—at 909.9 to 1. He wouldn't fork over the $11.

An aversion to gambling.

Perhaps his aversion to change stems in part from the trauma of his having to move to the Washington, D.C., area from Omaha as a young man. But I suspect that he also avoids risk so passionately because he feels such strong loyalty to his shareholders. He is determined that they not lose any money at all. His original shareholders did him the service of trusting him; many were friends and still are, and many are also relatives.

In fact, while Buffett seems an affable, gentle person, I think one thing that riles him—besides public criticism—is the suggestion that he is not an extremely risk-resistant investor.

Would a risk-averse investor own so few stocks? Here is his response:

"Many pundits would . . . say the strategy [concentrating on a few companies] must be riskier than that employed by more conventional investors. We disagree. We believe that a policy of portfolio concentration may well decrease risk if it raises, as it should, both the intensity with which an investor thinks about a business and the comfort-level he must feel with its economic characteristics before buying into it."

The kind of investment that Buffett prefers is, to use a word he often bandies about, "certain." As in, "I would rather be certain of a good result than hopeful of a great one." And: ". . . we are searching for operations that we believe are virtually certain to possess enormous competitive strength ten or twenty years from now. A fast-changing industry environment may offer the chance for huge wins, but it precludes the certainty we seek."

What odds does he want?

In 1965, he has written, there might have been a 99 percent probability that if he had borrowed money to invest, the results would have been good.

Buffett wrote, "We wouldn't have liked those 99:1 odds—and never will. A small chance of distress or disgrace cannot, in our view, be offset by a large chance of extra returns. If your actions are sensible, you are certain [!] to get good results. . . ."

CHAPTER 9

Buy Screaming Bargains

This is the cornerstone of our investment philosophy: Never count on making a good sale. Have the purchase price so attractive that even a mediocre sale gives good results.

—Warren Buffett

Buffett remains mum about stocks he is buying or is about to buy, but he has been pretty open about explaining his general investment strategy. His strategy, unfortunately, is not so simple as it may first appear. He uses a number of different gauges and sometimes buys stocks that don't seem to fit his criteria very snugly. And he is a qualitative as well as a quantitative investor, using not just science and numbers, but art.

Still, he has one vital rule: Try to buy entire companies, or their stock, cheap. That will provide the "margin of safety" that Benjamin Graham was so intent upon. If something goes amiss, you won't lose much—because a margin for error (or just bad luck) has been built in.

Alas, it's not easy to distinguish between a stock that's cheap and a stock that's fully priced or even overpriced. A few years ago a portfolio manager showed me a "screaming bargain," a good company with simply unbelievably wonderful numbers: UST. Formerly U.S. Tobacco.

In other words, a seeming screaming bargain might just turn out to be a problem stock. And the numbers alone won't help you decide which is which.

Of course, one way of dealing with this is to buy a number of stocks that seem to be screaming bargains. Enough of them should turn out to be the genuine article, providing you with a decent profit.

But that's not Buffett's way. He wants to identify true screaming bargains in advance, and not take a chance that some of his choices won't work out. He wants near certainty. Yes, there are screaming bargains out there, and that is what Buffett is searching for—the occasional, sometimes very occasional, screaming bargain.

In any case, one should remember, as the poet Richard Wilbur said, there are 13 ways (at the very least) of looking at a blackbird. There is no magic mathematical formula that will enable you and your calculator to identify the stocks that Buffett might buy next. Still, there are some relatively simple screens, as we shall see, that can help investors identify promising companies; and the more screens that a particular stock passes, the merrier an investor may wind up being.

What exactly is a "screaming bargain" that Buffett is searching for? One definition is a cheap stock of a financially healthy company selling an ever-popular product, employing excellent salespeople and gifted researchers, with a splendid distribution network. All managed by capable people.

To evaluate the financial health of a company and whether its stock is cheap or not, you can check its return on equity, book value, earnings growth, ratio of debt to equity, and the current value of its future cash flow. All are useful; none are surefire. Which explains why it is good for an investor to have an edge, to know a little more about an industry or a particular stock than someone who just goes by the numbers.

Rules of Thumb

Let's begin with one of the most important gauges of a company's prosperity:

Look for companies with high and growing return on equity (ROE).

"Equity" is the net worth of all of a company's assets. To calculate "return on equity," divide the equity into net income, also called "operating earnings." (Net income is calculated after removing preferred stock dividends—but not common stock dividends.)

ROE = net income/(ending equity + beginning equity/2)

This formula calculates ROE for a specific time period, typically a year. You add the value of the company at the beginning of the period to the value at the end of the period, then divide by two to get the average yearly value of the company.

Example:

ROE = $10,000,000/($35,000,000 + $45,000,000/2), or 22.2 percent

You must be careful about the number on top, the numerator—there are many ways to calculate it. Buffett excludes from yearly earnings any capital gains and losses from a company's investment portfolio, along with any unusual items. He wants to focus on what management did with the company assets during what might be an ordinary year.

A company's yearly return on equity tells you whether its management has been using its assets profitably and efficiently.

"The primary test of managerial economic performance," Buffett has written, "is the achievement of a high earnings rate on equity capital employed (without undue leverage, accounting gimmickry, etc.) and not the achievement of consistent gains in earnings per share."

What's wrong with "consistent gains in earnings per share"? A company could use a portion of its earnings in Year One to invest conservatively (say, in a bank account) for Year Two, then use that for Year Three, and so on. Every year, record earnings, right? Sure, but eventually the return on equity would drop to the bank deposit's rate of interest.

A company could, of course, zip up its earnings by boosting its debt, too. By borrowing a lot of money to invest, by boosting its equity-to-debt ratio, a company could readily increase its return. Not kosher, Buffett believes. "Good business or investment decisions will produce quite satisfactory economic results with no aid from leverage," he has said.

Not that he is totally dubious of debt. If there's a fine opportunity available, he wants the money to take advantage of it—even if he must borrow. As he has said, "If you want to shoot rare, fast-moving elephants, you should always carry a gun."

To increase return on equity, according to Buffett, a company can increase sales or make more of a profit from sales, lower the taxes it must pay, borrow money to invest or to expand, or borrow money at lower interest rates. It could buy another company that has been doing well. Or sell off a losing division. Or buy back shares. Or lay off employees whose absence would not affect the bottom line.

A rising ROE is a good sign, especially if it's high compared with its competitors.

By and large, returns on equity average between 10 percent and 20 percent. ROEs over 20 percent (certain industries tend to have higher ROEs than others) are impressive, but this might be largely because of a brisk economy. And as companies grow larger, their ROE tends to decline. Companies with consistently high returns on equity are uncommon. Still, high returns on equity will sooner or later translate into a higher stock price.

The Value Line Investment Survey and Standard & Poor's Stock Reports will give you the data you need, or you might check such web sites as Business.com and MSN MoneyCentral Investor.

Look for those rare companies with regular 15 percent growth in their earnings.

Buffett wants a minimum of 15 percent to compensate him for taxes, the risk of inflation, and the riskiness of stocks in general. Simple math will help you determine whether a stock may bless you with 15 percent or more a year. Look at (1) its current price, (2) its earnings growth rate in the past few years, or (3) look up analysts' estimates on various financial web sites. Remember that the 15 percent return should include dividends.

Earnings growth can be misleading. What if revenues grew faster, meaning that profits actually declined? Or if earnings grew because of the sale of assets? What if the company's prosperity is already reflected in the stock price? Check the company's current price-to-earnings ratio, compare it with its competitors' ratios, and compare it with its historical price-to-earnings ratio.

Look for companies with high profit margins.

Well-managed companies are always trying to cut costs, and a rising profit margin may indicate that costs have indeed come down. The question is: Will the profit margin be sustainable? Maybe the price of a raw material, like paper, came down temporarily. Or the company enjoyed a one-time tax write-off.

Of course, some companies always have high margins (movie studios), while others tend to be relatively low (retail stores).

Look for a company whose book value has been growing regularly.

At the beginning of his annual reports, Buffett does not trumpet how much, or how little, Berkshire's stock has risen. He talks about its "book value," what the company is worth per share, or what the owners would receive if Berkshire went bankrupt, the company was sold, and every shareholder received a little piece.

Since Buffett took over Berkshire in 1965, book value has grown a remarkable 24 percent a year. Book value may not be a perfect gauge of value, but it's better than a stock's price, which depends on the economy, the stock and bond markets in general, and investor psychopathology.

"The percentage change in book value in any given year is likely to be reasonably close to that year's change in intrinsic value," Buffett has said.

Companies whose book value has not changed over the years tend to be stodgy old companies, like U.S. Steel. Their stock prices are, at best, stable. Companies whose book value has been increasing regularly tend to be fast-growing companies, and their stock prices tend to soar alongside the growth in book value.

A company can raise its book value by boosting its profits (cutting costs, introducing popular new products or services), by acquiring profitable companies, and by having high returns on its assets. Berkshire is unusual in that its book value rises whenever the stocks it owns rise in price.

But book value can also climb if a company issues more shares, diluting the value of current shareholders' stock, so be mindful of the tricks a company can play.

Buy companies without worrisome debt.

A debt/equity ratio of 50 percent or lower is considered the industry standard, although many other measures are available. A rising debt/equity ratio may be a cause for concern. Also be wary of a big jump in accounts payable—bills that haven't been paid.

Buy companies whose cash flow indicates that they are cheap in comparison to what they will be worth down the road. In short, their intrinsic value is high.

The firm of Tweedy, Browne, whose investment philosophy resembles Buffett's, has published a paper entitled, "The Intrinsic Value of a Growing Business: How Warren Buffett Values Businesses," quoting—and then expanding—on what Buffett has already said about his favorite strategy.

"The value of any stock, bond, or business today," wrote Buffett, "is determined by the cash inflows and outflows—discounted at an appropriate interest rate—that can be expected to occur during the remaining life of the asset."

In other words, the value of a security or a business is the cash it generates from now on. But because cash in the future is worth less than cash you get now (you can invest cash you get now, and very safely, in government bonds), you must lower the value of the future cash you might get ("discount" it) by the amount of interest on that money that you did not receive. Ten dollars ten years from now might be worth paying only $7 for now—depending on the interest rate you use. The higher the current interest rate, the less you would pay now for the $10—because the more interest you would have forgone while waiting to collect the $10.

Next, a practical definition from Buffett of "intrinsic value," or what a company is actually worth.

> Let's start with intrinsic value, an all-important concept that offers the only logical approach to evaluating the relative attractiveness of investments and businesses. "Intrinsic value" can be defined simply: It is the discounted value of the cash that can be taken out of a business during its remaining life.
>
> The calculation of intrinsic value, though, is not so simple. As our definition suggests, intrinsic value is an estimate rather than a precise figure, and it is additionally an estimate that must be changed if interest rates move or forecasts of future cash flow are revised. Two people looking at the same set of facts, moreover—and this would apply even to Charlie and me—will almost inevitably come up with at least slightly different intrinsic value figures.

Intrinsic value is rarely the same as market value, the value of all of a company's outstanding stock. Market value can be influenced by investor psychology, the economic climate, and so forth. A closed-end mutual fund, for example, may sell for more than, or less than, or exactly for what its underlying assets are actually worth. (Such a fund, traded as a stock, owns a variety of securities.) Usually such funds sell at discounts, although no one is quite sure why.

In another talk, Buffett has pointed out:

> If you had the foresight and could see the number of cash inflows and outflows between now and Judgment Day for every company, you would arrive at a value today for every business that was rational in relation to the value of every other business.
>
> When you buy stocks or bonds or economic assets, you do so by placing cash in now to receive cash later. And obviously, you're looking for the highest [rate of return]. . . .
>
> . . . Once you've estimated future cash inflows and outflows, what interest rate do you use to discount that number back to arrive at a present value? My own feeling is that the long-term government rate is probably the most appropriate figure for most assets . . .
>
> . . . When Charlie and I felt subjectively that interest rates were on the low side, we'd be less inclined to be willing to sign up for that long-term government rate. We might add a point or two just generally. But the logic would drive you to use the long-term government rate.
>
> If you do that, there is no difference in economic reality between a stock and a bond. The difference is that the bond may tell you what the

> cash flows are going to be in the future—whereas with a stock, you have to estimate it. [With most bonds, you are promised a specific return year after year.] That's a harder job, but it's potentially a much more rewarding job.
>
> Logically, if you leave out psychic income, that should be the way you evaluate a firm, an apartment house, or whatever. And in a general way, Charlie and I do that.

By "in a general way," he means not slavishly. It's not the only way he estimates what a company is worth.

Here's an easy example that Buffett gave: Let's say that you have a bond, or an annuity, that pays you $1 a year—forever—and that long-term interest rates are currently 10 percent. What is your annuity worth? Well, 10 percent of what is $1? Answer: $10.

But what if that annuity pays you 6 percent more every single year? From $1.00 to $1.06 to $1.12 to $1.19 and so forth. Now your annuity is worth more: $25 rather than $10. Obviously, the more an investment grows in the future, the more you should be willing to pay for it.

Tweedy, Browne has further explained how the numbers work. What would you pay now to receive $1 in 12 months if you wanted a 10 percent return? Answer: $0.90909 cents. That's calculated by subtracting the money you *didn't* get during the year while you were waiting

($1 – $0.090909 = $0.90909.)

What would you pay now to receive $1 in two years if you wanted a 10 percent compounded rate of return on your money over two years? Answer: 82.65 cents. Obviously, the longer you must wait to receive your money, the less you would pay for that future money today.

To estimate the intrinsic value of common stocks, you would estimate the future cash flow of a company a certain number of years from now, then figure out what you would pay for the stock today for that cash flow in the future.

If you try to value a company whose cash earnings are expected to grow fast, you might find that even a very high purchase price is warranted. As Tweedy, Browne points out, if Coke's earnings were to grow at a 15 percent annual rate for the next 50 years, each $1 of current earnings would grow to $1,083.65 over 50 years. The current intrinsic value, assuming a 6 percent discount rate, would be $58.82, or about 59 times current earnings.

Buffett has owned Coke when it had a very high p-e ratio of 65.

But if Coke's future earnings increase at a 15 percent yearly rate, then a 65 p-e ratio "may turn out to be a bargain." In short, "The math tells you that long-run earnings growth is worth a lot." Hence the wisdom of buying and holding winners.

In Chapter 20, as we will see, in order to compile a list of stocks Buffett might approve of, Standard & Poor's analyst David Braverman estimates a company's free cash flow five years from now, being guided by its recent growth in earnings. Then, to discount the cash flow that investors would receive in five years, he divides the cash flow by the current yield on 30-year Treasuries, coming up with a current valuation. Any stock selling for more than that, he discards.

Tweedy, Browne acknowledges the value of this method of calculating intrinsic value, but notes that you must be dealing with companies whose future cash flows are somewhat predictable—Coca-Cola, for example, rather than Laura Ashley's dress business.

CHAPTER 10

Buy What You Know

Buffett has certain favorite phrases, such as "margin of safety." Another is "circle of competence." He tries to invest only in companies and industries about which he is especially knowledgeable, such as insurance companies, where he has an edge. If he is going to buy a house, he wants to know a lot about the community (taxes, safety, reputation of the schools, local controversies) and the neighborhood (could a gas station go up next door? are schools within walking distance?). If he is going to play any card game, for money, he wants to be knowledgeable about the rules and thoroughly familiar with time-tested winning strategies.

To specialize in certain types of investments—convertible bonds, pharmaceutical stocks, closed-end mutual funds, semiconductor stocks, fast-food restaurants, whatever—seems to be a perfectly obvious and perfectly sensible investment strategy. If you know a little more than other investors about one stock or one industry, you will have a small advantage that, once in a while, could prove profitable; the advantage will be compounded by the self-confidence you enjoy, which might bolster your courage to buy more when others are selling and to sell when others are clamoring to buy.

Buffett happens to know a lot about banks. In the early 1990s, when savings and loans across the nation were in hot water, Wells

Fargo's stock suffered along with everyone else's. One respected analyst was fiercely negative about the stock; another, buoyantly optimistic. Buffett knew that Wells Fargo was an exception. Management had resisted making risky loans to foreign countries; it had lots and lots of cash in reserve. Buffett dived in.

Specializing in one or more industries is especially suitable for people who happen to labor in that particular line of work. Computer programmers might incline toward technology stocks, journalists in media, physicians in health-care stocks. As one doctor boasted to me, he was aware of which companies always seemed to be coming up with important new products, which companies had the most knowledgeable salespeople, which companies were the most respected by physicians in general.

So, why don't investors in general establish a niche and remain there?

There are social pressures on people to become Renaissance men and women, to be familiar with painting, history, music, astronomy, wine, horse racing, cards, baseball, and everything else under the sun. All-around people, not nerds specializing in computers, mutual funds, or residential real estate.

Even actors who can play different roles get special adulation, a remarkable example being Robert De Niro, who has portrayed everyone from a boxer to a mobster to a bus driver to a protective parent.

Versatility is certainly desirable and admirable; no one wants to be a nerd.

But versatility isn't easy to achieve. When Jussi Bjoerling, the great operatic tenor, was scolded for being so wooden on stage, he scornfully replied, "I am a singer, not an actor."

And if, as an investor, you want to carefully avoid gambling, to avoid taking enormous risks, you should specialize in your stock selections and not try to cover the waterfront. Yes, you should have a well-diversified portfolio, but perhaps by buying mutual funds in those areas you're inexpert in. For the individual stocks in your portfolio, you might determine what you are good at, or what you want to be good at, and cultivate your garden.

Buffett deliberately and thoughtfully has specialized; he has not tried to impress other people with his versatility:

- He has generally avoided investing in foreign stocks.
- He has also kept away from technology stocks, although he was savagely abused for this early in 2000, before the technology disaster struck.

- He has avoided commodity-type companies, those that produce a product that others can easily emulate and where the resulting intense competition keeps profits down.

Staying out of Technology

Explaining why he has avoided technology stocks, Buffett wrote:

> If we have a strength, it is in recognizing when we are operating within our circle of competence and when we are approaching the perimeter. Predicting the long-term economics of companies that operate in fast-changing industries is simply beyond our perimeter. If others claim predictive skill in those industries—and seem to have their claims validated by the behavior of the stock market—we neither envy nor emulate them. Instead, we just stick with what we understand. If we stray, we will have done so inadvertently, not because we got restless and substituted hope for rationality. Fortunately, it's almost certain there will be opportunities from time to time for Berkshire to do well within the circle we've staked out.

In 1998 and 1999 Buffett resisted suggestions as well as tirades that Berkshire invest in technology stocks, explaining that he and Charles Munger "believe our companies have important competitive advantages that will endure over time. This attribute, which makes for good, long-term investment results, is one Charlie and I occasionally believe we can identify. More often, however, we can't—at least not with a high degree of conviction. This explains, by the way, why we don't own stocks of tech companies, even though we share the general view that our society will be transformed by their products and services. Our problem—which we can't solve by studying up—is that we have no insights into which participants in the tech field possess a truly *durable* competitive advantage."

For the general public, a sensible alternative would be to buy a lot of technology stocks—via a mutual fund, perhaps. But buying a dozen or two dozen tech companies, betting on an entire industry, while reasonable, is not typically Buffett's strategy. It's too much like gambling.

Buffett has quoted an appropriate maxim: "Fools rush in where angels fear to trade."

CHAPTER 11

Do Your Homework

One of the most common mistakes made by investors is to neglect local enterprises in favor of distant concerns. This is often very foolish, especially on the part of the small investor, because it is much easier for him to get the essential facts in regard to a local bond or stock.

What perverse trait of human nature makes us overlook the near-by opportunity? Why is all the romantic glamour monopolized by far away things?. . . The man with a thousand dollars to invest displays exactly the same pathetic but very human trait that the boy or girl who supposes they would be much happier if they could get away from home. . . .

A man in Cleveland wants to know about a picayune, irresponsible, fly-by-night promoter in New York. There are dozens of strong banking and brokerage firms in Cleveland. A resident of Maryland wants to know about a swindling bucket shop in a certain Western State. Does he not know that some of the oldest and strongest investment dealers in investment securities hail from Baltimore?

—from *Putnam's Investment Handbook*, by Albert W. Atwood, Lecturer at Columbia University (New York: G.P. Putnam's Sons, 1919)

There are legendary stories of Buffett's being asked to invest in one thing or another, and making up his mind with the speed of summer lightning. In one instance, a businessman, Robert Flaherty, phoned Buffett at home in 1971 to ask if he would be interested in buying See's Candy Shops, a chain of chocolate stores in California.

"Gee, Bob, the candy business. I don't think we want to be in the candy business." Then silence.

Flaherty and his secretary tried to call Buffett again, but the secretary mistakenly called him at his office. When she finally reached him at home, after a few minutes, the first thing that Buffett said was, "I was taking a look at the numbers. Yeah, I'd be willing to buy See's at a price." He bought it for $25 million.

Sometimes, when the numbers are good and the business is fine, Buffett will act quickly. But otherwise he becomes an ordinary gumshoe, trying to find out everything he can about a company.

As a student at Columbia Business School, he learned that Ben Graham was chairman of Government Employees Insurance Company in

Washington, D.C. On a Saturday, Buffett took a train to Washington and went to GEICO's offices in the now-deserted business district.

The door was locked. He kept knocking until a janitor appeared. Buffett asked: "Is there anyone I can talk to besides you?"

The janitor agreed to take him to a man working on the sixth floor, who turned out to be Lorimer Davidson, financial vice president. He and Buffett talked for four hours.

Recalled Lorimer, "After we talked for 15 minutes I knew I was talking to an extraordinary man. He asked searching and highly intelligent questions. What was GEICO? What was its method of doing business, its outlook, its growth potential? He asked the type of questions that a good security analyst would ask. . . . He was trying to find out what I knew."

Buffett was impressed. He then visited some insurance experts, who told him that the stock was overpriced. He came down on the side of GEICO, and put most of his savings, $10,000, in the stock. When he returned to Omaha to work with his father, the first stock he sold was GEICO. Today, of course, Berkshire Hathaway owns all of GEICO.

A Gumshoe

As a gumshoe, Buffett is not like Nero Wolfe, never budging from his New York City brownstone and his orchids, letting Archie Goodwin go out and do all the in-person investigating. Buffett goes out into the field. He gets his hands dirty.

Byer-Rolnick manufactured hats. Buffett visited Sol Parsow, who owned a men's shop in Omaha where Buffett bought his suits. What did Parsow think of that company? Said Parsow, "Warren, I wouldn't touch it with a 10-foot pole. Nobody is wearing hats anymore." Certainly President Kennedy wasn't.

Buffett listened. He didn't buy.

Not long after, Buffett became interested in a company in New Bedford, Massachusetts, that made suit liners. He went back to Parsow. "Sol, what's going on in the suit industry?" "Warren, it stinks," was the reply. "Men aren't buying suits."

Buffett should have listened. Instead, he went ahead and kept buying shares of Berkshire.

Thinking of buying shares of American Express during a time when that company was involved in a scandal, Buffett visited Ross's Steak House in Omaha. He stationed himself behind the cashier and watched as customer after customer continued using American Express cards. He checked with banks and travel agencies in Omaha, and yes, they were still selling American Express traveler's checks. He found that American Express money orders were still popular with supermarkets and drugstores. He even spoke with American Express's competitors.

Buffett then bought in.

When Buffett became interested in Disney stock, he dropped in to a movie theater in Times Square to see Disney's latest film, *Mary Poppins*. He looked around the theater; he was the only adult not accompanied by a child. He also noticed how rapt the audience was when the film began. Later, Buffett actually visited with Walt Disney himself on the Disney lot and was struck by his enthusiasm about his own work.

Going out into the field, or at least making a lot of phone calls, is a good way to get an edge over other investors. Tom Bailey, who founded the Janus funds in Denver, would tell his analysts to visit the supermarkets and other stores in town and find out what customers were buying.

A smart former Fidelity money manager, Beth Terrana, once told me about visiting a company she was interested in and interviewing its chief financial officer. The CEO decided to listen in on the meeting, and remained for two hours. Terrana decided not to buy the stock. One reason: Didn't the CEO have anything better to do?

In general, money managers want company officers to have a clear game plan for the future. They want to emerge from a meeting with the managers knowing a lot more than they knew before, having a better appreciation of the problems and the possibilities. Sometimes, listening to someone explain things, you quickly recognize that the person has fresh, persuasive insights that you had been lacking; sensible explanations for what had previously been annoying mysteries. That can build a lot of confidence.

As mentioned, whatever industry you already know a little about is a good place to consider investing. A local company, or a national company with a local office, is also a good place to look. In your hometown, you will meet employees, competitors, suppliers, customers. The local newspaper will carry stories, "scuttlebutt," as Phil Fisher called it.

Investing in your own employer may not be a wonderful idea because you don't want to keep your nest egg and your job security in the same basket. But if you deeply admire your employer, the risk of putting your savings where your job is may be worth it.

Employees of Microsoft aren't complaining about the fortunes they made there.

Find out everything you can about a company before you invest. That way, not only will you know more than other people who trade the stock; you'll *know* you know more. Value investors, when they see a stock they like go down, buy more shares.

Read the annual report and the 10-K; read the Value Line Investment Survey, Standard & Poor's "The Outlook," brokerage reports; check the web site; speak with shareholder relations. Try out the product or the service.

You might even visit stores and speak to salespeople.

That's what Lise Buyer, a former analyst for T. Rowe Price Science & Technology, used to do in Baltimore. Every month she would bop around the computer shops. "What's selling?" she would ask a clerk. "What's hot? What's being returned? What are people saying? What are they looking for? What are they complaining about?"

"Don't those salespeople," I asked, "figure out that you're a pro?" "Yes," she conceded with a smile, "sometimes they do, but by the time they figure out who I am, they're gone. There's a big turnover in computer stores."

If you were looking for a house to buy, you would compare different houses in different neighborhoods. You would inspect any house you are interested in from top to bottom, even looking in the basement for water stains on the walls. You would speak with the owners ("Does the roof leak?") and check with neighbors ("Any flooding septic tanks hereabouts?"). You would hire a home inspector and a termite inspector. You might pay for a formal appraisal. You would dicker about the price. And then, after three months, you would buy. And you would normally buy to hold.

Warren Buffett buys stocks the way he buys houses. And he's lived in his Omaha house a long, long time.

CHAPTER 12

Be a Contrarian

If you want to outperform the stock market, to do better than the Standard & Poor's 500 or the Dow Jones Industrial Average, you must be willing to be different. There's nothing terribly wrong with doing as well as the market by buying an index fund—if you're an individual investor. But professionals are hired to beat the index, or at least to do as well while incurring less risk.

You can beat the index by:

- Moving from stocks to cash or to bonds at a time when you think stocks are overvalued, or by stocking up when you think stocks in general are cheap
- Concentrating on buying stocks that seem cheap because investors are too pessimistic and impatient—whereas, because of your special knowledge, you know better
- Concentrating on buying thriving companies that don't seem excessively expensive because investors aren't sufficiently optimistic (the growth strategy)
- Avoiding the common, almost irresistible, psychological mistakes that other investors make

- Taking advantage of other investors' misconceptions, and betting big against prevailing opinions. As Buffett once remarked, "I will tell you the secret of getting rich on Wall Street. You try to be greedy when others are fearful and you try to be very fearful when others are greedy." Contrarian investing in a nutshell.

Investors, being of average intelligence and average perspicacity, can jump to the wrong conclusions and misinterpret the evidence. That's when shrewd investors can clean up.

How often are the mass of investors extremely wrong? Not often. That's why Buffett and Munger talk about a few great opportunities that may come along in a lifetime, a few really fat pitches.

Where do you find grossly mispriced stocks? Some money managers scout around for new acquisitions amid the list of stocks hitting new lows for the year.

Where *don't* you find underpriced stocks? In conversations at cocktail parties. If everyone is boasting of how much money they made in Internet stocks for example, the end is near. Writes James Gipson of the Clipper Fund: "The cocktail party test is an unscientific but useful test of conventional wisdom." This celebrated contrarian continues: "The best investment policy is to avoid what everyone else is buying; the best social policy is to be discreet about it." You don't want to offend people; you also don't want them to steal your ideas.

In my own case, the best investment decisions I ever made were to hold on, not to sell, even when I was plenty worried. When Johnson & Johnson stock tumbled after someone poisoned a bottle of Tylenol, I hung on. The price went down maybe 10 points, then rebounded, thanks to the company's energetic efforts to snuff out the flames. No, I wasn't smart enough or self-confident enough to buy more shares. But I felt sure that this, too, would pass.

When the Clintons came into office and prepared to shake up the drug industry, I resolutely held onto all my health-care stocks, recognizing the vast power of the health-care industry in this country. Again, I wasn't smart enough or courageous enough to buy more shares. I recall giving a tip to a woman who asked for investment advice: Vanguard Health Care Portfolio, I told her. Disgusted, she turned away. She had lost enough money on health-care stocks, she said over her shoulder. Probably the only really worthwhile stock tip I've given in my entire life.

It may not be generally recognized, but Buffett has a genius for bucking trends. In 1975, at the end of the crash of 1973–1974, he was buying everything he could lay his hands on; he was a child let loose in a toy store. In 1987, before the crash, he was complaining that there was little to buy. In 1999 and 2000, he was skeptical of the stock market in general.

The first time I heard of Buffett was when he was buying GEICO in 1976, when the company seemed close to bankruptcy. The stock had been $42 in 1974; now it was below $5. I was then a resident of New Jersey and a GEICO customer; GEICO sought a rate increase in New Jersey and was denied. I then received a notice that GEICO was leaving the state and would no longer offer me a policy. For someone named Warren Buffett to be buying GEICO stock at that time, I thought, was very, very strange.

The Contrarian Personality

Being a contrarian seems to require a certain personality type. Contrarian investors are in the habit of being skeptical of the conventional wisdom. When the market is going up, for example, their joy is restrained: There's less for them to buy, and it's time to consider selling. When the market is sinking, their spirits soar: Macy's is having a bargain sale.

Apparently the investing public can make big mistakes because people have trouble dealing with complex, conflicting information—such as on the direction of interest rates or the direction of the stock market. People like to simplify things, to overdramatize things, to jump to easy conclusions.

Contrarians are ready at all times to secede from the majority, to express their sourly skeptical views. Buffett, unlike Ben Graham, now believes that buying great companies slightly cheaply is a good strategy, and that one need not fear that the next bear market and the next depression are lurking around the corner.

Of course, being contrarian requires a good deal of self-confidence, too. That probably comes from having a good self-image (it helps, psychologists tell me, if your mother loved you); and from previous and profitable lessons gleaned about the folly of other investors.

But it also helps to not have too much confidence. As Gipson has pointed out in his book *Winning the Investment Game* (New York: McGraw-Hill, 1987), "Too much confidence can be as dangerous as too little. Just as an insecure investor is prone to rely on consensus thinking, an overconfident investor is liable to think he can do no wrong after a period of unusually good profits. . . . The investor who runs a little scared and is prepared to question assumptions, recheck analyses, and recognize mistakes early is likely to fare better."

Contrarian investors, he also writes, never feel comfortable when they make their best buys. As a contrarian Neuberger Berman manager once confessed to me, he tries to ignore the queasy feeling in the pit of his stomach, holds his nose—and buys.

But Gipson is flat out wrong when he argues that "When it comes to making money and keeping it, the majority is always wrong." More people invest in index funds these days than in any other kind of stock fund—and they are doing the right thing. But Gipson is flat out right when he claims that unusually successful investing, as Ben Graham said, often entails just selling to the optimists and buying from the pessimists.

Be Confident

Buffett is forever fretting about losing money and making mistakes, but when he's sure, he's sure. He waits and waits, and when his pitch comes he swings for the seats. He is modest in confessing his lack of knowledge; he is bursting with confidence on those occasions when he is sure of himself. At one point in his career, American Express was most of his investment portfolio.

Self-confidence is something value investors need. Very often their strategy doesn't work, and for long periods of time. And while they may be willing to continue carrying the flag with bombs exploding all around them, the people they work for or with may not be so patient and forbearing. In 1999 some value managers actually lost their jobs—and many others began moving further and further toward the growth side of the continuum by nibbling on high-priced technology stocks. Buffett himself was savagely abused by certain individuals for not having dived in headfirst into technology. "What's wrong, Warren?" was the memorably misleading cover line on an issue of *Barron's*.

Those who dived in, not surprisingly, wound up hitting bottom.

Ignoring the Herd

It's not just in his investing style that Buffett is unconventional. He has no qualms that his stock stands out from the herd because of its high price. Or that its name conveys nothing. Or that his annual meetings are so different from other annual meetings. Or that Berkshire has so small a staff. Too many people, he believes, confuse the "conservative" with the "conventional."

He himself doesn't pay much mind to the voice of the people. He isn't interested in stock tips.

"In some corner of the world they are probably still holding regular meetings of the Flat Earth Society," Buffett has written. "We derive no comfort because important people, vocal people, or great numbers of people agree with us. Nor do we derive comfort if they don't."

CHAPTER 13

Buy Wonderful Companies

Here are examples of stocks or entire companies that Buffett has purchased, all of which have turned out to be big winners.

Government Employees Insurance Company

In 1976 Buffett accumulated almost 1.3 million shares of GEICO, an auto insurance company, at an average of $3.18 per share. GEICO was in big trouble at the time. It was actually close to bankruptcy. In 1976 the company reported a loss of $1.51 per share. The year before it had lost $7.13 per share.

Apparently the root cause of the trouble was that GEICO was insuring too many problem drivers, whose claims were keeping the company from being profitable. A sign that a company is overextended: Its sales are more than three times its equity, the value of the stocks all shareholders own. GEICO's insurance sales were $34 per share in 1975, almost 16 times shareholders' equity.

Meanwhile, its income from investments was a meager $0.98 per share. If the company could at least break even on its insurance underwriting and stop losing money, a purchase price of $3.18 per share would be only a little more than three times the earnings of $0.98 a share. A terrific bargain.

Besides, there were reasons to be optimistic. The company had hired John Byrne, a former manager of Travelers Insurance Company, as its new president. Beyond that, GEICO had an edge: It sold auto insurance very cheaply. Unlike almost all other auto insurance companies, GEICO sold directly to the public, bypassing insurance agents and their sales commissions. That gave GEICO a clear advantage over other insurance companies, which would antagonize their current agents if they decided to skip over them and sell directly—and more cheaply.

Could another insurance company come along and compete with GEICO? Unlikely. Yes, there was a "moat," as Buffett would call it. Even if a new company entered the business with low prices, GEICO could lower its own prices. A new company obviously would have a formidable task taking business away from GEICO.

Byrne proved to be a magician. Among other things, he dumped bad insurance risks wherever possible, including everybody in New Jersey—including me. Result: Between 1976 and 1995 GEICO sales shot up from $575 million to $2,787 million, and sales per share rose from $16.84 (adjusted for the issuance of convertible preferred stock in 1976) to $206.44 (adjusted for stock splits).

In 1996 Berkshire Hathaway bought most of the remainder of GEICO's shares, at $350 a share. This price valued the shares at 20.1 times earnings, which was reasonable. From 1976 to 1996 the compounded increase in the stock's price was around 27.2 percent a year.

The Washington Post Company

Buffett had paid an average of $4 a share for the Washington Post by June of 1973. The Post owned not just the leading newspaper in the nation's capital, but *Newsweek* magazine, three television studios, and one radio station back then. What was the Washington Post really worth? Buffett checked what other newspapers, magazines, TV, and radio stations had recently been sold for and figured that the Post was worth $21 a share.

A daily newspaper that has no major competition from another daily, Buffett believed, enjoys a keen edge. People get accustomed to the newspaper and its columnists; they are unlikely to switch to another newspaper, even if its price is a nickel or a dime less. Newspapers, after all, are relatively cheap to buy and put out; it is the advertising that supports papers.

Under capable leadership (remember the Watergate reporting?), the Washington Post Company blossomed. Between 1972 and 1998, sales compounded at 9.1 percent a year and sales per share at 11.8 percent. Earnings per share soared 15.5 percent a year, from $0.52 to $21.90. The stock's price-earnings ratio expanded from 7.7 in 1972 to 26.4 in 1998, rising from $4 a share in 1973 to $578 a share at the end of 1998. The compounded increase in the stock's price over 25 years was 22 percent.

Coca-Cola

When news reports announced that Buffett had purchased 6.3 percent of the stock of Cola-Cola, some people were puzzled. In 1989 the stock seemed overpriced—and it was certainly not something Ben Graham would have bought. Buffett had acquired the stock in 1988 and 1989 at an average price of $43.85 a share. That was 15.2 times the 1988 earnings per share of $2.88.

It was a big bet. Coke then represented 32 percent of Berkshire's stockholder equity (as of the end of 1988) and 20 percent of Berkshire's stock market valuation.

Still, Coke is the best-known brand name in the world and the world's largest producer and marketer of soft drinks. It sells almost half the soft drinks consumed on the entire planet, in almost 200 countries, and easily outsells its main competitor, Pepsi-Cola. Best of all, it still has a tremendous number of potential customers abroad.

Coca-Cola, Buffett said, was a stock he could comfortably hold onto for 10 years. In talking about Coke, he even evoked one of his favorite words: "certainty."

"If I came up with anything in terms of certainty," he has said, "where I knew the market was going to continue to grow, where I knew the leader was going to continue to be the leader—I mean worldwide—and where I knew there would be big unit growth, I just don't know anything like Coke."

Coke clearly had a moat around it—a moat filled with a certain carbonated beverage. Its 1997 after-tax profits per serving were less than half a cent, or just 3 cents from a six-pack of Coke. Yes, there are competitors—beyond just Pepsi-Cola; but competing against Coke on price, taste, and marketing is not a winner's game.

Coke boasted in 1989 that it would require more than $100 billion to replace Coke as a business. Commented Buffett, "If you gave me $100 billion and said take away the soft drink leadership of Coca-Cola in the world, I'd give it back to you and say it can't be done."

At the end of 1998, Coke's price (adjusted for splits) was $536, or 47.2 times 1988 earnings per share of $11.36. The price-earnings ratio had expanded from 15.2 in 1988 to 47.2 in 1998. From 1988 to 1998, an investment in Coke returned around 28.4 percent a year.

In recent years Coke has suffered: troubles in Europe, a strong dollar. The p-e ratio recently was only 38.9. In 2000 the price sank to $42—and it hadn't been that low since 1996. Still, in 2001 most of Coke's troubles seem to be past, and Value Line was predicting a brisk pickup in profits. "Coke is still an extremely strong company, with one of the world's best-known brand names and considerable financial strength," wrote Value Line's Stephen Sanborn, "and its longer-term prospects are favorable."

As a stock, it sounds like one that Warren Buffett might buy.

American Express

Tweedy, Browne, the investment adviser, boasts that it invested in American Express a year or two before Buffett himself bought shares. Yet, ironically, Chris Browne has written that Tweedy, Browne's investment was the result of a "Buffett 101" type of competitive analysis.

In the early 1960s American Express seemed to be on the ropes. A keen competitor, the Visa card company, was running ads showing owners of fancy restaurants who had announced that they had stopped accepting the American Express card. (The American Express card is a "travel and entertainment" card. Cardholders are expected to quickly pay what they have charged; they pay a yearly fee. American Express itself assesses stores a higher percentage on items charged than credit cards do. Visa cards are credit cards. Its cardholders have free time before they must pay what they owe. Originally, there was no yearly fee for credit cards.)

American Express had also become involved in a sordid salad–oil swindle. A subsidiary owned a warehouse in Bayonne, N.J. In the early 1960s the warehouse began receiving tanks of vegetable oil from a company called Allied Crude Vegetable Oil Refining. The warehouse gave Allied Crude receipts for the vegetable oil, which the company used as collateral to obtain loans.

Then Allied Crude filed for bankruptcy. And the creditors tried to get the collateral, the vegetable oil in those tanks. Alas, there wasn't much oil in those tanks. It was mostly seawater. The whole thing had been a fraud; someone—Anthony De Angelis, by name, who later went to jail—had bet heavily on vegetable oil futures and lost. Some $150 million was owed to creditors.

American Express had actually done nothing wrong. Still, to protect its name, the company magnanimously agreed to absorb the losses. The company, which had not omitted a dividend payment in 94 years, was rumored to be on the verge of bankruptcy.

"The news about American Express was terrible," Tweedy, Browne has written. The stock's price had dropped to nine or ten times earnings—and earnings might decline.

The essential question, as Tweedy, Browne saw it, was whether the American Express card remained competitive.

It was a situation where success bred success, failure bred failure. If more people used the card, and asked businesses if they accepted the card, more restaurants and other companies would accept it; if more restaurants and other companies accepted it, and put the notices on their windows, more people would use it.

But if fewer businesses accepted the card, fewer people could use it—and even fewer businesses would accept the card.

Now, Tweedy, Browne reasoned, a $100 dinner tab may cost a restaurant $10 for the price of the food. Gross profit: $90. That is before the cost of the cooks, waiters, rent, insurance, taxes, and so forth. American Express was charging restaurants 3.2 percent of the tab, or $3.20. Visa was charging only 1.75 percent, or $1.75.

Would a restaurant be willing to lose a little money in return for the big bucks that accompanied the American Express card?

Business customers favored the American Express card. Would restaurant owners fear that these patrons in particular might bypass their restaurants if they didn't welcome American Express cards?

Many American Express cardholders also had Visa cards, of course. But few businesses gave their employees Visa cards for their expense accounts. American Express had 70 percent of the corporate expense-account market. "The only corporate card in most persons' wallets was the American Express corporate card."

Tweedy, Browne did a small telephone survey of the restaurants patronized by one of its managing directors. Would these restaurants stop accepting the card? A restaurant in Lambertville, New Jersey had stopped accepting the card. The management had then noticed a decline in business-related dinners. Management promptly changed its mind. "We heard the same kind of thing in talking to other business owners," Tweedy, Browne reported.

So, one question had been answered: American Express wasn't about to be kicked out of restaurants all over America.

The next question was: Was there a moat around American Express? Or would Visa and MasterCard move into the corporate expense-account business?

Tweedy, Browne decided that they would be "somewhat reluctant competitors in the business credit card field" because of the economics of the situation.

The profits that banks make on Visa and MasterCard mainly come from charging sky-high interest rates on their customers' unpaid bills. If Visa and MasterCard customers paid off their debts in time, they would owe nothing—and wouldn't be especially desirable customers.

If Visa and MasterCard pursued the corporate expense-account business, these businesses, Tweedy, Browne assumed, would not tolerate having their employees charged sky-high interest rates.

"Thus, it seemed to us that American Express's dominant corporate-card position was a linchpin, a big moat that ensured acceptance of The Card by business establishments, and thereby protected American Express's economic castle."

Beyond that, Tweedy, Browne learned that:

- Cardholders had a higher opinion of American Express cards than credit cards; it had more cachet.
- Cardholders also considered American Express the more virtuous card because the balance had to be paid off every month, and there would be no interest charges to pay. If you needed a quick loan, Visa or MasterCard was what you used. "Even though an individual can pay off his or her Visa or MasterCard balance each month and never incur interest charges, several individuals we spoke with did not think of it this way. Here was more moat." And, of course, the moat the merrier.
- American Express, which was behind in its Frequent Flier program, was about to catch up.
- Corporate accounting departments found the American Express statements they received easy to understand and easy to work with.

- American Express gave some businesses that used its card special breaks on its travel business, such as discounts. "More moat."

In short, by doing some "Buffett 101" type of qualitative research, Tweedy, Browne got a beat on buying American Express stock.

Its definition of that kind of research: "Trying to see the whole picture, all of the moving parts and how they interact and affect each other, not just one piece of the puzzle."

CHAPTER 14

Hire Good People

After some . . . mistakes, I learned to go into business only with people whom I like, trust, and admire. As I noted before, this policy of itself will not ensure success: A second-class textile or department-store company won't prosper simply because its management are men that you would be pleased to see your daughter marry. However, an owner—or investor—can accomplish wonders if he manages to associate himself with such people in businesses that possess decent economic characteristics. Conversely, we do not wish to join with managers who lack admirable qualities, no matter how attractive the prospects of their business. We've never succeeded in making a good deal with a bad person.

—Warren Buffett

A "bad person" in this context is anyone who isn't wholeheartedly working on behalf of his or her shareholders, the real owners of the business. Someone whose mental energies are concentrated on his or her own financial well-being, his or her next job, or his or her future comfortable retirement.

The ideal people that Buffett wants in the way of management are people who behave as if they themselves were the owners. He wants them to be fanatics—to work their heads off, to live, breathe, and eat the business. And, of course, to be capable, and there's no better evidence of that than they have already been running the business and boosting the business's cash flow.

Of course, the ordinary investor is not in a position to check out the quality of management as thoroughly as someone like Buffett. But the ordinary investor can read the annual reports; attend annual meetings; read profiles of management people in *BusinessWeek*, *Fortune*, and *Forbes*, and perhaps see interviews with them on television. Granted, mistakes may be made. I myself was very much impressed after interviewing Lucent's former chairman at a shareholders' meeting before Lucent all but dropped off the face of the earth. But I was also so impressed by hearing the chairman of Johnson & Johnson talk (he criticized his company as well as himself) that I bought more shares.

The management of a company cannot work miracles. Or, as Buffett has nicely put it, "I've said many times that when a management with a reputation for brilliance tackles a business with a reputation for bad economics, it is the reputation of the business that remains intact."

But good managers can work near-miracles. They can develop a sensible plan and a reasonable timetable. Like top money managers, they can sit down with a flood of information, some conflicting, and decipher the fundamental trends and the most reasonable course of action. They can make logical decisions and get things done. They can improve morale. Reward competence. Cajole and persuade people. Look out for the company's best interests instead of just looking out for themselves.

Ron Baron, the fund manager, tells of buying stocks to a large extent simply because he was so confident in the new management. One manager had taken a failing hospital system and, astonishingly, turned it around; he then took over another hospital system in trouble. Investing in him, and the hospital, was, in Baron's view, almost a slam dunk. Mario Gabelli, another well-known fund manager, has put up on his office walls blown-up photographs of executives who had turned their companies around—while, of course, Gabelli funds owned their stocks.

Some other signs that the management of a company warrants respect:

- *They may buy back shares when the price seems low.* This encourages investors (even management, clearly, thinks the price is low); it reduces shares outstanding, thus helping favor demand over supply. (Alas, many companies announce share buybacks—and never do it. And some buy back shares even when they're *not* especially cheap.)
- *They are cost-conscious, up and down the line.* I once asked a corporate executive whether it's really important how conscientiously an employee fills out his or her expense account. Does the company really care if an employee takes a cab or public transportation? Dines at a five-star restaurant, with overflowing wine, or eats in his or her hotel room? Stays at the Ritz or a perfectly decent motel? His answer: "How an employee spends the corporation's money through his expense account indicates how he'll spend greater amounts of the corporation's money if he ever is given the opportunity."
- *They are forthright.* Like Berkshire itself. Buffett has told his own shareholders, "We will be candid in our reporting to you, empha-

sizing the pluses and minuses important in appraising a business. Our guideline is to tell you the business facts that we would want to know if our positions were reversed. We owe you no less."

- *They act like owners.* In some cases, because they were once the owners. They are obsessed with their businesses.
- *They are scrupulously fair.* Time and again, Buffett has reminded his shareholders that Berkshire is punctilious about dealing with them honorably. Unlike other companies, which (before the Securities and Exchange Commission issued a regulation on the subject) tipped off their favorite analysts and clients about developments that they had not told their own shareholders, Buffett has no favorites. "In all our communications," he wrote, "we try to make sure that no single shareholder gets an edge. We do not follow the usual practice of giving earnings 'guidance' to analysts or large shareholders. Our goal is to have all our owners updated at the same time."

Hire Warren Buffett

Warren Buffett runs Berkshire Hathaway by practicing what he preaches:

- **For years he and Charlie Munger have been paid very low salaries, especially for heads of a Fortune 500 corporation. "Indeed," commented Buffett, "if we were not paid at all, Charlie and I would be delighted with the cushy jobs we hold."**
- **He and Munger eat their own cooking; most of their money is in Berkshire. "If you suffer, we will suffer; if we prosper, so will you. And we will not break this bond by introducing compensation arrangements that give us a greater participation in the upside than the downside" (via stock options).**
- **When Berkshire split into A and B shares, Buffett told shareholders, "Berkshire is selling at a price at which Charlie and I would not consider buying it." That is like Joe Torre disparaging the chances of the Yankees winning the pennant: "Our ballplayers are too old and too rich." But Buffett wanted to be fair with potential Berkshire buyers. So he also used the occasion to point out that the brokers' commissions on the B shares would be only 1.5 percent—extraordinary for an initial public offering.**
- **Berkshire is probably the only corporation that lets its shareholders (A types) designate where they want Berkshire charity money to go. Why should corporate executives send all the money to their own alma maters?**
- **Berkshire shareholders don't pay taxes on dividends the company receives from companies like Coca-Cola and Gillette; Berkshire pays them.**

People Buffett Has Admired

All the businesspeople whom Buffett has admired seem to have emerged from the same Ebenezer Scrooge-like mold. They remind one of the Jean Cocteau film in which a young man keeps falling in love with women with the same face. (Much of the information that follows comes from Roger Lowenstein's biography, *Buffett: The Making of an American Capitalist*, New York: Doubleday, 1995.)

- Buffett's grandfather, Ernest, would lecture 12-year-old Buffett on the virtues of hard work when the young man helped out in the family grocery store. Ernest would also deduct two cents from his grandson's salary, just to convey to him the onerousness of government taxes.
- The legendary Rose Blumkin could not write and could barely read. She was born in Russia and lived in poverty—she and seven brothers and sisters slept in one room. Her family came to the United States in 1917, then settled in Omaha in 1919. She began selling furniture out of her basement, and eventually—in 1937—rented a storefront and started Nebraska Furniture Mart. Her motto: "Sell cheap and tell the truth."

She worked every day of the year. Never took a vacation. She screamed at her staff ("You dummy! You lazy!"). Her store was a huge success. Her explanation: "I never lied. I never cheated. I never promised I couldn't do. That brought me luck."

A local paper asked her what her favorite film was. "Too busy."

Her favorite cocktail? "None. Drinkers go broke."

Her hobby? Driving around and checking what other furniture stores were selling and for what prices.

Buffett, who bought Nebraska Furniture Mart, called her one of his heroes.

- Ken Chace had been chosen by Buffett to run Berkshire Hathaway, the textile mill. He never knew why—until the day he resigned. Then Buffett told him, "I remember you were absolutely straight with me from the first day I walked through the plant."
- A self-made man, Benjamin Rosner, owned Associated Cotton Shops, a chain of dress shops, which Buffett bought in 1967. Rosner was a work addict and, toward his employees, a slave driver. He once counted the sheets on a roll of toilet paper he had bought, just to make sure he had not been cheated.
- Jack Ringwalt was the majority owner of National Indemnity, an insurance firm in Omaha, which Buffett eventually bought. Ringwalt had entered the business during the depression by insuring risks that his competitors didn't want to touch, such as insurance for taxicabs,

lion tamers, and bootleggers. Like Buffett himself, he actually was risk averse. "There is no such thing as a bad risk. There are only bad rates," he told Buffett. (If you charge enough, you can remove the gambling aspect from something that's seemingly risky.) When Ringwalt went out to lunch, he left his coat in the office even in winter—just so he wouldn't have to check it and pay a charge.

- Eugene Abegg ran Illinois Bank & Trust in Rockford, Illinois. He had taken over the failing bank during the depression, and through intensely hard work built it into $100 million in deposits.
- Thomas S. Murphy, head of Capital Cities/ABC, saw to it that the giant company had no legal department and no public relations department. He was so frugal that when he had his headquarters painted, he didn't paint the side that no one could see, the side that faced the river. When he took over ABC, he closed the private dining room at the New York City headquarters.
- Roberto C. Goizueta of Coca-Cola had been buying back stock with excess cash. He also insisted that his managers account for the return on their capital.
- Carl Reichardt, chairman of Wells Fargo, the San Francisco bank, had sold the company jet and frozen the salaries of the other top executives during bad times. And he avoided real risks, like making loans to Latin American countries.

CHAPTER 15

Be an Investor, Not a Gunslinger

The stock speculator who cannot keep even the best of stocks for more than a few days because he does not get any 'action' out of them, that is, because they do not rise immediately in price, is a pitiable object. He often needs as much sympathy as the hopeless drunkard, the drug addict, or the cripple.

I have known speculators who had bought stocks which everyone knew were certain to appreciate in value and which in the course of a few months or even a few weeks did rise considerably, and in many cases increasing their dividend payments. But just because the stocks did not go up within a few days after they had been acquired the speculators became disgusted with them and let them go.

—Albert W. Atwood, *Putnam's Investment Handbook,* 1919

One explanation of Buffett's extraordinary success as an investor is that he, along with most other value investors, resists the temptation to be a gunslinger. He doesn't continually buy and sell. He buys *to* hold—and buys *and* holds.

Berkshire is not just risk averse. It's activity averse.

Said Buffett, "As owners of, say, Coca-Cola or Gillette shares, we think of Berkshire as being a nonmanaging partner in two extraordinary businesses, in which we measure our success by the long-term progress of the companies rather than by the month-to-month movement of their stocks. In fact, we would not care in the least if several years went by in which there was no trading, or quotation of prices, in the stocks of those companies. If we have good long-term expectations, short-term price changes are meaningless for us except to the extent they offer us an opportunity to increase our ownership at an attractive price."

When Buffett buys a stock, his favorite holding period, he has famously said, is forever. He has confessed that he makes more money by snoring than by working.

Before buying a stock, he asks himself: Would I want to own this business for 10 years? He doesn't slavishly follow the stock ratings in Value Line or Standard & Poor's. Those ratings are for only one year, not 10 years. And he stalwartly resists the vast conspiracy out there to get investors to buy, buy, buy, and to sell, sell, sell.

Chris Browne of the Tweedy, Browne funds has noted that Coca-Cola might not be a good buy right now. But if someone were asked to compile a list of stocks almost certain to do well over the next 20 years. . . .

There are other sensible and profitable ways to invest, of course, besides buying good companies and holding on. But for the lesser investor, buying good companies and just hanging in there is not impossibly difficult and challenging—and the tax benefits are nothing to sneeze at either. Buying good companies and tenaciously holding on doesn't require the accounting knowledge of a CPA, the investment knowledge of a CFA, or the up-to-the-minute information of an analyst. Just buying the Dow Jones Industrial Average is a sound and simple way for the lesser investor to do well—granted that this index, like others, every once in a while kicks out disappointing companies.

The Benefits of Sitting Still

Most investment strategies benefit when their managers buy and sell less frequently. For these reasons, among others:

- Value managers tend to stand pat; when growth managers play cards, they are always saying, "Hit me." Growth managers may have a harder time because they must make more frequent decisions.
- A high turnover means higher commission costs.
- A high-turnover portfolio is linked with low tax-efficiency (your gains are not shielded from Uncle Sam, which they would be if you held on). This isn't invariable. A manager whose portfolio has a high turnover may deliberately offset gains with losses, to boost tax-efficiency.

Over time, despite the experience of recent years, value stocks have done better than growth stocks—although this has been vigorously disputed in certain quarters. It can be tricky to define value stocks and growth stocks, and to decide when growth stocks cease to be growth stocks and value stops being value; the time period you study can also influence the outcome.

In any case, if value stocks do better in the long run, it may be simply because they tend to pay higher dividends. George Sauter, who runs the Vanguard index funds, believes that once taxes are taken into consideration, growth and value do the same. John Bogle, who founded the Vanguard Group, also believes that, in the long run, growth and value will come out even.

Another view is that it takes more courage, more sophistication, and more self-confidence to be a value investor. That's why some observers are convinced that most lesser investors are growth oriented; most professionals are valued oriented. (It's true that professional money managers like to talk like value investors: Their clients want to hear the value story, to be told how averse their money managers are to losing money.)

So it may be that value managers are rewarded more generously because they deserve to be better rewarded. The more pain, the greater the gain.

Why Investors Become Gunslingers

Many investors, especially unseasoned ones, buy and sell almost with the abandon of men switching television channels with their remotes. Buffett has referred to this as a "gin rummy managerial style," where you keep drawing new stocks, holding some for a while, quickly discarding others. Fast, furious, and—no doubt—fun.

In 1999 investors in general kept their stocks for an average of eight months, down from the two years that investors had kept stocks ten years earlier. Investors held Nasdaq stocks (generally smaller companies, along with technology issues) for only five months, down from two years. Even mutual fund investors are keeping their shares for fewer than four years versus eleven years a decade ago.

In a well-known study of 60,000 Charles Schwab investor–households from 1991 to 1997, Brad Barber and Terrance Odean, professors of management at the University of California at Davis, found that households that traded the most earned an annualized net return of 11.4 percent, while those who bought and sold infrequently earned an impressive 18.5 percent.

Beyond that, an April 1999 study of 10,000 individual investors by Odean found that the stocks that were bought to replace the stocks that had been sold performed *worse*. Investors lost 5 percent of their money on these trades (commission costs included).

The fact that momentum investing as an investment strategy has been so popular in recent years is perhaps the result not only of a prosperous economy and a soaring stock market, but of the greater number of ordinary investors who participate in the stock market. More Americans now own stocks than ever before. Also, online trading has lowered the commissions that investors must pay and made it easier to trade.

Lesser investors may buy a stock for the flimsiest of reasons. Because it's fallen far from its high. Or somebody on the TV series *Wall $treet Week* has just recommended it. Or—most commonly—because the stock has been going up.

"Momentum" investing—buying what's hot—is what beginners do. If you assembled a group of children, or inexperienced investors in general, and asked them which stocks they would choose, they would surely answer: stocks that have been doing well lately. Buying hot stocks, in short, is normal.

People tend to repeat whatever has been successful in the past; to bet on whatever has been working. We extrapolate. Extrapolation is generally a wise strategy. If we like a particular food or restaurant, we will return to that food or restaurant; if a friend proves a friend in need, we will seek his or her help again. Objects in motion, as Sir Isaac Newton observed, tend to remain in motion.

So, when we turn from investing in CDs and money market funds to investing in stocks, we naturally choose to buy stocks on a tear, the favorites. Warren Buffett has pointed out that if we were buying a loaf of bread or a bottle of milk, we would buy more when the price went down. If the price went up, though, we would buy less, or shop elsewhere. Why don't we do that with stocks? Why aren't more of us value investors?

The answer is: because we're not consuming those stocks we buy; we're planning to resell them, at a still higher price. Quickly. If we were buying stocks to hold for 10 years, as Buffett recommends, we might buy more of them as their prices went down, and less as their prices went up.

More Explanations

If the general public is indeed more growth oriented than value oriented, further explanations are easy to find.

- *Beginning investors are typically not aware that buying a variety of blue-chip stocks*, especially when they're a bit off their feed, *is a sound, conservative investment strategy*. It won't prove to anyone that you're smart, resourceful, or imaginative. But it's a sensible way to go if you want to retire rich.

A lawyer specializing in wills and estates once told me that when he examined the assets of well-to-do people who had recently departed, he found that many had bought stocks like Coca-

Cola, Merck, Exxon, and General Electric in their 20s—and hung on and on.

Studies of self-made investment millionaires confirm that they tend to be buy-and-hold investors. Charles B. Carlson, author of *Eight Steps to Seven Figures* (New York: Doubleday, 2000), reports that "The majority of millionaires surveyed hold stocks for at least five years. Many hold for ten years or more." (He interviewed more than 200 such people.)

- *Young people tend not only to buy hot stocks; they tend to trade them faster, too.*

Partly it may be on account of their metabolism. Your body slows down as you age; you yourself probably become more conservative, more worried about possible injury.

Then, too, it may be that as we grow older, life sometimes becomes more complex and difficult; our portfolio has swollen, our sources of income are varied, our pension plans are all over the place, we've had any number of jobs (and spouses)—it's hard to keep track of everything. Form 1040EZ is a thing of the distant and loving past. Besides, you want your survivors to have an easy time cleaning up the mess you left. Not to mention the erosion of your IQ points, making it difficult for you to track so many different investments.

The young may also not know that it can take a while for other investors to wise up and recognize a good company for what it's really worth. You can buy a stock for $20, knowing it's worth $40, and watch it retreat to $10 and stay there. (Fortunately, when it's finally recognized, it may shoot up like a rocket.)

The point is that if you're right, you're right. The fact that a stock you bought, which you thought was a screaming bargain, then went down and stayed down for a while, is not proof that you made a mistake.

No one, of course, should "fight the tape"—refuse to accept the reality of what a stock or the stock market is really doing. But viewing the tape with skepticism is sometimes a wise course. The problem is that beginning investors may not have the experience, or the self-confidence, to recognize that the stock market's day-to-day judgments are not always infallible. Perhaps because they believe in the efficient market hypothesis.

- Another reason people trade so much: *They bring along the habits they developed from gambling, from betting on baseball teams, football teams, horse races, and*—above all—*card games,* like poker, which some people claim to be the true national pastime. And when we gamble, we tend to put money on the previous winners. The race is not always to the swift, the battle to the strong, commented Damon Runyon, the newspaperman, but that's the way to bet. To bet on the tortoise, you would want towering odds.

• *By the same token, value investing is more sophisticated, more advanced.* The beginning investor doesn't normally think of betting on dark horses, on fallen angels, on the walking wounded. It takes thought, experience, and education to know that investing in companies in hot or at least lukewarm water can be profitable and relatively safe. Is the first stock anyone buys a value stock?

It takes a person some investment experience, or education, to learn that it may be better to buy a decent company at a low price rather than a glamorous company at a very high price. And that even the stocks of glamorous companies can be vastly overpriced, while struggling companies can be cheap and the better buy. (But strong companies in general do deserve some extra points.)

True, value investing, can prove to be anything but roses and wine. Other investors look askance at you ("You bought—what?"); your boss may question you sharply; and if you're a money manager, your shareholders may throw poisoned darts in your direction. Chris Browne of Tweedy, Browne, who writes an erudite and witty quarterly report, recalls receiving a letter from a shareholder accusing him of spending so much time writing his reports just to disguise how poorly his fund had been doing lately. (The fund rebounded nicely after 1999.)

• *Human beings tend to stress the short-term, to emphasize what has happened recently.* Politicians take tough, unpopular steps in their first year of office—raising taxes, say—and count on the last three fat years to bail them out. In the last year, in fact, they may go on a hiring binge and cut taxes. We concentrate on what's been happening in the stock market in recent months and years, but either ignore or don't know what happened years ago.

So it's easier for most people to buy hot stocks, stocks on a tear, rather than to do something so peculiar as to bet on unpopular, widely despised stocks.

• *Do investors buy and sell quickly because of lack of confidence?* They bought American Antimacassar for the flimsiest of reasons, and now that it has gone nowhere, they may have little confidence in their original judgment. Perhaps they bought it on a magazine's recommendation. And if they were more familiar with the stock, and had a number of good reasons for having bought it in the first place, they might not get so antsy. (Value investors, who tend to know their stocks thoroughly, are tempted to buy more shares when the price goes down.)

As a matter of fact, there's evidence that people in general, and investors in particular, tend to be too confident. Around 80 percent of the drivers in Scandinavia (or anywhere else, I'm sure) think that they're above average—when only 50 percent can be above average. Tests on U.S. citizens find that, given general questions to answer, they think their answers are correct far more often than they really are.

"Investors have become overconfident about their prowess in choosing stocks that will go up," observes Patricia Q. Brennan, a financial professor at Rutgers University in New Brunswick, New Jersey. "They attribute the good returns to themselves, the bad ones to their advisers, rather than to a stock market that has been rising. One of the results of this overconfidence is that they underestimate the risks they are taking."

But if investors are overconfident, why do they sell stocks to buy other stocks? Maybe they have gains on the stocks they sell, suggests Chris Browne. Or maybe they don't sell their losers and simply keep buying new stocks. That would help explain why so many people wind up with "messy portfolios," a huge, unwieldly godawful grab bag of this and that.

In the Odean study, men didn't fare so well at investing as women, presumably because men trade too frequently. Women hold their stocks longer, perhaps because they simply lack the confidence that men have—another uplifting example of modesty's being rewarded. A supplementary explanation is that this has something to do with the male and the female roles. Men historically spent more time outside the home, exposed to the elements and vulnerable to all sorts of dangers. Perhaps a need to continually move around, to avoid the elements and to avoid becoming prey, was bred into their genes.

Trading, in fact, seems more masculine. We have many words in praise of active, energetic, dynamic people; many other words denigrate those who are lazy and slothful. Idle hands are the devil's playthings.

Growth investing, with its quick ups and downs, is more exciting, more interesting. Gin rummy, after all, does have its good points. Many people are in need of novelty. That's why we have cycles in so many areas of human endeavor. Sociobiology is popular; then it fades; then it returns to favor. Technology stocks are the new thing;

then investors lose interest; then they rebound. Growth and value investing alternate days in the sun.

Enthusiastically showing me his collection, a child I know, Kevin, was enchanted with Pokemon cards a few years ago. Then he turned his back on them. "They're for little kids," he said, disgusted.

An ancient Greek explained why he was the only resident of his town not to vote for Aristides the Just: "I was tired of hearing him always called Aristides the Just."

Also, Chris Browne has noted that it's hard for "energetic, intelligent, well-educated, highly paid and self-confident individuals [money managers in general] . . . to sit tight and do nothing." Even though the evidence is that index funds, which rarely change their holdings, outperform most managers who spend their days shuffling their deck of stocks.

Buying and selling gives these people, Browne claims, "the illusion of control." They think they are doing something worthwhile, that they are "in charge."

"Why would investment management firms want to pay high salaries to people who do not appear to be doing very much, and who do not appear to have much control over what they are doing? Investment management firms, in general, must believe that lots of activity is useful because they are willing to pay for it, and high compensation ensures that lots of activity will be provided. Everyone involved must believe that it all makes sense."

Being a value manager and sitting still may be interpreted as laziness. The manager of Vanguard Windsor II, James P. Barrow, once told me, perhaps somewhat seriously, that he feels guilty getting paid to do so little. Doesn't your boss want you always to be working? Doesn't your boss love it if you work through lunch hour—assuming he or she gives you a lunch hour?

Another reason Browne furnishes for all this hyperactivity: Too many investors and institutions, when they judge a money manager's performance, don't pay enough attention to after-tax returns. If it's a tax-favored investment, that's another story. But estimates are that 60 percent to 70 percent of money invested in stocks is owned by tax-paying people and corporations. And buying and selling tends to increase taxes you owe.

Besides, there are a lot of good mutual funds out there, and buying more and more of them can be difficult to resist. The same is true of stocks. There are wonderful companies out there, and don't they deserve a place in your portfolio along with those excellent stocks you already own? Still, as Buffett has pointed out, if you let a fat pitch cross the plate and you don't swing, there's no umpire to call a strike. Why did he say that? Because we tend to feel that we must swing at fat pitches—and buy all the good stocks.

A good rule is: You don't have to buy every good stock, or every good mutual fund, or marry every attractive woman (or man).

• *There are economic reasons for having investors trade frequently.* Stockbrokers are paid by commissions, and the more their clients trade, the more money they make.

Bob and Rosemary Bleiler of Paramus, N.J., wanted to buy Disney stock many years ago, after they visited Disney World. The young broker they sat down with discouraged them—but then "permitted" them to buy 50 shares instead of the 100 they originally wanted. The stock did very nicely. Six months later, the young broker phoned. It's time to sell, she told them. Lock in your profits. They were reluctant. "That's what you do—you get in and you get out," she told them.

What she didn't tell them was that they were celebrating after having made goodly profit, but she was just a wallflower at their party. She couldn't join in the festivities unless they sold—and paid her a second commission when they bought something else. (Had they bought 100 shares of Disney then and kept it, the Bleilers calculate, they would have made $37,000.)

• *Wall Street analysts also foster a gin-rummy investment climate.* While they may be reluctant to issue a sell recommendation, they focus on whether a company they cover will meet its quarterly earnings estimates, and whether or not it will outperform over the next year. Analysts, like money managers, are expected to justify their salaries—in their case, by producing important, hard news.

So are the media, which continually convey a flood of the latest business news, all of it worth knowing, much of it worth ignoring. But if a CNBC announcer reports that one analyst has changed his or her rating of American Antimacassar from "buy" to "hold," the implication is that you should do something about this vital piece of information. "All the noise that Wall Street produces," money manager Michael Price once said to me disgustedly.

Newspapers must have big headlines to balance small headlines, so some stories get played up. Financial programs on TV and radio must fill up their time. Besides, overplayed sensational stories get better read. We journalists don't play up stories just to sell newspapers, as critics contend. We overplay stories to get them read. A very human desire, especially common among writers.

Journalists also want to be read continually. A newsletter editor I know changes his recommendations of mutual funds every so often, so readers will inevitably conclude that they cannot dispense with his newsletter. Otherwise, they would miss his vital buy-and-sell decisions.

Forbes magazine changes its honor roll of best mutual funds so extensively every year that its portfolio has done rather poorly. Changing funds once a year, on an arbitrary date, is not sound investment strategy. But if the honor roll remained virtually the same every year, how eager would readers be to see it?

The agreed-upon wisdom in the media seems to be that investors should quickly lock in good stocks—and quickly get rid of deteriorating companies. They probably should—if they are growth investors. And the media focus on growth investors. Not sophisticated growth investors, but unsophisticated growth investors.

Even a newsletter that Warren Buffett himself reads, the "Value Line Investment Survey," caters to traders. It focuses on how a stock may perform over the next year.

In the January 12, 2001, issue of "Value Line," three of the 100 most timely stocks were removed because their earnings declined relative to other companies' earnings, and three others—with growing earnings—replaced them. Of the 300 second-most-timely stocks, there were 16 changes.

Whereas "Value Line" is growth oriented, concentrating on stocks with increasing earnings, Standard & Poor's "The Outlook" also will recommend value stocks, stocks of companies that have been suffering but that seem underpriced. Still, even "The Outlook" has a short-term outlook. In its January 10, 2001 issue, nine stocks were upgraded (to top rating or second); nine were downgraded; coverage for ten new stocks was initiated.

Examples of the reasoning behind upgrades: Pittston Company "will benefit from a greatly improved environment in which to divest the company's coal operations." eBay "will see greater relative activity in a slowing economy as buyers seek better deals and sellers want to raise money." Circuit City Stores' "decision to move more slowly on store remodeling is a plus."

The reasoning behind downgrades: Tiffany & Company's "disappointing holiday season sales and resulting lower earnings estimates leave shares fairly valued" (down from above average). Park Place Entertainment: "Slowdown in U.S. economy could translate into weaker business for gaming company."

Still, "Value Line," in its analyst reports, will sometimes consider the long-term investor. AptaGroup gets only a 4 (below average) rating, but the analyst writes: " . . . patient investors might find its 3- to 5-year potential capital gains interesting." Rock-Tenn Company is ranked 4: "... we think patient investors should consider this issue." At the opposite end, a stock rated 2 (above average), Insituform Technology, has unappealing prospects: "long-term appreciation potential is limited, though, since we expect a somewhat lower, more-normal price-earnings ratio" in three to five years. Kaufman & Broad is rated 1, but "given the run-up in the stock's price, this issue offers below-average long-term appreciation potential."

Needless to add, following the stock market intensively can make investors very nervous. It's hard to hold onto a stock for 10 years when you are regularly receiving bad news about that stock. Days when stocks go down are almost as frequent as days when they go up.

In fact, if homeowners knew what the value of their homes were day after day, instead of at intervals of many years, perhaps they would not have hung on so patiently. What if a home had been worth $250,000 in 2000, then only $225,000 in 2001? Would the homeowner have sold in a panic?

It's natural for the media to focus on growth investors, people concerned about the next quarter's earnings. Those are the people most interested in the news. Not that value investors aren't interested in news, but in less.

What would a newsletter for value investors be like? A virtually unchanging portfolio with reports on the same stocks again and again.

One reason Buffett can buy and hold with such equanimity is that he doesn't get distracted. He doesn't care whether the Grand Pooh-Bah at this-or-that company is talking doom-and-gloom, or that the Grand Pooh-Bah at that-or-this company is singing "Happy Days Are Here Again." He doesn't guess where interest rates are going now, speculate about the implications of the trade deficit, estimate the economic consequences of a tax cut, fret about what the 60-day moving averages show, or whether dividend yields are historically high or historically low or historically average. To quote Buffett,

> If we find a company we like, the level of the market will not really impact our decisions. We will decide company by company. We spend essentially no time thinking about macroeconomic factors.
>
> In other words, if somebody handed us a prediction by the most revered intellectual on the subject, with figures for unemployment or interest rates, or whatever it might be for the next two years, we would not pay any attention to it.
>
> We simply try to focus on businesses that we think we understand and where we like the price and management.

• Another reason why people may trade so often: *It's a survival from earlier times*. Even into the twentieth century, many gambling parlors passed themselves off as brokerage houses. Customers didn't actually invest in companies via their stocks. They bet on whether stocks would go up by a certain number of points. And the bet lasted only a short time. These gambling parlors were called bucketshops.

"There is no room for doubt as to the character of the bucketshop," wrote John Hill Jr. in his book *Gold Bricks of Speculation: A Study of Speculation and Its Counterfeits, and an Exposé of the Methods of Bucketshop and "Get-Rich-Quick" Swindles* (Chicago: Lincoln Book Concern, 1904). "It is a gambling den, and nothing else. It is generally a dishonest gambling den, for there are few, if any, bucketshops whose frequenters have fair treatment. The patron puts his money into the pretended purchase or sale of stocks, grain or other commodities, at prices posted on the blackboard, which are, or purport to be, the figures at which securities or commodities are selling on the floor of the stock or produce exchanges. He bets that the price will vary in his favor before it will go one point against him."

But the bucketshops' proprietors, while seemingly selling something like options, actually manipulated the prices so that customers almost always lost.

"Thus, in defiance of law and decency, the 'future delivery' transactions on grain and cotton exchanges and the cash transactions on the stock exchanges have been counterfeited in bucketshops, with disastrous results to the reputation of exchanges and legitimate brokers and commission merchants. . . .

"While the whole scheme is one that should call forth public protest, especially from the agricultural classes [who frequented bucketshops more], its novelty in a small community where entertainment and excitement are lacking draws all classes to the counterfeit 'boards of trade.' "

The author, who was with the Chicago Board of Trade, concludes that "One sometimes wonders if avarice is our national curse."

These old-time gambling parlors possibly have had some influence upon modern brokerage houses and their practices. Anthropologists call old practices that continue in a new form "survivals."

Professional Advice

An unusual stockbroker is Barbara F. Piermont in Florham Park, New Jersey, who recommends that her clients buy good blue-chip stocks and hold onto them. A 30-year veteran, she acknowledges that one reason so many other investors buy and sell is that their stockbrokers want them to—because they are paid through commissions. So is she, but "I don't live on them. And I have lots of clients, who are happy to send me more clients."

She has discouraged her clients from pursuing hot companies, like the dot-coms. "I like slow and steady stocks, and I want my customers to be investors, not traders."

To persuade her customers not to trade so much, she urges them to set goals they want to reach. Focusing on the long-term seems to make people less inclined to gamble in the here and now.

It's the New Generation, she believes, who trade so much, especially after normal trading hours, after watching CNBC or the news headlines. Some hot new stock is touted; they buy it and hold it a few days; they then suffer buyer's remorse and unload it. "Quick money," she calls it.

Blue chips under a temporary cloud, she suggests, may be good buys. Or if a blue chip announces good news (higher earnings, the settling of a lawsuit, a big new contract) and the price unaccountably doesn't reflect the news, consider adding that stock to your portfolio.

A compromise she suggests for some of her clients: Set aside 5 percent to 15 percent of your money for trading, and put the rest in "stable stuff." You might use any excess profits from your gambling portfolio to put into your serious portfolio. But don't take profits from your serious portfolio to refinance your gambling portfolio. (A mutual fund authority, Alan Pope, has recommended that people have two portfolios of mutual funds: one for serious money and one for "crap-shooting money.")

Where did she get the idea to recommend that her clients buy and hold blue-chip stocks?

Henry and Phoebe Ephron were writers (Nora Ephron, author of the novel *Heartburn*, is their daughter), and at a party Mrs. Ephron, who knew nothing about investing, happened to meet Bernard Baruch, the famous investor. (Among investors of the distant past, he is one of the very few whose writings are still worth reading. It was Baruch who said, "Buy straw hats in January." He confessed that he always sold too soon. He also said that the only people who buy at the bottoms and sell at the highs are, of course, liars. Baruch is reported to have told Will Rogers to exit the stock market before the Crash of 1929, advice for which Rogers was always grateful.)

At the party, Mrs. Ephron heard Bernard Baruch give someone advice. Invest in a company that makes a product that people use, then

A Possible Cure

How to cure yourself of trading too much? James B. Cloonan, chairman of the American Association of Individual Investors, has confessed that "I still sell stocks too quickly." His solution: "to maintain an artificial portfolio of all stocks I sell, using the sale price as the purchase price. I then monitor that portfolio to see how it performs."

throw away, Baruch said. (Baruch once asked Ben Graham to become partners with him, but Graham declined.)

Mrs. Ephron went home and thought about it. Then she went to bed. In the middle of the night, she woke up with an idea. She had two daughters. She decided to invest in the company that made Tampax.

She did. And when she died years later, Mrs. Piermont learned from a friend, Mrs. Ephron's thousands of shares of Tampax were worth a fortune.

"That stuck in my mind," says Mrs. Piermont. People should buy companies with products in inexhaustible demand and just hold on.

More from Buffett on Buying to Hold

When Berkshire owns stocks of outstanding businesses with outstanding managements, Buffett has said, "Our favorite holding period is forever. We are just the opposite of those who hurry to sell and book profits when companies perform well but who tenaciously hang on to businesses that disappoint. Peter Lynch aptly likens such behavior to cutting the flowers and watering the weeds."

"Lethargy bordering on sloth," as Charlie Munger once put it, "remains the cornerstone of our investment style."

Buffett, as he has regularly reminded his shareholders, doesn't care what happens to the economy (apart from sometimes allowing him to buy stocks cheaply) or to the prices of the stocks he owns. With companies like Coca-Cola and Gillette, "we measure our success by the long-term progress of the companies rather than by the month-to-month movements of their stocks. If we have good, long-term expectations, short-term price changes are meaningless for us except to the extent they offer us an opportunity to increase our ownership at an attractive price."

On another occasion: "We continue to avoid gin rummy behavior." True, Berkshire closed its textile business after 20 years, but "only because we felt it was doomed to run never-ending operating losses. We have not, however, given thought to selling operations that would command very fancy prices nor have we dumped our laggards, although we focus hard on curing the problems that cause them to lag."

In a famous passage during one annual report, Buffett revealed that he considered Capital Cities/ABC, GEICO, and the Washington Post permanent holdings. "Even if these securities were to appear significantly overpriced, we would not anticipate selling them, just as we would not sell See's or the *Buffalo Evening News* if someone were to offer us a price far above what we believe those businesses are worth.

"This attitude may seem old-fashioned in a corporate world in which activity has become the order of the day. . . ."

Buffett may have contradicted himself here. He had also told his shareholders, "Sometimes, of course, the market may judge a business to be more valuable than the underlying facts would indicate it is. In such a case, we will sell our holdings. Sometimes, also, we will sell a security that is fairly valued or even undervalued because we require funds for a still more undervalued investment or one we believe we understand better."

Of course, as Buffett explained, Berkshire would not "sell holdings just because they have appreciated or because we have held them a long time."

Attempting to deal with this contradiction, Buffett went on to say that yes, Berkshire would sell overvalued businesses—apart from Coca-Cola, Gillette, and Capital Cities/ABC.

This inertial attitude derives, no doubt, partly from a desire to reassure managers of Berkshire businesses, partly from loyalty, partly from sentiment, and partly for business reasons. If you sell jim-dandy Business A and pocket a lot of money, you must find a jim-dandy Business B that's for sale. And if the buyer of Business A overpaid, you yourself might be forced to pay through the nose for Business B—because prices have gone up everywhere. As Buffett pointed out, a business that is "both understandable and durably wonderful" is "simply too hard to replace."

"Investment managers," Buffett went on, "are even more hyperkinetic: Their behavior during trading hours makes whirling dervishes seem sedated by comparison. . . . Despite the enthusiasm for activity that has swept business and financial America, we will stick with our 'til-death-do-us-part policy. It's the only one with which Charlie and I are comfortable, it produces decent results, and it lets our managers and those of our investees run their businesses free of distractions."

On another occasion: "Our stay-put behavior reflects our view that the stock market serves as a relocation center at which money is moved from the active to the patient." The idle rich remain rich; the energetic rich don't.

In one talk, Buffett condensed three of his investment themes, buying good companies cheap, not biting off more than they could chew, and inactivity. Buying "superstars . . . offers us our only chance for real success. Charlie and I are simply not smart enough, considering the large sums we work with, to get great results by adroitly buying and selling portions of far-from-great businesses. Nor do we think many others can achieve long-term investment success by flitting from flower to flower."

More of the same advice: "If you aren't willing to own a stock for ten years, don't even think about owning it for ten minutes." Naturally, a Wall Street expression that Buffett loathes is "You can't go broke taking a profit." He's justified, of course. People do tend to sell their winners too soon and to hold their losers too long. But some investors hold their winners so long that they become losers. A compromise piece of advice might be: "You can't go broke taking a few chips off the table."

The Gunslinger's World

Of course, many momentum investors are sophisticated, smart, and successful. There are famous gunslingers. Among them are Fred Alger of the Alger Funds, Kenneth Heebner of the CGM funds, and a variety of Janus managers, several of whom trained with Alger.

An impressive newcomer among gunslingers is Andrew C. Stephens of Artisan Mid Cap. The average stock fund manager's portfolio had a turnover of 103 percent in the year 2000. The average large-growth stock manager a turnover of 148 percent. Stephens' fund had a turnover of 236 percent in 1998, 203 percent in 1999, and 246 percent in 2000. Yet in 1998 his fund beat the S&P 500 by 4.79 percentage points, in 1999 by 36.85 percentage points, and in 2000 by 45.09 percentage points.

If you buy fast-growing, healthy companies rather than companies that are sleepy if not downright sickly, you must be ready to unload them at the first sign of serious trouble—their growth is slowing. Their earnings will probably sink, and their price-earnings ratio will probably become compressed, because investors no longer have such rosy views of their future. Growth investors talk about something called the Greater Cockroach Theory. If you see one, others must be lurking nearby; one earnings disappointment, one piece of bad news, suggests that others are on the way.

The smaller the fast-growing companies you buy, the more rapidly they are likely to falter and fade. The people running smaller companies tend to have less talent on their bench, less money, less experience; they also risk being put out of business by their bigger, merciless rivals. That's why the investor who focuses on small, fast-growing companies must also be quick on the trigger, ready to sell what's been hot and has begun cooling off before others wise up.

When Morningstar checked whether various funds would have been better off just leaving their portfolios alone for an entire year, or whether they improved matters by moving in and out, the conclusion was mixed.

Trading large-cap stocks "hardly seems worth it." In most cases, managers who puttered with their portfolios added little to their returns. Small-cap portfolios, especially those buying growth stocks, benefited the most from any fiddling around with their portfolios.

CHAPTER 16

Be Businesslike

While Buffett is clearly an unusually decent gentleman, with rare exceptions he has remained firmly businesslike. He is assigned the task of making good money for his shareholders, and while he allows room for compassion toward other interested parties, shareholders come first.

This somewhat stern businesslike attitude has governed not just Buffett's investment career, but is reflected in his personal life. Business is business, wherever it is transacted. It was a lesson he may have learned from his father and from Ben Graham.

As the publisher of one magazine I worked for liked to put it, "We are not an eleemosynary institution."

Berkshire Hathaway, the textile mill, was, after all, a company that Buffett was emotionally attached to. He assured people that he was opposed to ending the business, laying off its workers, hurting the economy of New Bedford, Massachusetts. But he did—unhappily. That was the money manager's dilemma at its most raw: Are you more loyal to the investors who own the business or to the employees of the business? When push came to shove, Buffett, predictably, sided with the owners.

But not without misgivings and not without straying a bit from his mandate.

Here is what he wrote in 1978 in his annual report: (1) Our "textile businesses are very important employers in their communities; (2) management has been straightforward in reporting on problems and energetic in attacking them; (3) labor has been cooperative and understanding in facing our common problems; and (4) the business should average modest cash returns relative to investment." Besides, "As long as these conditions prevail—and we expect that they will—we expect to continue to support our textile business despite more attractive alternative uses of capital."

In other words, while the business was just okay, Buffett preferred to continue holding on because of his obligations to the community, management, and labor—and because his own shareholders would get a decent cash return, although better investments were available elsewhere. The money manager as upright human being.

It turned out that Buffett was wrong about Berkshire's modest cash returns. Foreign competition was slaughtering the industry in this country. In 1980 the textile mills began consuming enormous amounts of cash. "By mid-1985 it became clear, even to me," Buffett wrote later, "that this condition was almost sure to continue." Nor could he find a buyer.

He went on: "I won't close down businesses of subnormal profitability merely to add a fraction of a point to our corporate rate of return. However, I also feel it inappropriate for even an exceptionally profitable company to fund an operation once it appears to have unending losses in prospect." Adam Smith wouldn't approve of his not closing down a not-very-profitable business, he went on, and Karl Marx wouldn't have approved of his not supporting a dying industry. But "the middle ground is the only position that leaves me comfortable."

Many other U.S. textile-mill owners had shut their plants sooner: They had the same information he himself had, but "they simply processed it more objectively." He had ignored the advice of the philosopher Auguste Comte: the "intellect should be the servant of the heart, but not its slave."

Buffett has declared that "Good profits are not inconsistent with good behavior." But when they are, profits must come first.

Other instances of Buffett's adherence to a semitough businesslike philosophy:

- After Buffett invested in the *Buffalo News* and experienced all sorts of trouble, the paper's chief competitor, the *Courier-Express*, suddenly folded. At a meeting of managers soon after, someone asked about profit sharing for employees in the newsroom.

Roger Lowenstein, Buffett's biographer, comments that "On its face, this seemed reasonable." The employees had done what was expected of them.

Replied Buffett, "There's nothing that anyone on the third floor [editorial] can do that affects profits." A dubious notion. The more skilled newspaperpeople could go elsewhere, lowering the quality of the paper. But, after all, in Buffett's mind shareholders come first. Lowenstein wrote that Buffett "was merely living up to his brutal-but-principled capitalist credo."

• Early in his career, Buffett began buying Dempster Mill Manufacturing, a farm equipment manufacturer in Beatrice, Nebraska. In 1961 he bought a controlling interest and became chairman. He wasn't a huge success at persuading the management to cut the inventory and shrink the costs. Then he hired someone, Harry Bottle, to come in and take over Dempster. Bottle cut costs drastically. Some 100 people were let go, and in Beatrice, Buffett was roundly criticized.

A friend teasingly asked Buffett, "How can you sleep at night after firing all those people?"

Said Buffett, for whom this was a sensitive subject, "If we had kept them, the company would have gone bankrupt. I've kept close tabs and most of them are better off."

• When Buffett became chairman of Salomon during its troubles in the early 1990s (a trader had tried to trick the Treasury into giving him more than his allotment of securities), he was outraged at the bonuses the executives were raking in. They wound up with almost 75 percent of the company's profits, which explains why shareholders were so unhappy. Among companies in the S&P 500, the return on Salomon's stock was 445th. A wonderful company but a lousy stock, Buffett called it. Then, in an advertisement in the *Wall Street Journal* and other giant newspapers, Buffett denounced Salomon's pay scale and announced that he was taking $110 million away from the bonus pool for 1991, even though profits had climbed (before the scandal). Salomon laid off 80 executives and 200 support staff. Managers' bonuses were cut 70 percent. Eventually the company turned around.

• Buffett put in a bid to bail out Long Term Capital Management, the hedge fund, when it was in the midst of its death throes. The U.S. government finally rode to the rescue with a loan, fearing the repercussions in the financial markets if the company went belly-up. But before then, Buffett had put in a bid for all of Long Term Capital Management's assets, a bid so lowball that everyone was shocked. But it was vintage Buffett.

In Business and Family

In intrafamily relations Buffett has also been Scrooge-like, insisting that his family members be self-reliant. Once his sister, Doris, to make quick money, had taken the reckless step of selling options on stocks she didn't own, and wound up $1.4 million in debt. Buffett reorganized a family trust so she would get monthly income, but he refused to pay off the debt. Doris had to default.

When daughter Susie got married and became pregnant, she wanted to expand the tiny kitchen in her townhouse in Washington, D.C. Cost: about $30,000. She asked her father for a loan, at current interest rates. He said no. "Why not go to the bank and take out a loan like everyone else?" Why should he show favoritism to his daughter? (The answer should have been obvious.)

Son Howie wanted to be a farmer. Buffett, in an unusually magnanimous gesture, offered to buy a farm (with a rather low maximum limit) and rent it to his son on standard terms. Howie finally found a farm that cheap—after knocking himself out seeing a hundred of them.

"[W]hen even close friends asked him for money, and for worthy causes," writes Lowenstein, "Buffett sent them packing."

An Exception

Still, on at least one occasion in his career Buffett (and Munger) let sentiment sneak into their cold business world.

Both Buffett and Munger were big owners of Blue Chip Stamps, and both decided to buy shares of Wesco Financial of Pasadena, California, which owned a savings and loan. Then Wesco announced that it would merge with another California savings and loan, Financial Corporation of Santa Barbara. Buffett and Munger tried to stop the merger, whose terms they felt were decidedly unfair to Wesco. Munger visited Louis R. Vincenti, Wesco's president; Buffett visited Elizabeth Peters, Wesco's largest shareholder. Buffett succeeded in persuading her to vote with him against any merger.

When the merger was called off, the stock began falling. Buffett and Munger could have loaded up on cheap shares then, but instead they decided to pay the higher price that had prevailed before the merger fell through—something they had been responsible for. Said Munger, who like Buffett was a straight arrow: "We decided in some quixotic moment that it is the right way to behave."

The Securities and Exchange Commission (SEC) thought something was rotten about the whole deal.

In questioning Munger later on, an SEC lawyer asked: "Why would you intentionally pay a higher price for something you could get for less?" Said Munger, "We wanted to look very fair and equitable to Lou Vincenti and Betty Peters." Lawyer: "What about your shareholders? Didn't you want to be fair to them?" Munger: "Well, we didn't feel our obligation to shareholders required us to do anything which wasn't consistent with leaning over backwards to be fair."

When Buffett was asked about his responsibility to Blue Chip shareholders, he replied that "I own a fair amount of the stock." The lawyer asked whether it would have looked bad if he had bought Wesco stock cheaply right after the merger fell through. "I think someone might have been sore about it," he replied. Buffett also testified that he wanted to remain on good terms with Vincenti, Wesco's president. "If he felt that we were, you know, slobs or something, it just wouldn't work."

In 1976 after a two-year investigation, the SEC charged that Blue Chip had propped up the price of Wesco by insisting on buying shares at a higher than market price. Blue Chip was ordered to pay $115,000 to various Blue Chip shareholders who, the SEC decided, had been hurt because Buffett and Munger had been buying shares artificially high.

It was just a slap on the wrist, but it's what happens when businessmen try to act like gentlemen.

In short, investors out to emulate Buffett's investment style should be steadfastly businesslike. Ethical investing may have its place, but what you are seeking, first and foremost, is profitability.

Just because an investor favors a particular company's pro-female or pro-minority policies, or because he or she once worked there and the company was benevolent, are not sufficient reasons to continue investing in it—unless it's a good investment in its own right. Even the fact that a company's stock has blessed you with enormous returns in the past is no reason for you to remain loyal if the company is fast going down the drain.

The old Wall Street warning, A stock doesn't know that you own it, wouldn't be repeated so often if people didn't bring so much emotional baggage to their investment portfolios.

If you want to show everyone how smart you are, join Mensa. Don't try to prove it in the stock market. And if you want to give vent to your compassion and loving-kindness, send checks to charitable institutions directly. Don't try to express your humanity by increasing the likelihood that you will make bad investments.

Avoiding bad investments, though, does not mean that you must glom onto seemingly good investments that might offend your sense of ethics, like tobacco or armaments companies. You can, as Buffett does, wait for other good pitches. Just don't swing at bad pitches—even if the pitcher is your sister, daughter, or son.

CHAPTER 17

Admit Your Mistakes and Learn from Them

Agonizing over errors is a mistake. But acknowledging and analyzing them can be useful, though the practice is rare in corporate boardrooms. There, Charlie and I have almost never witnessed a candid post-mortem of a failed decision, particularly one involving an acquisition. . . . The financial consequences of these boners are regularly dumped into massive restructuring charges or write-offs that are casually waved off as "nonrecurring." Managements just love these. Indeed, in recent years it has seemed that no earnings statement is complete without them. The origins of these charges, though, are never explored. When it comes to corporate blunders, CEOs invoke the concept of the Virgin Birth.

—Warren Buffett

One recurring theme of the Berkshire annual reports is: Buffett makes a lot of mistakes. As he wrote in the 2000 annual report, "I'm the fellow, remember, who thought he understood the future economics of trading stamps, textiles, shoes, and second-tier department stores," referring to seeming blunders he had made in the past.

In the reports, the litany of mistakes tends to come right up front. The 1999 report discusses "just how poor our 1999 record was. . . . Even Inspector Clouseau could find last year's guilty party: your Chairman." He describes the mistakes; he tries to figure out why he made them; and he assesses the consequences of those mistakes.

Admitting mistakes and trying to learn from them seems to be an attribute of gifted investors—and of gifted people in general. Let's look at how Buffett has discussed some of his mistakes in the past:

- In the 2000 annual report he confesses, "I told you last year that we would get our money's worth from stepped up advertising at GEICO in 2000, but I was wrong. . . . The extra money we spent did not produce a commensurate increase in inquiries. Additionally, the percentage of inquiries that we converted into sales fell for the first time in many years. These negative developments combined to produce a sharp increase in our per-policy acquisition cost." (He gives more details about the problem, pointing out that a key competitor, State Farm, has resisted raising its prices.)

- Why didn't he repurchase shares of Berkshire Hathaway when they were cheap?

"You should be aware," he has said, "that, at certain times in the past, I have erred in not making repurchases. My appraisal of Berkshire's value was then too conservative or I was too enthused about some alternative use of funds. We have therefore missed some opportunities. . . ." Granted, he continued, he did not miss out on making a great deal of money.

- "I clearly made a mistake in paying what I did for Dexter [a shoe company] in 1993. Furthermore, I compounded that mistake in a huge way by using Berkshire shares in payment. . . ."
- (Talking about Berkshire Hathaway textiles): "We also made a major acquisition, Waumbec Mills, with the expectation of important synergy. . . . But in the end nothing worked and I should be faulted for not quitting sooner."
- "Shortly after purchasing Berkshire, I acquired a Baltimore department store, Hochschild, Kohn, buying through a company called Diversified Retailing that later merged with Berkshire. I bought at a substantial discount from book value, the people were first class, and the deal included some extras—unrecorded real estate values and a significant LIFO cushion [potential tax deduction]. How could I miss? So-o-o—three years later I was lucky to sell the business for about what I paid. . . ."
- "Late in 1993 I sold 10 million shares of Cap Cities at $63; at year-end 1994, the price was $85¼. (The difference is $222.5 million for those of you who wish to avoid the pain of calculating the damage yourself.)"

"Egregious as it is, the Cap Cities decision earns only a silver medal. Top honors go to a mistake I made five years ago that fully ripened in 1994: Our $358 million purchase of USAir preferred stock, on which the dividend was suspended in September. . . . This was a case of sloppy analysis, a lapse that may have been caused by the fact that we were buying a senior security [owners of preferred stock must be paid dividends before owners of common stock] or by hubris. Whatever the reason, the mistake was large."

• Another mistake: Buying Gillette preferred instead of Gillette common. "But I was far too clever to do that. . . . If I had negotiated for common rather than preferred, we would have been better off at year end 1995 by $625 million, minus the 'excess' dividends of about $70 million."

Learning from Mistakes

Not learning from your mistakes, of course, may mean that you may repeat those mistakes or make similar mistakes.

Learning means: recognizing that it was a mistake, despite any excuses that you might have been tempted to make, and pledging to recognize such a situation in the future and to avoid making the same or a similar mistake.

One of the worst investors of our time was the late Charles Steadman, whose Steadman funds year after year lost money. Steadman Oceanographic lost around 10 percent of its value every year for 10 years. Such consistency, even among poor-performing mutual funds, is rare. What Steadman, a lawyer who was not unintelligent, did wrong was: (1) buy story stocks, those that had exciting tales to tell, such as a company that claimed to breed disease-free pigs; (2) buy stocks with no persuasive numbers behind them; and (3) make the same mistake again and again. He must have had a powerful need to impress people by reaping extraordinary profits from colorful companies. Or he was simply unable to resist the allure of story stocks. Perhaps he had once made a killing on a story stock, and yearned to feel once again the ecstasy of that experience, the giddy sensation of far greater wealth, of soaring self-confidence and self-satisfaction.

People who can confront and analyze their mistakes seem to have deep-seated self-confidence. They know that, despite their lapses, they are still worthwhile, talented individuals—and perhaps even gifted in whatever line of activity they made their mistakes. (Or they have just trained themselves, or been trained, to endure the pain of self-criticism, recognizing the benefits.)

Charles Bosk, a sociologist at the University of Pennsylvania, has conducted a series of interviews with young physicians who had left neurosurgery-training programs. Either they had been let go, or they had resigned. What, he wondered, separated these young doctors who went on to become surgeons from those who had faltered and stumbled along the way?

It wasn't so much a resident's intelligence or dexterity, Bosk decided, as much as the person's ability to confront the possibility, the causes, and the consequences of his or her mistakes, and to take steps to keep them from recurring. Quoted in *The New Yorker* magazine (Aug. 2, 1997), Bosk said:

> When I interviewed the surgeons who were fired, I used to leave the interview shaking. I would hear these horrible stories about what they did wrong, but the thing was that they didn't *know* that what they did was wrong.
>
> In my interviewing, I began to develop what I thought was an indicator of whether someone was going to be a good surgeon or not. It was a couple of simple questions. Have you ever made a mistake? And, if so, what was your worst mistake?
>
> The people who said, 'Gee, I really haven't had one,' or 'I've had a couple of bad outcomes, but they were due to things outside my control'—invariably those were the worst candidates.
>
> And the residents who said, 'I make mistakes all the time. There was this horrible thing that happened just yesterday and here's what it was.' They were the best. They had the ability to rethink everything they'd done and imagine how they might have done it differently.

Possibly these surgeons had not made mistakes, in the sense that they had done something that they should not have done—or not done something they should have. Just as you can buy a stock that goes down without your making a mistake—you couldn't have known about, say, a new lawsuit—a surgeon can have a bad outcome that is not his or her fault. Perhaps the patient had health conditions the surgeon and hospital weren't aware of. But assiduously checking into the causes of mishaps in general—stocks of yours that plummet, patients who have bad results—even if the mishaps aren't your mistakes, can be as beneficial as trying not to repeat mistakes that result from a failure on your part.

Peter Lynch has admitted that he would sometimes buy a stock at \$40, sell it at \$50, then buy it again at \$60. He didn't fear the pain of humiliation, of experiencing a decline in his self-esteem, by his publicly acknowledging that he had done something he should not have—sold that stock at \$40. (If I had seen that the stock rose briskly after I sold it, I would out of shame never have looked at its price again.) By the same token, Gentleman Jim Corbett, the heavyweight champion boxer, was said to have been very polite to other men. No one would suspect him of being afraid of them. No one would think Peter Lynch was not a gifted investor, despite occasional lapses. And, of course, no one thinks less of Warren Buffett for his compulsively studying his so-called mistakes.

He plays bridge the same way. "When he makes a stupid mistake," Carol Loomis has written, "he tends to be hard on himself. 'I can't believe that I did that,' he said recently after one hand. 'That was incredible.' "

CHAPTER 18

Avoid Common Mistakes

Once, when Warren Buffett was asked to explain his success as an investor, he gave a simple answer: "I'm rational." He generally doesn't make the emotional, silly, and illogical mistakes most investors are prone to making.

Not long ago, I sold $20,000 shares of SBC and bought two $10,000 positions in Berkshire Hathaway and Pfizer. I still had $20,000 left in SBC. But when I look at my stocks now, I'm delighted that Berkshire and Pfizer have risen—and even pleased that SBC has fallen—because all of these steps confirm how clever I am. I have to remind myself that I'm still behind because I have lost more money in SBC than I have gained in Berkshire and Pfizer.

Psychologists have devised a term for behavior like mine, where I try to fool myself into thinking what I did was very clever: "stupidity." Another term they use is "recency": People tend to overemphasize things that have happened recently. If there's a flood nearby, people will buy more homeowners' insurance; if a stock has been going up and up, people are likely to jump on the bandwagon.

Like all other psychological mistakes, recency can serve a useful purpose. Maybe floods are getting more common these days; maybe that stock will continue going up because (1) some professional investors are gradually buying big positions and (2) new investors keep discovering it. But focusing on recent purchases, and overlooking the stocks that have been in a portfolio for years, can be a costly mistake.

Related to recency is "extrapolation," the human tendency to think that whatever has been happening will continue to happen; the number that comes after 1, 3, 5, and 7 is 9. Extrapolation is a useful guide in life. A good restaurant deserves a return visit; a friend who gives useful advice is worth consulting again. But it doesn't always work in the stock market, where a stock or the market itself can become excessively expensive, where the number that comes after 1, 3, 5, and 7 may be minus 12.

A recent and *striking* event can have a far greater impact on our psyches. A recent airplane crash may lead us to buy more airplane insurance; a recent decline in the stock market can cause us to panic and sell.

Obviously, we investors are a neurotic lot. Just consider how many investors think that they don't really have a loss unless they sell a losing stock; and how many other investors believe that an individual bond is better than a bond fund because you can't lose money on an individual bond if you don't sell it before maturity (assuming that it doesn't default). It's the same fallacy: An individual bond that's worth less is a loser even if you don't sell it.

Yet, ironically, a popular theory for many years has been the efficient market hypothesis, the notion that stock prices are reasonable because all information is distributed quickly and equally, and all investors are intelligent and logical. The evidence seems to fit better with the Nutty Investor Theory, the notion that stock prices are frequently too high or too low because a great many investors are illogical.

To do well in the stock market, as Buffett has, it helps enormously just to resist the common psychological mistakes that other investors make.

Perhaps the single most important mistake is recency/saliency/extrapolation, which drives markets up too high and drives them down too low. "The major thesis of this book," writes a noted value investor, David Dreman, in *Contrarian Investment Strategies: The Next Generation* (New York: Simon & Shuster, 1998), "is that investors overreact to events. Overreaction occurs in most areas of our behavior, from the booing and catcalling of hometown fans if the Chicago Bulls or any other good team loses a few consecutive games, to the loss of China and the subsequent outbreak of McCarthyism. But nowhere can it be demonstrated as clearly as in the marketplace."

Other common psychological mistakes include:

LOSS AVERSION. People seem to hate losses twice as much as they love winners. They will accept a bet where the odds may be 2 to 1 in their favor, but no less. Many experiments have confirmed this. I myself presented this case to a group of investors: In your company cafeteria you overhear the president and chairman talking about how wonderful things are. Earnings are going up; a new product is flying off the shelves; a big competitor is in big trouble. Do you buy more shares? About half would, half wouldn't. Again, you're in your company cafeteria. You already own the stock. You overhear the president and chairman lamenting how lousy things are. Earnings are down; a new product has bombed; a big company is beating you up big-time. Do you sell? *Everyone* would sell.

I once asked Richard Thaler, a leader in behavioral economics, to explain the origin of loss aversion: It's an inheritance from our primitive days, he said, when losses—of food, shelter, safety—imperiled your very life.

LOVE OF GAINS. Investors are also prone to selling too quickly; instead of selling their losers and letting their winners ride, they hold onto their losers and sell their winners. Perhaps they are afraid that their gains will vanish if they wait too long. A bird in the hand . . .

THE PATHETIC FALLACY. A term coined by art critic John Ruskin, it entails endowing inanimate objects with human qualities. For instance: not selling a stock because when you were an employee the company treated you generously, or because a favorite relative bequeathed it to you, or because the stock once blessed you with princely returns and you don't want to be an ingrate by selling it. A stock, as the saying goes, doesn't know that you own it. (Also called "personalization.")

SEPARATING MONEY INTO DIFFERENT CATEGORIES. This can occur when, for example, you've doubled your money on American Antimacassar, and that prompts you to invest your profits more aggressively because it was easy money rather than money you worked hard for.

COGNITIVE DISSONANCE. It can be painful to change your mind, to substitute one set of beliefs for another. That may be why analysts tend to be slow in upgrading a stock that has a positive earnings surprise, and to be slow in downgrading a stock with a negative earnings surprise. Related to this is the "endowment effect": People tend to accept evidence that supports whatever they already believe (a stock that they own is a good buy) and reject evidence that conflicts with what they believe (a stock they own is a dog).

AVOIDANCE OF PAINFUL MEMORIES. I would never consider buying Intel because the very name reminds me that I foolishly sold the stock 20 years ago. I have trouble buying any stock or mutual fund that cost me money in the past.

CONTAMINATION. Some stocks get hurt because others in the same industry have been hurt. But a company in one industry could prove immune from the epidemic, and even benefit later on if its competitors lose their shares of the business. Shrewd investors like to zero in on companies in a suffering industry that seem to be immune, the way Buffett bought Wells Fargo during a period of bank troubles and has been glomming onto companies with asbestos problems recently. (Sometimes called "false parallels.") By the same token, some stocks take off because they're in a favored industry, such as Internet stocks, even though they may be exceptions. This is called the Halo Effect.

COMPLEXITY. In some situations, even sophisticated investors aren't sure what to do. There are lots of good reasons to buy, lots of good reasons not to buy. One money manager, Brian Posner, told me that that's what he looks for—complicated situations, where by intense study he can gain an edge over other investors.

TOP-OF-THE-HEAD THINKING. I once got a solid tip from a friend in the medical arena that Pfizer, the pharmaceutical company, was in a lot of trouble. It had manufactured a heart valve that was defective, and everyone with such a valve might sue. I sold my 100 shares of the stock at $79 and smugly watched as the news got out and the price starting dropping—$78, $76, $74, $72. Then, over the course of the next year, Pfizer went to $144. You've heard that happiness is a stock that doubles in a year? I have a neat definition of the word "misery."

A year after I sold my Pfizer, I asked Ed Owens, portfolio manager of Vanguard Health Care Portfolio, to tell me about something he was proud of having done recently. He mentioned buying all the shares of Pfizer that he could lay his hands on. Didn't he know about the defective heart valve? Yes, of course, but he and his analysts figured that if everyone with a defective heart valve sued, it would knock just one point off Pfizer's price. Meanwhile, the company had all sorts of promising drugs in its pipeline, including one with a funny name: Viagra.

THINKING INSIDE THE BOX. So many investors, having lost money on Internet stocks, for example, feel that they must regain their money by holding onto their Internet stocks. But, as Buffett has said, you don't have to make it back the same way you lost it.

ANCHORING. People seem hungry for any sort of guidance. Tell them the date when Attila the Hun invaded Europe, and they will use that off-the-wall number to guide them in estimating the population of Seattle or Timbuktu. In the stock market, people will anchor on a stock's yearly high, or the price at which they bought it. If the high was $50, they will think it must be cheap at $25 (especially if they are adherents of the efficient market hypothesis). If they bought it at $50, then it declined, they may wait until it reaches $50, then unload it.

THE HERD INSTINCT. Many people will go with the flow—even good investors, one of whom once told me that he will buy only on an uptick. Often the voice of the people is indeed the voice of God; if I was in a theater and everyone began running madly for the exits, I would try to beat them out the door. Often, though, especially in the stock market, the voice of the people is plain wrong. Of course, people also have a tendency to be stubborn, to ignore the crowd. There's a fine line between courage and stubbornness.

OVERCONFIDENCE. Lawyers, drivers, physicians all think that they are better than they are—in winning cases, in avoiding accidents, in diagnosing illnesses. Positive thinking can be beneficial. You apply for jobs for which you don't have the requisite experience; you enthusiastically undertake projects where you may be over your head. But overconfidence can also lead investors in particular to take too much risk, to overestimate their knowledge and skill, to trade too much, to stubbornly refuse to sell.

THE SUNK COST FALLACY. People will send good money after bad. If you've spent $500 getting an auto repaired, it's very painful to junk the car and buy a new one but somewhat less painful to put more money into the car. By the same token, some people are tempted to buy more shares of a stock that has gone down—perhaps also to prove to themselves that they weren't dopes for buying it high.

OVERLOOKING SMALL EXPENSES, ESPECIALLY IF THEY ARE REPEATED. Small leaks, as Munger likes to say, sink great battleships. Gary Belsky and Thomas Gilovich, in their book *Why Smart People Make Big Mistakes—And How to Correct Them* (New York: Simon & Schuster, 1999), call this "Bigness Bias." Or, as Harold J. Laski, the political analyst, once pithily observed, Americans tend to confuse bigness with grandeur.

THE STATUS QUO BIAS. People apparently would rather do nothing rather than do something that would be a mistake. They are happier holding onto a stock that loses half its value than they are selling stock one and buying stock two, which also loses half its value. This is reinforced by folk wisdom: out of the frying pan into the fire.

CONFUSING THE CASE RATE WITH THE BASE RATE. If you look at one case, the answer may seem to be X; but if you look at many cases similar to that case, you may see that the usual answer is Y. A well-known example: In college, Jane was interested in books. Is she more likely to be a librarian now or a salesperson? Answer: Salesperson, because there are far more salespeople in the United States than librarians. In the stock market, investors may think that a particular Internet stock is bound to succeed, paying scant attention to how many other similar Internet stocks have fallen by the wayside.

NOT DISTINGUISHING BETWEEN WHAT'S IMPORTANT AND WHAT'S TRIVIAL. Psychological tests indicate that when investors are given far more information, they become more confident—but not better investors. Perhaps only the very best investors can distinguish the wheat from the chaff. During World War II, the U.S. Army Intelligence broke the Japanese war code and began deluging General George C. Marshall with decoded messages. He finally exploded in frustration: Stop sending me so many trivial messages.

CHAPTER 19

Don't Overdiversify

As an investor Buffett prefers to have a concentrated portfolio, one with relatively few securities in comparison to the amount of money invested.

A concentrated or "focused" portfolio has a number of clear-cut advantages:

- You can become familiar with 25 companies far better than 50; you can also track their activities more easily. (More than one portfolio manager has said that 70 is the most stocks he or she can follow.)
- You can zero in on your very favorite stocks—not your second favorites.

In short, you can choose better stocks for a concentrated portfolio and, because you have more time and energy to study this more limited portfolio, you can follow your investments more intensively.

Of course, it is possible to make a case against a concentrated portfolio:

- A mistake could be more costly. If you own 100 stocks with each representing 1 percent of your portfolio, a 50 percent decline in one stock would lower your portfolio by only 0.5 percent. If you owned 50 stocks, the decline would be 1.0 percent.

- It can be hard to distinguish between your favorite and your second-favorite choices. Several fund managers have told me that they cannot tell in advance which of the stocks in their portfolios will do exceptionally well and which might crater.
- A large position in a stock, or a medium-sized position in a thinly traded stock, can be hard to unwind without driving the price down.
- An incontrovertible benefit of an index fund is its wide diversification across different stocks in different industries. Not many actively managed funds actually do better than large-company index funds (although this may be largely because index funds are so cheap to run).

The sensible conclusion is that, for most investors, a concentrated portfolio is a perilous undertaking, and they might be better advised to build a well-diversified portfolio.

A concentrated portfolio, on the other hand, could be suitable for an unusually capable investor; the skill of that investor may offset any added risk brought about by the narrowness of the portfolio. The fastest horses can carry the heaviest weights.

For the average investor, having a concentrated portfolio—say, of six or seven stocks—could spell disaster. The ordinary investor should diversify across a variety of different stocks and different industries. In this case, at least, the ordinary investor should blithely ignore Buffett's recommendation.

Buffett has apparently recognized that his recommendation that people own only six or seven stocks might be ill advised. In one talk, he actually advocated that investors consider index funds.

A Look at Performance

A study of concentrated mutual fund portfolios that Morningstar conducted (October 2000) found, not surprisingly, that they were more likely to have extremely good, or extremely bad, records.

Some focused funds, like Janus Twenty, have enjoyed spectacularly fine results. (The fund, despite its name, might own 50 stocks.) Clipper, a concentrated fund run by James Gipson, has also excelled. (See Chapter 29.) But Yacktman Focused, run by a well-respected value investor, Donald Yacktman, has suffered horribly during most of its life.

Morningstar editors have conducted two enlightening studies of concentrated portfolios. In the first, they examined funds with 30 or fewer holdings over a three-year period. The funds were limited to those investing mostly in U.S. securities, but they could be sector funds, specializing in, say, health care. There were 75 such funds.

Compared with very similar funds (large-company value versus large-company value, for example), the concentrated funds tended to be top performers—or bottom performers. Not average.

The winners, like Strong Growth 20 and Berkshire Focus, might have invested heavily in technology stocks. Or, like Clipper, Oakmark Select, and Sequoia, they might have mostly avoided technology. But there was apparently a tendency for the winners to have made big bets. Amerindo Technology had more than 40 percent of its assets in one stock, Yahoo, in 1998. Oakmark Select's choosing cable stocks helped account for its good fortune.

Still, it is important to remember that only a three-year period was chosen. Big bets might not pay off as well over longer time periods.

"Essentially," Morningstar concluded, "the differences in performance boil down to stock-picking." In other words, money managers with fine records tended to continue doing well with focused portfolios.

Most of the concentrated funds, Morningstar also found, were more volatile than other funds. Marsico Focus soared 34 percent in late 1999; it fell more than 18 percent between March and May of 2000. During these periods, Marsico Focus diverged from other large-growth funds by around 10 percentage points. PBHG Large Cap 20 rose 75 percent in the last quarter of 1999, then dropped more than 20 percent between March and May of the following year.

Surprisingly, even concentrated value funds were unusually volatile. Sequoia fell 16 percent between December 1999 and February 2000, then gained 21 percent between March and May 2000. During these periods, its performance diverged from the performances of other large-value funds by 10 percentage points. (I suspect that recent years have been unusual for value funds, and that concentrated value portfolios would tend, like value funds in general, to be less volatile than concentrated growth funds.)

In its second study, Morningstar looked at quasi-concentrated funds: those that had at least 50 percent of their assets in their 10 largest holdings. They found that it wasn't a bad idea at all for somewhat diversified funds to concentrate their assets in their top holdings. In other words, for a fund to compromise: to have a lot of different stocks, but to tilt toward its favorites. (Exception: sector funds. Those that overweighted their top 10 holdings tended to do miserably. Morningstar's puzzling explanation: " . . . most likely because most stocks in a sector often move together." Perhaps it's just harder to bet on differences between similar stocks.)

Another finding from this second experiment: It paid to buy and hold. Top-performing funds like Janus Twenty "hold onto winners longer than their competitors do, so individual positions are allowed to mushroom in size as they perform better. Thus, their contribution to a fund's performance is more meaningful."

The better-performing funds among the quasi-concentrated funds also tended to be a little more volatile than their peers, which isn't surprising.

The overall conclusion that one can draw from Morningstar's studies is just what one might expect: Concentrated portfolios can be perilous. Concentration, states Morningstar, "produces extreme performance, but it isn't actually better on average."

In Sum

No doubt, the better the investor you are, the less you need to diversify. Unfortunately, the cruel fact is that there is a law for the lion and a law for the lamb; a law for geniuses like you-know-who and a law for Joe Schmos like you and me.

Buffett can get away with having a concentrated portfolio. In fact, it helps account for his glittering record. He knows his companies backward and forward. While you and I have been wasting our lives watching football games and reading John Grisham novels, he's been reading balance sheets. You know what he does for fun? Reads quarterly reports.

I recall hearing Phil Rizzuto, the light-hitting former Yankee shortstop, talking on television. Someone mentioned to him that Ralph Kiner's advice to other hitters was: Always swing as hard as you can. (Ralph Kiner hit a lot of home runs.) Replied Phil Rizzuto, in shock: "Holy cow, that's about the worst advice I've heard in my whole life!" It was advice suitable for Mr. Kiner, not for Mr. Rizzuto.

You and I and Phil Rizzuto—let's face it—should be very content with singles. Ralph Kiner and Warren Buffett, on the other hand, have been among the very small percentage of humanity qualified to swing for the fences.

Buffett, who is, after all, very smart, has acknowledged as much. He has said that he sees nothing wrong with investors putting money into index funds. He was referring to "an investor who does not understand the economics of specific businesses [but who] nevertheless believes it in his interest to be a long-term owner of American industry. That investor should both own a large number of equities and space out his purchases [practice dollar-cost averaging]. By periodically investing in an index fund, for example, the know-nothing investor can actually outperform most investment professionals. Paradoxically, when 'dumb' money acknowledges its limitations, it ceases to be dumb."

CHAPTER 20

Quick Ways to Find Stocks That Buffett Might Buy

Warren Buffett buys stocks that he considers to be sure things. He has an aversion to gambling, and wants the odds to be five or ten or even 100 to one in his favor—which is not normally considered gambling. That's one reason why an investor should be wary of putting money into stocks that seem to meet a few of Buffett's investment criteria. Buffett himself would tend to reject any stocks with even a faint whiff of doubt, emulating his mentor, Ben Graham. And he would try to research the heck out of any company, like the fanatics he admires.

He also uses qualitative, non-mathematical criteria to judge companies—in particular, the quality of management. The ordinary investor, unfortunately, has limited access to top business people. If Warren Buffett phoned the XYZ Corporation and asked to speak to the CEO, he would not be referred to "shareholder relations," the way you and I would. And talking to management and evaluating management can provide strong evidence, or even just subtle clues, as to whether to buy a stock.

In short, buying stocks that, from the numbers alone, might interest Buffett is not as safe a strategy as an investor might believe. Finding stocks that seem to fit Buffett's criteria is useful for anyone seeking to emulate Buffett, but that should be only a starting point. Buffett expert Robert Hagstrom suggests that you then obtain annual reports and 10(k)s, study what analysts have to say, read interviews with management, and so forth. And, I would add, the less extra research you do, the more such Buffett-type stocks you might buy.

The lesser investor had better think not only of diversifying, but of leaving a ship that begins to take on a lot of water—and certainly not holding on forever.

A final warning: Edwin Walczak, who runs a mutual fund that follows Buffett's approach, Vontobel U.S. Value (see Chapter 28), reports that if you get five Buffett imitators in conversation, each will hold a basket of stocks that the others don't.

Robert Hagstrom

With these warnings, the reader should know that there is a web site that lists Buffett-type stocks, chosen by criteria set up by none other than Robert Hagstrom. (See Chapter 20.)

To reach the web site, go to Quicken.com

Hagstrom is quick to warn visitors that the stocks listed—which have been chosen by Quicken, using Hagstrom's formula, and not by Hagstrom himself—aren't a royal road to riches.

He writes: ". . . even if you use the tenets outlined in One-Click Scorecard and you do the follow-up research necessary before buying a stock, it is not likely that you will generate [a] 23 percent average annual gain over the next 30 years. Even Mr. Buffett admits that the possibility of his repeating this long-term performance is remote."

Still, Hagstrom adds that "I do believe that if you follow these tenets you will stand a better chance of outperforming the market."

The web site lists well over 100 stocks that have passed at least six of the criteria recommended by Hagstrom. Your "next step should be an evaluation of a company's management," he advises. "This is just a starting point." As Hagstrom sees it, Buffett studies four essentials about a company: (1) the company itself, (2) the management, (3) the financials, and (4) the asking price—in that order.

The site also provides the visitor with information about the various companies and a company profile.

In February 2001, these were the first 20 stocks listed on the web site, their order determined by how high their apparent "discount to intrinsic value" was.

	Company	*Discount to Intrinsic Value*
1.	Wesco Financial Corp.	98.6
2.	ECI Telecom Ltd.	95.5
3.	Koss Corp.	92.8
4.	Mesabi Trust CBI	92.6

5.	Xeta Technologies	92.0
6.	Cohu Inc.	91.5
7.	W Holding Company	91.1
8.	American Power Conversion	91.1
9.	General Employment ENT	87.0
10.	Cognex Corp.	86.6
11.	Pre-Paid Legal Services	86.4
12.	D.R. Horton Inc.	86.3
13.	ILG Industries	85.6
14.	Telefonos de Mexico SA L	84.6
15.	Jones Pharma Inc.	83.6
16.	Chittenden Corp.	83.1
17.	Orbotech Ltd.	83.1
18.	Communications Systems Inc.	83.0
19.	Dell Computer Corp.	82.8
20.	Royal Bancshares PA A	81.6

David Braverman

Another person who has picked up the gauntlet is David Braverman, a senior investment officer at Standard & Poor's and the leading analyst who covers Berkshire.

Since Braverman began constructing such portfolios (in February 1995), the Buffett-like stocks he has chosen have returned 255 percent (without dividends or transaction costs, through January 2001) compared with only 174 percent for the S&P 500 Index.

Here are the five criteria that Braverman used in screening the 10,000 stocks in the S&P Computstat data base:

1. High "owner earnings," which is essentially free cash flow—net income after taxes, plus depreciation and amortization of debt, less capital expenditures. A company had to have at least $20 million in free cash flow.
2. A net profit margin of at least 15 percent.
3. A high return on equity, or net income (before payment of preferred dividends), as a percentage of the value of stock outstanding. Braverman screened for a recent quarterly ROE over 15 percent, and an ROE of at least 15 percent for each of the past three years. (Buffett considers profit growth relative to growth in the capital base more meaningful than just growth in earnings.)
4. A high return on reinvested earnings. Each dollar of earnings retained by the company should produce more than a dollar of market value. To meet this test, Braverman looked for compa-

nies whose growth in market capitalization surpassed growth in retained earnings over the past five years.

5. No overvalued stocks. Free cash flow was projected five years out, under the assumption that cash flow grows at the same rate as earnings. To come up with a maximum valuation, Braverman then divided the estimated free cash flow by the current yield on the 30-year Treasury bond. Stocks selling above their projected valuations were thrown out.

The stocks listed below are not necessarily those that Buffett would buy. In choosing stocks, as mentioned, Buffett employs qualitative criteria as well—the nonmathematical as well as the mathematical, the heart's reasons as well as the head's. Also, Braverman did not eliminate technology stocks, like Microsoft, although Buffett has steadfastly avoided them.

Stock	*Current Price*	*Current P-E Ratio*
AmeriCredit	35	15.2
Biogen	68	4.5
Bristol-Myers Squibb	62	25.6
Brown & Brown	39	—
Citrix Systems	26	28.0
Dionex Corp.	36	—
Franklin Resources	41	16.7
Gannett Co.	67	17.4
Gentex Corp.	25	—
IPALCO Enterprises	24	14.1
John Nuveen	55	—
Lee Enterprises	32	—
Lincare Holdings	58	21.5
Linear Technology	43	31.2
Mackenzie Financial	19	—
MGIC Investment	56	9.7
Microsoft	61	33.9
Oracle Corp.	17	4.7
Orbotech	38	—
(T. Rowe) Price	36	15.7
SEI Investments	41	37.3
Tellabs	43	19.9
Verizon Communications	48	15.2
Watson Pharmaceuticals	56	25.2

CHAPTER 21

William J. Ruane of Sequoia

William J. Ruane (Photo courtesy of Bachrach).

What the Yankees are to baseball and what Beethoven is to symphonic music, Sequoia is to the world of mutual funds. Simply the best. If you had invested $10,000 in Sequoia in 1970, your money would have been worth $1,315,850 at the close of the year 2000. Since 1970 Sequoia has beaten the S&P 500 by an average of 2.7 percentage points a year. (See Figure 21.1.)

Alas, Sequoia bolted its door to new investors in the year King John signed the Magna Carta (or maybe it was only as recently as 1982).

The chairman of the Sequoia Fund is William J. Ruane. Silver-haired, fair skin, pleasant and charming, speaks slowly and carefully. Easy to get along with.

FIGURE 21.1 Sequoia Fund's Performance, 1994–2001.
Source: StockCharts.com.

Ruane's office is in the General Motors/Trump Building—on 59th Street and Fifth Avenue—with green marble and white marble in the lobby. Across the street from the Plaza, à la Vieille Russe, FAO Schwarz, Bergdorf Goodman. Ruane's 47th-floor office—simple and classic, much dark wood, no Quotron machine, no Bloomberg—has a gorgeous view of Central Park and parts north. Tasteful, conservative, interesting furniture. On an end table is Roger Lowenstein's biography of Warren Buffett. (It called Ruane "a straight arrow.") In a bookcase: James Kilpatrick's biography of Buffett, along with many investment books, stuff about Harvard, photos of family, books by Adam Smith, a biography of Bernard Baruch.

At 75 Ruane is still busy, still searching for good stocks; he divides his time as well as he can, but puts his family first. He's chairman of the board of Ruane, Cunniff & Co.; Richard T. Cunniff, 78, is vice chairman; Bob Goldfarb, 56, is president and has been CEO for the past three years.

A thread in our conversation: How impressed he is with Goldfarb, who has been a partner for 30 years and who is, in Ruane's estimation, the second-best money manager he has ever encountered. (No, he doesn't know many other money managers personally because "this wonderful candy store" he's been running is not in the Wall Street mainstream, but he reads about them.) "Buffett has no peer in brilliance, but Bob Goldfarb's next on my list," Ruane asserts. "He has the right approach and his talent is unique. He's a brilliant investor."

Benjamin Graham, the legendary Columbia professor who wrote the 1930s classic, *Security Analysis*, "provided the framework for Bob and my thinking and approach, and for many others," Ruane says. "We have great respect for quantitative [math] analysis. Financial reports are critical; the numbers tell you so much. With the amount of information made available by law, you can get an awfully good idea of what a company's about."

Still, Philip Fisher, author of *Common Stocks and Uncommon Profits*, "brought in new dimension, and all of us have found it instructive." Fisher (Chapter 5) argued that buying and holding blue-chip stocks was a fine strategy.

Finally, Buffett's teachings through his annual reports and so on "have continually advanced the foundation of security analysis established by Graham.

"In Graham's day, the depression and after," Ruane went on, "you could find lots of values by quantitative research—and it's still true to an extent. In the 1950s and 1960s, though, book value became less important than the quality of earnings power—more determinant of value.

> I can't emphasize that enough, that value as an entity also embraces growth. People ask: Are you growth or value? People don't fully appreciate the fact that growth is absolutely part of the value equation. But value is the ultimate yardstick.
>
> What it's all about is the market value of a stock. You multiply the price of a share by all the shares outstanding, minus the preferred stock, then calculate the real value, the intrinsic value, based on its earnings power. And if the market value is below the intrinsic value, you've got it.

He himself will buy stocks that aren't cheap. If a company has a high growth rate, "I'll pay up for it. Value may be the bottom line, but growth is a factor. The quality of earnings matters."

Ruane studied engineering during World War II in the U.S. Navy. After the war, he found that his aptitude for the practical application of engineering, working for General Electric, was such that he was not likely "to have a stellar career in that field."

He then went to Harvard Business School, where he studied under George Bates, who used the "case method" (real-life examples, not textbooks). "But Bates insisted that we read two books: *Where Are Their Customers' Yachts?* by Fred Schwed Jr. and Graham and Dodd's *Security Analysis*."

Ruane began aiming for a career as a security research analyst and eventually one of a money manager. He came to New York in 1949 and worked for Kidder, Peabody, "a great firm in those days." As a starter he was given three clients to handle—and a total of $15,000 to manage.

Then he learned that Ben Graham let outsiders audit his class at Columbia. "I called up and they said fine—this was in 1950. It was a seminar course, with 15 Columbia students and five stockbrokers." Ruane first met Buffett then; Buffett was taking the course.

"It was a great experience. The seminar was made completely fascinating by the interplay between Ben and Warren Buffett, who together made the sparks fly."

What can he tell me about Graham? "I didn't know him well, but he was a wonderful teacher, bright and fair. One afternoon he called me up for coffee; he was in New York on his way to California. He had read a book in Portuguese and liked it so much that he wanted to translate it, so he dropped in on a publisher that day. His interests were so diverse. He lived well, but not on a major scale. He was not just a genius in the field of economics, but he was brilliant in many other ways and, on top of that, he was a very kind guy."

Didn't Graham's investment rules change over the years?

"The world changes, and you must change with it. There's been a shift from working capital to earning power as the prime determinant of value. The current value of all future dividends, discounted back. Clean earnings power. You look for stocks with a special strength or niche or moat. You want growth that's somewhat predictable over five, eight or ten years. And after you've done that much homework, why not own a lot of it? If your assumption was right, you can continue to hold on."

Like Ruane, Goldfarb went to Harvard; in 1971 he walked in the front door looking for a job. "There were three or four of us then, and we made him an employee. We had no doubt about him at all. He's been a major factor in the fund's doing so well."

Questions and Answers

Q. If I ever manage to get my hot little hands on one sniveling share, can I buy more?

W.R. Yes. Unless you try to buy $1 million worth, as someone once tried to.

Q. Will Sequoia ever reopen to new investors?

W.R. Very doubtful. We have a commitment to our board of directors that accepting additional money is not in our shareholders' interest. As it is, we don't have enough good ideas to keep fully invested. Even originally, money was coming in faster than we had good ideas.

A flood of new money couldn't be invested profitably—that's one reason the fund remains closed. Another reason: "Potential shareholders of size want to see you and hear you, and that would take up too much of our time."

Ruane, Cunniff & Company now manages $4 billion–$5 billion in private accounts as well as Sequoia, which has about $4 billion in assets.

Sequoia is discriminating about the stocks it buys. "I believe in concentration," says Ruane, "and we bought just five new stocks in 2000."

Sequoia is 33 percent invested in Berkshire Hathaway. "But we didn't buy it for 20 years—for various reasons. Then we looked at it in 1989, took a good look at it, and decided that it was an attractive stock."

We talked about the Trading Madness, the vast conspiracy to persuade the investing public to buy and sell as frequently as possible. He mentioned watching CNBC, where "some people recommend stocks selling at many times their growth rates and analysts predicting 15 percent–20 percent growth for 20 or 30 years. It doesn't happen in the real world." He referred to an article by Carol Loomis in an issue of *Fortune* providing evidence that hardly any companies do that well regularly.

Q. Why all this turnover?

W.R. It isn't just brokers who are out to make money. It's also fueled by an enormous frenzy by thousands of money managers who are twisting and turning to try to be in the right place at the right time, with little thought of the underlying investment's merits.

Q. What mistakes have you made?

W.R. I've sold too early so many times. You should sell only when there is a significant change in a company's fundamentals. You know it when it comes along. But while the world changes, it doesn't change that much in five-year periods. Wall Street will sell a stock to a point where it's way out of whack. For example, in the late 70s, Gillette was selling at 6 or 7 times earnings. The p-e grew to reflect its basic fundamentals.

The 50s to the 80s were a great time; investors didn't appreciate the value of internal compounding. The arithmetic was fabulous. Many companies selling at low p-e's had a high return on equity.

Sequoia's golden years were the mid-70s. In 1975 the fund rose 62 percent, and in 1976 it rose 72 percent. After the horrendous bear market of 1973–1974, he recalled, "Stocks were being given away.

"But more and more, stock prices became realistic. Their prices became significantly related to interest rates. I don't think the market is very overpriced now, but I'm not finding as much to buy. The market was dirt cheap in '78."

Not that all investors are much wiser these days. With wonderment in his voice, he mentioned that on March 1, 2001, the market was down 210 points, yet it ended up higher. "It's hard to know what's on some people's minds as the pack flows one way and then the other on any particular day."

Q. Didn't you once say that return on equity was the key clue that a company was doing well?

W.R. Return on equity tells you how profitable a company is, but it doesn't tell you if the company is static, what the opportunity is for reinvesting its earnings for growth, for a continuing high rate of return.

Q. What about index funds?

W.R. They're wonderful for people, although a year ago when the S&P was 30 percent in tech and tech was overpriced, that index fund wasn't the best place to be. Still, if you want to be in the market and you have no particular knowledge (and it's hard enough if you *do* have particular knowledge), an index fund is probably the best way to invest.

Basics

Minimum Investment: Closed
Phone Number: 212-832-5280
Web Address: www.sequoiafund.com

Q. What about momentum investing? Buying securities that have been going up?

W.R. It's not investing.

Q. What other advice do you have for ordinary investors?

W.R. Put half your money into an index fund, and have the other half in good three–four year bonds or Treasuries, and keep rolling it over. You shouldn't have to think about the quality of your bond investments. If you're not a pro, don't fool about with those things.

He also urges investors to have a decent reserve fund, one that will last three or four years. In Treasuries. "I really believe, as I get along, that if you have a liberal reserve, you will continue to do intelligent things with stocks even when you're under pressure."

Advice from Albert Hettinger of Lazard Freres

Says Bill Ruane, "I got some fine advice, which I treasure, in 1957 from a great mind: Albert Hettinger of Lazard Freres. He's not well known now, but he was one of the finest investors of the mid-century. He had four general rules, which I've never forgotten."

1. Don't use margin. If you're smart, you don't have to borrow money to make money. If you're dumb, you may go broke.
2. Buy six or seven securities you know well. Have a concentrated portfolio. But don't have only one or two securities.
3. Pay no attention to the level of the stock market. Concentrate your attention on individual stocks. Market-timing has led to enormous mistakes.
4. Beware of momentum. Stocks and markets tend to go to extremes both on the upside and the downside.

CHAPTER 22

Robert Hagstrom of Legg Mason Focus Trust

The Legg Mason Focus Trust Fund, managed by Robert G. Hagstrom, was originally intended to closely reflect Buffett's investment strategy in a mutual fund, one with a low minimum first investment. But as the fund has evolved, it seems to have moved more toward the growth end of the spectrum, under the guidance of the celebrated money manager Bill Miller, who runs various Legg Mason funds.

Hagstrom, 41, has a B.A. and an M.A. from Villanova University. He is a Chartered Financial Analyst and a money manager as well as the author of excellent books on Buffett's investment strategy, such as *The Warren Buffett Way* (New York: John Wiley & Sons, 1995). As is his wont, Buffett hasn't commented on the books, but his partner, Charlie Munger, has recommended them to Berkshire shareholders. Hagstrom has also identified the major mathematical criteria he believes that Buffett uses to screen stocks, and more than 100 of them are listed on the Quicken web site. (See Chapter 20.)

The Focus Trust Fund began in 1996, the name apparently deriving from Buffett's comment to Hagstrom that his is a "focus" portfolio. At the time there were only a few concentrated funds, such as Clipper, Longleaf Partners, Janus Twenty, and Sequoia.

When I first interviewed Hagstrom, in 1995, he acknowledged that his fund wasn't an exact replica of Berkshire's stock portfolio. Focus Trust owned shares of William Wrigley Jr., which Berkshire didn't; the fund didn't own Coca-Cola or Gillette because "they've run up so far." Hagstrom was also avoiding UST, a favorite of Buffett's: "The possible liability lawsuits frighten us." Among the entire areas that Hagstrom was avoiding: technology.

A year after the fund was launched, assets were still only $20 million. "Fortunately, I knew Bill Miller," Hagstrom told me recently, "and he agreed that Legg Mason was the perfect place to take a focus-type, low turnover fund." In 1998 the fund changed its name to Legg Mason Focus Trust.

With only 17 or so stocks, the fund is certainly concentrated. But Hagstrom, unlike Buffett, has been willing to venture into technology, and under Miller's guidance he put one-third of Focus Trust into New Economy-related stocks.

Thanks to the tech wreck, Focus Trust had a miserable 2000, down 22 percent. But for the first two, three, and four years of its existence it outperformed the S&P, quite an accomplishment considering how miserably other value funds had been faring and how splendidly the growth-oriented S&P 500 had been performing. By the end of 1999, in fact, Focus Trust had beaten the S&P 500 by 18 basis points (0.18 percent) a year. The fund was also impressively tax-efficient, with a 98 percent score as opposed to only 96 percent for Vanguard 500 Stock Index. (Investors kept 98 percent of their total returns out of Uncle Sam's clutches.) See Figure 22.1.

Questions and Answers

Q. What happened in 2000?

R.H. In 2000, we got clobbered. We were overweighted in technology. We had nothing in oil, nothing in drugs, nothing in utilities [sectors that excelled].

Q. Hasn't Buffett himself become less and less of a Grahamite? More and more a follower of Fisher—more growth-oriented?

R.H. This shift on Buffett's part has been no doubt a result of the influence of his partner, Charlie Munger. Still, Buffett continues to seek a "margin of safety," trying to buy assets cheaply, and zeroes in on the companies he buys, not on what's going on in the markets in general ["bottom up" and not "top down"]. He simply seeks valuable businesses with favorable long-term prospects and capable managers. But low price-earnings ratios and low price-book

FIGURE 22.1 Legg Mason's Focus Trust's Performance, July 1998–April 2001.
Source: StockCharts.com.

ratios, and high dividend yields, aren't special concerns to him now. That wasn't characteristic of Graham. The Graham strategy—low p-e ratios, low price to book—wasn't consistently successful after the 70s and early 80s.

Q. Can an ordinary investor truly emulate Buffett and do well by buying only a handful of stocks?

R.H. If you concentrate on 15 or 20 good stocks with low turnover, it's my experience that you will do well. Your relative performance will be dramatic. The trouble is that any investment strategy will fade sometime, and ordinary investors, along with professionals, will have their endurance tested.

Basics

Minimum first investment: $1,000 (it's the same for IRAs).
Phone: (800) 822-5544.
Web Address: www.leggmason.com.

Most fail. The influence of the market and other investors is so great. Even if a money manager steadfastly carries the banner, his or her followers may retreat.

Morningstar in January 2001 rated Legg Mason Focus Trust "average" compared with other stock funds, "below average" compared with other large-blend funds. The fund was overweighted in retail, financials, and technology. The turnover in 1999 was 14 percent, in 1998 21 percent, in 1997 14 percent, and in 1996 8 percent.

CHAPTER 23

Louis A. Simpson of GEICO

Louis A. Simpson (Photo courtesy of GEICO).

Buffett has said that the person who might take over Berkshire Hathaway when he leaves—he was 70 in the year 2001—is Louis A. Simpson, 63, a reclusive value investor who has run GEICO's investment portfolio since 1979.

Simpson, according to Buffett, invests in almost the same way he does. "Lou takes the same conservative, concentrated approach to investments that we do. . . . ," to quote Buffett. "His presence on the scene assures us that Berkshire would have an extraordinary professional immediately available to handle its investments if something were to happen to [Munger] and me."

Unlike all the other investment managers who run Berkshire's subsidiaries, Simpson has a totally free hand, indicating how much trust Buffett places in him.

One can learn which stocks Simpson owns in his GEICO portfolio by checking with A.M. Best, which rates and tracks insurance companies.

Forbes magazine (October 10, 2000) has reported that Simpson is a "slightly more daring investor—one who's not afraid of tech buys or portfolio turnover." Most of the time his portfolio has trailed Buffett's, but not by much. In 1999, when tech stocks were in their glory, Simpson's portfolio actually did better.

From late 1979 into 1996, when GEICO was still traded publicly, Simpson's average yearly return was 22.8 percent versus Berkshire's 26.5 percent—as against the Standard & Poor's 500's mere 15.7 percent. Using data from A.M. Best, Forbes estimated that GEICO earned 17 percent in 1999, while Berkshire just about broke even.

Simpson's portfolio is more concentrated than Buffett's, probably because he has less money to invest—$2 billion versus $40 billion. Recently Berkshire Hathaway owned twenty-eight stocks; GEICO, only nine. According to Morningstar, the average large-cap value fund owns 89. One of Simpson's stocks, Shaw Communications, even has a high p-e ratio, at 61.

Simpson also seems to buy and sell positions more frequently than Berkshire, *Forbes* reports, although this, too, may be because of the smaller size of his portfolio.

In 1999 Simpson bought two stocks, Jones Apparel and Shaw Communications, representing almost a quarter of his entire portfolio. He tossed out Manpower, the employment agency for temps. In 2000 he bought GATX and Dun & Bradstreet. In 1999 Berkshire also bought some stocks, but they were small pickings—just 5 percent of the portfolio.

In 1997 Simpson bought Arrow Electronics and Mattel; in 1998, he sold them both. He bought TCA Cable in 1998 and sold it in 1999.

Whereas Buffett won't buy technology stocks—he points out, quite correctly, how difficult it is to identify today those companies that will be powerhouses five or ten years from now—Simpson has. But he has glommed onto seemingly cheap tech stocks.

Berkshire in 2000 had half of its portfolio in the financial sector; Simpson was in the same ballpark, having 25 percent of his portfolio in Freddie Mac and U.S. Bancorp.

Like Buffett, Simpson is a fanatic. He gobbles up financial statements and annual reports as if they were crime novels. And like Buffett he's sure of himself as far as investing goes. He, too, lives far away from the madding Wall Street crowd—in Rancho Santa Fe, California, which is near San Diego.

Simpson was born in Chicago. He taught economics at Princeton in the early 1960s, then moved to Shareholders Management, a mutual fund run by the controversial Fred Carr. Simpson left after a half-year, apparently because Shareholders Management's wildly risky investment strategy had landed the company into hot water.

Ten years later he interviewed for the GEICO job. After Buffett talked with him for four hours, Buffett said, according to *Forbes*, "Stop the search. That's the fella."

He's said of Simpson that he has "the ideal temperament for investing." He "derived no particular pleasure from operating with or against the crowd." He has "consistently invested in undervalued common stocks that, individually, were unlikely to present him with a permanent loss and that, collectively, were close to risk free."(Martin Whitman, the investor, claims that Buffett's greatest strength is his ability to identify good people.)

"Simpson seems to have the ideal temperament for Buffett," Robert Hagstrom told me. "He views stocks as businesses, he wants to concentrate, and his portfolio has a low turnover. And he doesn't have any anxiety about his stocks being out of favor."

The heir apparent himself has outlined his investment strategy in a GEICO report:

- "Think independently." He's skeptical of Wall Street; he reads widely and voraciously.
- "Invest in high-return businesses for shareholders." He wants companies making money now and promising to continue making money. He interviews management to make sure they are shareholder friendly and not out to boost their incomes or their self-esteem by creating empires.
- "Pay only a reasonable price, even for an excellent business." Even a splendid company is a bad investment, he believes, if the price is too high. (Fisher might argue that the price of a splendid company would have to be *extremely* high.)
- "Do not diversify excessively."

GEICO's Recent Holdings	
COMPANY/BUSINESS	**PRICE-EARNINGS RATIO**
Dun & Bradstreet/financial rater	31
First Data/credit card processing	13
Freddie Mac/mortgage seller	17
GATX/railcar leasing	14
Great Lakes Chemical/chemicals	12
Jones Apparel/clothing	14
Nike/footwear	19
Shaw Communications/cable TV	61
U.S. Bancorp/banking	11

CHAPTER 24

Christopher Browne of Tweedy, Browne

Managing Directors, Tweedy, Browne (left to right): John Spears, Robert Wyckoff, Christopher Browne, Thomas Schrager, William Browne (Photo courtesy of Tweedy, Browne).

Even if someone is a Buffett buff, he or she may not know the name of the stockbroker who bought shares of Berkshire Hathaway for Warren Buffett.

The broker's name was Howard Browne, of the firm that is now known as Tweedy, Browne. It's a fine old firm, and it still practices Benjamin Graham-type investing, looking for (among other things) cheap cigar butts that have a few good puffs left in them.

The mutual funds the company runs, Tweedy, Browne American Value and Tweedy, Browne Global Value, have commendable records. In fact, Morningstar chose Global Value as its foreign fund of the year for 2000.

The family itself is different from other fund families for a variety of reasons.

- There are only two funds in the family—no sector funds, no fixed-income funds, no "market-neutral" funds, no funds du jour.
- Tweedy, Browne sticks to its knitting. The stocks of both funds have price-earnings ratios and price-book ratios far below the average Standard & Poor's 500 stock. Neither fund, naturally, has more than a trace of technology stocks.
- The fund family has a colorful history. It was launched as a brokerage firm in 1920 by Forrest Berwind Tweedy, and for years its biggest customer was no less than Ben Graham.

Another customer, later on, was Buffett, a student of Graham's at Columbia, who bought most of his shares of Berkshire Hathaway through Howard Browne, father of the two Brownes who run the fund today. (A third manager is John Spears.)

Howard Browne even gave Buffett desk space. Buffett would drop in and sip a soft drink—no, not Coca-Cola but Pepsi.

Buffett asked all his brokers not to buy the stocks he was buying. (If they did, that would raise a stock's price, forcing Buffett to pay more for the stock later on.) Apparently Browne's father was one of very few who listened.

Something else different about Tweedy, Browne: The managers are intellectuals. They study the academic data about investing. They have even published some splendid pamphlets: "What Has Worked in Investing" (answer: undervalued stocks) and "Ten Ways to Beat an Index" (a key way: buy and hold undervalued stocks). They even have an essay on how to invest like Warren Buffett. (See Chapter 9.)

Beyond that, Chris Browne just happens to be a felicitous writer. A taste: "As we have said in the past, we love technology, but we just don't love technology stocks. We also have a Web page, www.Tweedy.com, where we post any news about the firm. . . . A Web poacher took www.TweedyBrowne.com. We were too cheap to ransom it back." (But it's back anyway.)

The company's offices are on Park Avenue in New York City. Interviews with the shrewd and urbane Chris Browne, 53, are a pleasure.

Questions and Answers

Q. Why do growth and value stocks alternate days in the sun?

C.B. Those terms are hard to define. Growth guys claim that they buy all the neat companies and all the technology companies growing wonderfully. They say that we value guys invest in the hospice patients of corporate America. Rust-belt stuff. But Warren Buffett said that value and growth are joined at the hip. And the best growth people are also value people.

A lot of people who call themselves growth players buy stocks that are hard to value. Fiber-optic cable makers, for example. The whole technology market in recent years.

Sanford Bernstein did a study of pharmaceutical companies and technology companies during the past 20 years and found that they had the same long-term rates of return. The difference was that the technology leaders kept changing, but the pharmaceutical leaders remained the same. Technology stocks are far more likely to crash and burn. Everyone expects them to be so perfect, and with the least disappointment they're down 20, 30, 60 percent.

Some people confuse growth investing with momentum investing, where, if it's been going up, you buy it. But when the music stops, the question is whether you'll get a chair.

Everyone jumps onto the bandwagon; money gravitates to what has performed best recently. Nothing else explains the dot.com phenomenon. There was no fundamental financial reason for buying these stocks. And when they began to run out of cash, it caused the collapse.

You can buy and hold drug stocks for 10 or 20 years, but not tech stocks—except for IBM and Hewlett-Packard. It's difficult for tech stocks to defend their market position. Someone is always inventing something that goes twice as fast. These companies have to reinvent themselves every 10 years, but Coca-Cola makes Coke, and that's it.

Q. How do you choose value stocks?

C.B. To insulate us, we track purchases by company officers. We rate people who buy in importance, too: more if it's the chairman or the chief financial officer, less if it's an outside director. Ideally, we see a reasonable price-book ratio, a reasonable price-earnings ratio, and insiders accumulating shares.

We also follow the leads of smart people. Years ago, Wells Fargo was selling for $65 a share with no earnings. The Federal Reserve wouldn't believe that the bank had no problems with its real-estate loans, so the Fed had made the bank set aside extra reserves. That wiped out the earnings. Two respected bank analysts had totally different opinions: One said the bank's loans would blow up, the other said that idea was absurd. We didn't know whom to believe. Then Warren Buffett bought $600 million worth of shares. He didn't phone us to tip us off; but the news that he was buying was better than a phone call.

In 1993 Johnson & Johnson was selling at only 12 times earnings when Hillary-care was threatening the pharmaceutical industry. Then Tom Murphy at Capital Cities, a director at J&J, bought nearly 40,000 shares. We decided to make a significant investment—and we made good profits.

In general, it's better to be lucky than smart.

Q. What about Pharmacia? That's in both your portfolios.

C.B. It's had all sorts of problems. But it has the lowest ratio of price to sales of any major pharmaceutical. And they have enough white coats doing research, they're bound to find something. When Fred Hassan came over from American Home to take over Pharmacia, he and other key insiders bought more than 100,000 shares personally. We put this fact-set together and bought.

In general, we've found that if you pay attention to academic studies of stock market truths, plus particular fact-sets, plus you have a diversified portfolio, you'll have satisfactory rates of return.

Not many people pay attention to what has worked in the stock market—things like low price-earnings ratios, low price-book ratios, and the high price you might get in an open auction for the entire company. It's not that it's difficult to figure out. It's like pricing a house. What have similar houses been going for?

As value investors, our focus isn't on buying stocks that may beat the estimates by a penny.

Value people aren't the kind of guys you go drinking with. They're eccentric. Opinionated.

Growth people are all over the landscape in terms of investing. Will the drug sector do well over three weeks or not? They don't have strong opinions about anything. They don't adhere to principles. But they're good people to go out drinking with.

Growth investors may wind up with a lot of short-term capital gains. We have long-term gains. We held Johnson & Johnson for more than six years. We'd like to hold our stocks forever. We're biased toward nontaxable gains. Buffett is a good example: He never sells anything.

The three of us [C.B. and managers William H. Browne and John D. Spears] have $400 million of our own money in the stocks that our clients own and in the funds themselves. For us, April 15 is a national day of mourning.

We accept the fact that as value managers we'll have down periods, but over 20-year periods we'll be winners. The chances of hedge-fund jockeys beating the index over the next quarter for the next 20 years are pretty slim. They're inclined to confuse luck with intelligence.

We pay more attention to what we can actually accomplish. We look at the empirical data. There's little empiricism in this business.

Others sit down at a desk and ask themselves, What shall we buy or sell today? They're business types, looking for new products. If XYZ stock has faltered for three quarters, they're out of there. And because they work for someone else, they might be fired.

We stick to our guns. We don't have bosses who can fire us. The only people who can fire us are our clients.

Warren Buffett answers to no one. He can't be fired. He can do whatever the hell he wants.

Q. How does Buffett's strategy differ from Tweedy, Browne's?

C.B. We don't make as large a bet. We're more diversified. We have less confidence in our ability. Besides, if we weren't as diversified as we are, we could lose our accounts.

Q. What do you think of Buffett's strategy of buying good companies and owning them forever?

C.B. Buy blue chips? It sounds nice. Yet Lucent and AT&T were blue chips, and look at them now. Lucent is going to have to reinvent itself. Who knows?

The question Buffett asks is, Could I own this stock for ten years? If I were locked into a stock, what would I buy? I'd say some of pharmaceuticals, like Johnson & Johnson. Buffett wants a company with a moat around it, and Johnson & Johnson has a moat. No one is about to replace Band-Aids.

Q. What about Philip Morris stock? That wasn't a stock to buy and hold forever.

C.B. We got rid of it. It's not subject to market analysis. Who knows what will happen with the court system? It's got a nice, addictive product, it's cheap, and it does well in developing countries. When people in a developing country become affluent, they buy the best brand names: Coca-Cola and Marlboro. But as far as we're concerned, we'd rather buy something else.

Q. What do you think of index funds?

C.B. They're difficult to beat—both pre-tax and even more on an after-tax basis. But at this point, the S&P 500 is so tech oriented and so overweighted in a few stocks. No one creates a portfolio in terms of the weightings of an index. That skews the returns dramatically—five or ten stocks have been accounting for almost all of the returns.

Q. Why has your global fund been doing better than your U.S. fund?

C.B. In our U.S. fund, we don't have much in technology stocks—just telecoms. That has hurt us. Abroad, there are crazy indexes. The Swedish index is half Nokia. Five stocks make up 80 percent of the Dutch index. It's really wacko.

In our foreign fund, we have only 11 percent in U.S. stocks. And we're 100 percent hedged. We don't try to predict currency movements.

Q. What mistakes have you made?

C.B. Even if a stock fits your profile and you have good diversification, sometimes you run into a wall. It happens. The most difficult thing is, when you have negative news, to try to examine the stock on its new fundamentals. If it's still selling at a discount, we'll hang on. But if we think a lot more bad news may be coming, we'll get out. We tend to be not as forward thinking as growth managers. Value people tend to focus on the here and now as opposed to making predictions.

I sit on other boards, and the chairmen may say earnings will be 43 cents a share this quarter, and two weeks later it turns out to be 27 cents a share. They don't know.

God's the only great predictor, and he's not talking to many of us. And those who do talk to God don't ask the right questions.

Q. If you had to choose one stock to own for 20 years, what would it be? Johnson & Johnson?

C.B. As a game, we ask ourselves that. But we don't act on it. I can't tell you exactly, but it would probably be in the pharmaceutical industry. Look at the demographics, look at the rates of discovery in biomedical science. I'm on the board of Rockefeller University, and biotechnology research is very exciting. Research time is getting compressed.

In technology, obsolescence may take six months. In 1970 we bought a hand-held calculator for $350. It weighed three pounds. It had memory. Two years later, the company that made those calculators was in bankruptcy and Hewlett-Packard was giving calculators away as Christmas presents. Today, PalmPilots are wonderful, but the cost will have to come down. When Bill Gates starts making them, the price will go down and down.

Q. Why do so many investors make mistakes?

C.B. People tend to value action rather than inaction. That's why women are more successful investors than men. They're more cautious. They buy and sell less than men, and they get better results. Turnover is inversely related to investment results. Portfolio managers are always buying and selling stuff. They think they're making intelligent decisions, but the data suggest otherwise.

People feel that they must be doing something to justify their existence. Even if they don't feel that way, the people they report to feel that way. "No changes this month? What are we *paying* you for?"

Some people make a killing, and other people think they can, too—it's the confidence factor. Everyone thinks they will win the lottery, despite the fact that five million tickets are sold. It's pathetic, but they do.

There's so much noise, so much instant information, and people always react. We ourselves say, "That's nice, but not relevant." Other people buy at 10 A.M. and sell at 11 A.M. They make four points on the round-trip.

At other mutual funds, their results are compared to a benchmark, an index. So they feel that they have to be diversified like the index, always to have to be 10 percent in oils. We ourselves ignore industry categories.

Q. Have you ever been asked to put together a concentrated portfolio?

C.B. Yes, but when we try to identify the best stocks in our portfolio, we're always wrong. They're the ones that decline. So we find it very easy not to try to do what we know we can't do.

The American Value Fund

The American Value fund, launched in 1993, is unusually stable. Its beta is 0.77, meaning that it fluctuates only 77 percent as much as the S&P 500. Morningstar rates it "below average" for risk. The fund trades infrequently: Its turnover is usually less than 20 percent a year. (In 1995, it was 4 percent.) The fund's long-term record, Morningstar reports, "is solid, suggesting that this offering is a good option for investors with growth-heavy portfolios." (See Figure 24.1.)

Tweedy, Browne Global Value is a little less volatile than its U.S. counterpart, with a standard deviation of 15.9 versus 16.87. Its five-year record is also better: 19.13 percent a year versus 16.75 percent. The fund also has much more in the way of assets: $3.557 billion. Assets are heavily invested in Europe (42 percent), with only 12 percent in U.S. stocks

The funds share some of the same stocks.

FIGURE 24.1 Tweedy, Browne American Value Fund's Performance, July 1995–August 2001.
Source: StockCharts.com.

Basics

Minimum Investment: $2,500
Phone: (800) 432-4789
Web Address: www.TweedyBrowne.com
Fees: These funds are no-load funds.

CHAPTER 25

Martin J. Whitman of the Third Avenue Funds

Martin J. Whitman (Photo courtesy of Third Avenue Funds).

I asked Marty Whitman how his investment strategy differs from Buffett's—Whitman has known Buffett for 25 or so years.

"He's a control investor," he replied. He owns 100 percent of some of his companies, like See's Candy; he's an active member of the board of directors of certain companies that Berkshire has a large stake in, like Coca-Cola and Gillette. He recently approved of a change in the CEOs of both companies.

"We at Third Avenue," said Whitman, "are just passive investors. Not that we aren't influential."

What are Buffett's special gifts? "Of all the people I know," replied Whitman, "he has the most uncanny insights into people. He's an unbelievably good judge of people. It's a great talent. And he's a good financial guy, too."

How is Whitman himself at evaluating people? "I screw up. Boy!"

Whitman, a white-haired gentleman in his 70s, has a pleasant manner, a sweet smile, a fresh sense of humor, and a razor-sharp mind. He's outspoken, too—a journalist's dream.

At a Morningstar conference not long ago, he listened attentively while a youthful journalist recommended that everyone just invest in index funds. Value managers don't like to hear that. Marty was the next speaker. "I don't know who that young guy was," he said sweetly, referring to the *Wall Street Journal* writer, "but he's a complete idiot." Vintage Whitman. (Whitman rightly saw that the S&P 500, dominated by high-priced big-capitalization stocks, would fall into a deep hole in the year 2000.)

Another time, visiting New Jersey to give a talk, he and his driver got lost, although they managed to arrive at the lecture hall in time. He told the audience, "Finding good undervalued companies is hard, but finding Route 4 from the George Washington Bridge is sheer murder."

Another way Whitman and Buffett differ: "He won't do high tech, and I do a lot of high tech. We're both right. Tech has a high failure rate, a high strikeout rate. But when we do tech, we do 12–14 stocks among semiconductors—and that's very tough for a control guy," someone who wants to micromanage his portfolio. "I made a fortune in semiconductors, something he wouldn't touch. We knew going in that there might be dogs," but that's why they bought 12 or 14 of them.

Early in his career, Whitman went into bank and shareholder litigation—"a great training ground." He became interested in closed-end funds, and went after Equity Strategies, a fund whose net asset value was far below its intrinsic value, what the individual holdings in the fund were really worth. He took it over and opened it up, realizing the appreciation. "That's something people can't do these days," he said, "because of legal restrictions the closed-end funds have set up."

He's taught at the Yale School of Business for years, and recently began teaching at Columbia.

During a wide-ranging conversation in his office, Whitman told me that "it's ordained that some of your stocks won't do well. There are a lot of disappointments." He was wearing a purple sports shirt, slacks, and beaten-up sneakers—placed atop his desk. What the heck, it's his office and his company.

Questions and Answers

Q. What causes most of your own mistakes?

M.W. Faulty appraisals of management's abilities. We can really screw up. Assessing people happens to be Buffett's great strength. I know Buffett, and he's not such a genius. He doesn't know as much about finance as I do. But he's a great judge of people, especially management people. He'll agree with that.

Like many other value investors, Marty has little but contempt for growth investors. As he sees it, they buy high-priced stocks, wait until the market goes nuts and those stocks become even more high-priced—then sell.

M.W. The inmates are running the insane asylum. All "value" means is being price-conscious. Growth investors ignore the price, and put their weight on the outlook—speculating on the great times ahead.

A principal reason why value stocks in the long run do better than growth stocks is that you don't need a crazy stock market to bail you out. There can be mergers, buyouts, acquisitions—and you make money. That's why Alan Greenspan and the economy are "irrelevant": All you need do is buy good stocks cheap—and hang on. We ignore market risk.

Third Avenue Value was going great guns in 2000 because Whitman bought semiconductor stocks in 1997 and 1998, when they were ridiculously cheap. Otherwise, most of his portfolio wasn't doing much: "Sixty percent of it sucks, price-wise." See Figure 25.1.

He adds another reason why his portfolio is beating the band: "I'll spell it out. L-u-c-k."

Whitman, who's been in the business for nearly 50 years, likes to contradict people—perhaps that comes with the value territory, buying stocks that almost everyone else despises.

Q. Doesn't a value investor need lots of patience?

FIGURE 25.1 Third Avenue Value Fund's Performance, 1994–2001.
Source: StockCharts.com.

M.W. With individual stocks, maybe, but not with your entire portfolio if you're doing it right. Some of your stocks will be basking in the sun. I've never lost a night's sleep.

Q You're not a big fan of index funds?

M.W. It's far superior to speculating. But it's not as good as intelligent value investing. It's not even close.

For novice investors, I recommend mutual funds, where it's hard for investors to get roundly abused. And the part I like best, the promoters can get filthy rich. It's like having a toll booth on the George Washington Bridge. All cash—and you don't have to work very hard.

I suggest that the average investor buy a leading value fund, like Mutual Shares, Gabelli, Oakmark, Longleaf, Royce, or Tweedy, Browne. In all the years I've been in business the outside passive investor is always getting taken to the cleaners. IPOs. Tax shelters. Junk bonds. They buy what's popular. And that's a death sentence.

Q. What one stock would you recommend that a person buy and hold forever?

M.W. Capital Southwest, a diversified business development company run by someone I admire, Bill Thomas. I expect it to grow by 20 percent a year.

Basics

Minimum First Investment: $1,000
Phone Number: (800) 443-1021
Web Address: www.mjwhitman.com/third.htm
Fees: This is a no-load fund.

Q. What investment book would you recommend? Besides your own book, *Value Investing*?

M.W. Trouble is, no book emphasizes the quality of a company's resources before the quantity. Or advises people to buy cheap rather than to predict prices. To look for the absence of liabilities. And a generous free cash flow and other signs of strong financials.

Q. What really good question did I fail to ask you?

M.W. The advice I give kids at Yale who want to go into the field: Get training in an investment bank, in public accounting, as a private placement lender, or as a commercial lender. Learn the guts of the business.

Q. How important is the p-e ratio when you assess a stock?

M.W. Toyoda Automatic Loom Works has tremendous assets in securities, including Toyota, the auto company. Yet leading analysts writing about Toyoda ignore the assets and write about the high p-e ratio. Their brains are not in the usual biological place.

CHAPTER 26

Walter Schloss of Walter & Edwin Schloss Associates

Walter Schloss (Photo courtesy of John Abbott).

Walter J. Schloss worked as an analyst for Graham himself, and his record is powerful evidence that value investing is a sensible strategy. Schloss has been managing money since 1955. In that span, his investments have risen 15.7 percent a year; the Standard & Poor's Industrial Average (not the 500 Index) has climbed only 11.2 percent a year.

At age 84, Schloss still comes to work every day, sharing an office with the Tweedy, Browne folks on Park Avenue in New York City. When he and Christopher Browne go out to lunch, Browne—a man in his early 50s—has to quicken his step to keep up. And in an interview with me, Schloss was full of beans, quick thinking and contentious—for example, dismissing the naïve notion that anyone should buy and hold stocks indefinitely (I had said that ordinary investors might learn that from Buffett), denigrating index funds, and scolding me for mistakenly referring to Bill Ruane, who started the Sequoia Fund, as Charles.

Schloss is nowhere near so famous as Graham's most notable pupil, with whom Schloss shared an office when both worked for Graham back in 1957. Contented with his role in life, Schloss has never tried to make his firm especially large.

He and the Sage of Omaha remain friends. At first Schloss was dubious about letting me interview him. Then he decided, "I'll check with Warren." An hour later, he called me back: Buffett had told him that he didn't mind.

Like Graham, Schloss looks for good companies with cheap stocks, and he focuses almost exclusively on the numbers. He discouraged me from visiting him in person—he was busy, and didn't want me to make the trip—so I spoke to him on the phone.

Questions and Answers

Q. Benjamin Graham, I gather, was very much influenced by the crash of 1929 and the depression that followed.

W.S. Yes, the crash affected him a lot because he had spent a lot of money and suddenly he wasn't making any.

Q. Graham and Buffett never forgot how treacherous the stock market could be.

W.S. Yes, and Warren's father, too. His father was a stockbroker. I think he inherited that fear—a lot of us did.

Q. People don't remember much about the crash years.

W.S. They don't want to.

Q. 1929 wasn't actually that bad a year. The market was down only 17 percent.

W.S. It was if you had bought on margin, which people were doing as if they were the high-tech stocks of today. You could buy on margin with only 10 percent, so if the market went down a little bit, you could be wiped out. Stocks that might have been 90 went down to 2.

Now we have margin of 50 percent, but even with that speculators lost a lot of money with high-tech stocks. The stock market went back up at the end of 1929, then went down in March of 1930. It was a bear trap.

Q. I think Ben Graham fell into that trap.

W.S. I don't know. . . . But you learn by doing.

Q. Graham's rules for investing changed over the years, didn't they?

W.S. We live in a society that changes, so you can't be too strict about the rules you had 40 or 50 years ago. You can't buy stocks on the basis you did then. We would buy companies selling for less than their working capital, but now you can't do it. Those companies would get taken over. We use book value now.

Q. And other investors discover those cheap stocks, too?

W.S. You have 40,000–50,000 Chartered Financial Analysts looking for those stocks. I have a friend who came out of the Harvard Business School in 1949, I think it was, and he said that out of the whole class only four people went down to Wall Street. In the last couple of years, 80 percent or 90 percent went down to Wall Street.

Q. Do you think book value is the single best way to estimate the intrinsic value of a company?

W.S. No, no, I don't think it's the only way. It's a factor, though. The problem is, even if there's book value, a company may not really be worth a lot—a big old plant might be hard to sell, for example. The thing I would watch for is debt. If you look at the companies in trouble, like Xerox or Chiquita Banana, these companies had a lot of debt. And then when things go bad and they need more money, the fellows who lend money get scared and say, We don't want to lend you money any more. So what are they going to do, sell their plant? So I think that debt is one of the most important things to look for.

Q. Charles Ruane [another Graham disciple] has said that return on equity may be the most important factor.

W.S. He may be right. But his name is Bill, not Charles.

Q. That's what we journalists specialize in—getting names wrong. What purchases have you made over the years that you did especially well with?

W.S. We don't discuss what we've bought. Warren has to tell the SEC what he's bought and sold every year, so he has a year to accumulate stock [before the public finds out]. But we don't talk about what we're buying or what we've bought.

Q. Do you totally ignore how good a company's managers are, or—

W.S. I can't evaluate management. Theoretically, management is in the price of a stock. If it's a good company with good management, the stock sells at a high p-e. If the management is poor and people don't like the company, it sells at a lower p-e. And sometimes it's just in a bad industry. But I can't evaluate management. The price of a company may be a reflection of the way people think about the whole company at that particular point. You can look at management and you might say it's good because the stock is doing nicely with a good profit margin. We're a small investment company; we don't have time to go around talking to the people, talking to their competitors.

Q. What's the most common mistake that ordinary investors seem to make?

W.S. I think people trade too much, looking for short-term gains. But I don't think you should hold stocks indefinitely.

Q. You told me that you sold Bethlehem Steel . . .

W.S. It was selling at $37, and I sold it to buy this Western Pacific. At the time, Bethlehem Steel was in the Dow Jones Average. I think it's at $3 now. Western Pacific went out at around $163. So you can't just say that you're going to buy the good companies and hang onto them all the time. That sounds all right, but you might as well buy Berkshire Hathaway and let Warren worry about it.

But I don't think you should even be writing about the stock market. We've had a great bull market for 18 years; you'll never see a bull market like this again.

Q. Don't you think people can learn something valuable about investing from Buffett and other value investors?

W.S. If they haven't learned by now, I don't think they'll ever learn.

Q. Why do you have doubts about investing in index funds?

W.S. Because all you're saying is that you'll do as well as the market. That's not what you're really supposed to be doing. You're giving up. You're just saying, Okay, I'll do what the market does, period. You might be right, but then you have to value the stocks in the index—if you really want to be intelligent about it. You might say, these stocks are selling at a high price in relation to what I think they're worth, and if you think they're selling at a high price, it wouldn't be a good idea to buy an index fund. You're going to have to evaluate the market yourself.

Q. But you don't engage in any market-timing—

W.S. No, I'm not interested in timing.

Q. But if you didn't find anything worth buying, you'd sit in cash?

W.S. Yes.

Q. Why do value and growth investing seem to take turns basking in the sun or skulking in shadows?

W.S. That's a good question, and I don't know, and I won't even think about it, to tell the truth. I don't really care. But you get trends, and people want to do things, and suddenly they get into a mania, about growth stocks or high-tech stocks, and then they go in, and they don't work out, and then someone says, I think you should buy value stocks, and they do that for a while—I don't know the motivation.

People are sort of influenced by, I guess, CNBC, where these guys are touting stocks. They rarely tell you to sell stocks. And the brokers do another thing, of course, which is human nature—they recommend stocks that are going up because if you recommended a stock that was going down, and it kept going down, the customer would be unhappy with it. But if a stock is going up, everyone is happy with it because you're buying a stock that's doing nicely.

Q. Your investment style is very close to Ben Graham's, isn't it?

W.S. I try to be close to Graham in style. Ben Graham wasn't focused entirely on the stock market. He was a brilliant guy; he was able to translate Greek and Latin and all that. But investing was a challenge for him, and he met the challenge by writing books. And I think *The Intelligent Investor* is a great book, and if you were to tell people to read it, that would be a very good thing to do.

Q. Why has Warren Buffett been so successful?

W.S. Well, he's a very good judge of businesses, particularly financial businesses. You'll notice that a great deal of his money is in American Express, the banks, Wells Fargo, Freddie Mac. He's got companies where he can kind of project what they will do. But with industrial companies, the kind that we invest in, particularly the cyclical companies, you can't do that so easily. You have a good year, and then the next year is bad. Banks have been getting more and more money, and other industries have been cutting back. The textile industry has been destroyed. Coca-Cola is having a few bad years. How high is up?

I think Warren feels more comfortable owning financial companies. GEICO is another one of his financial companies. Warren is extremely good at making investments in companies where he can project what they'll do 10 years from now.

Q. Of every 10 stocks you buy, how many work out well and how many don't?

W.S. I don't know. I'd say about 80 percent work out. I don't really know.

Q. It can take four years for a company to work out?

W.S. On the average. That's not true of every company. If a company is having trouble, it may take six years to work out. And sometimes you buy a stock and it sort of catches fire, or somebody takes it over. And you didn't know that would happen. You get some lucky breaks and you get some poor breaks. Sort of a law of averages.

Q. You invest in what sized companies? Mid-caps?

W.S. Mid-caps and smaller rather than big companies. The big companies have been sort of pawed over by all the analysts. The analysts look at the 150 or 200 largest companies. If you're managing $50 billion, you can't fool around with buying a small company, where you might be able to buy only $100 million worth of stock. As for the high-tech companies, they're mostly small, but the speculation was that they had a great future. Well, maybe they do and maybe they don't, I'm not smart enough to know.

Q. Why are you in such good all-around health?

W.S. My father. My job in life is to beat my father. He was 103 when he died. Actually, I think it's just a genetic thing. I'm just very fortunate that I have some of his genes.

Q. Can you tell me more about yourself?

W.S. I like playing bridge and tennis, and I like the theater. We're New Yorkers, we were born in New York. It is a very stimulating place, it has a lot of museums. Anybody can do anything they want in New York; there are a lot of different alternatives. Some people don't like that. They like a quiet area where there isn't all that pressure. I don't mind the pressure. I kind of like it actually.

We're a low-key company; we're not a big company. I didn't want to be a big company, I didn't want to have a big staff, I didn't want the responsibility of hiring people and firing people. I wanted to keep my life simple. But I love working with my son, Edwin. We make a good team.

I came to Wall Street in 1934. In those years, there wasn't much going on. And then the war broke out and I spent four years in the army, and then I worked for Ben Graham for nine and a half years. So I've been around a long time, and it's been an interesting run.

CHAPTER 27

Robert Torray of the Torray Fund

Robert Torray (Photo courtesy of William K. Geiger).

Bob Torray and an investor who has had a decisive influence on Warren Buffett, Phil Fisher, seem to be blood brothers. They believe in buying fine companies when they're not especially expensive, then holding on and on.

Yet Torray has never read Phil Fisher's writings, although "I'm aware of him," he told me. "I'm keen on being my own guy."

The only investor whose opinion he values, he said, is his partner, Doug Eby.

Still, "Warren Buffett, whom I don't know, has had a profound effect on my thinking. No other investor can match his insight, humility, and accomplishments. There are others who have made a lot of money, especially in the tech area, but I believe they're not as well situated for the long haul. In most cases, their fortunes are tied to a single company. Things change—we see it every day. A lot of single-stock fortunes have evaporated recently, and it's likely there will be more. I don't see a chance of that happening at Berkshire. It owns too many businesses, and the ones that count are very solid."

An Unconventional Background

Torray's background is not what one would expect in a money manager. He majored in history at Duke University, getting his B.A. in 1959. He then went to law school for a year and a half, and clerked for a law firm that did work for the Securities and Exchange Commission. His boss there talked a good deal about stocks, and that made Torray interested.

He began working as a stockbroker for Alex. Brown and Sons in Baltimore in 1962, quickly moving over to managing pension funds, in Washington, D.C. In 1967 he went to Eastman Dillon Union Securities, in New York City, now part of PaineWebber. He founded his own firm in 1972, in Bethesda, Maryland. He opened the Torray Fund in 1991. (See Figure 27.1.)

At the beginning he invested in obscure, little-known companies, turnarounds, special situations, taking advantage of market cycles. A specialty of his was spur-line railroads, those whose lines were small and off-the-beaten path. "A tough way to make a living," he recalled, although he didn't do badly.

He still vividly remembers one of the very first stocks he ever bought: Agricultural Research and Development, a "story" stock. The story: It was developing a technique of breeding pigs immune to diseases. Torray bought 50 shares at $2. Soon the stock had soared to $250. Then the truth came out. The company owned a pig farm in Virginia, and in order to breed disease-free pigs it was slaughtering all of its pigs that got sick. Not especially scientific. The stock went to zero. Said Torray, "That made a big impression on me."

Modern Mistakes

What causes his mistakes these days? "I have a list as long as my arm," he said with a sigh. "They're all over the place. But the main cause is that the fundamentals of the stock weren't that good—and I convinced myself that they were."

Actually, he's convinced that mistakes are unavoidable and there's no cure. "If this business were easy, it wouldn't be such fun—and, of course, all the investment gurus would be retired multi-millionaires."

FIGURE 27.1 Torray Fund's Performance, April 1996–April 2001.
Source: StockCharts.com.

One company he bought faced lawsuits because of its use of asbestos. Management airily dismissed the whole subject as unimportant. The issue turned out to be a big problem. Torray sold the stock.

Another mistake he made years ago: He bought into a stock before he visited with management, something he rarely does. It turned out that the company was cooking its books—for example, billing for consignments it had made to Europe that hadn't been sold. Not surprising: The company's officers had stock options and bonuses that depended on the company's gross income. The chairman told Torray it wasn't his fault—other people at the company were responsible.

Then there was the $100 million acquisition the same company had recently made, buying a hearing-aid manufacturer. "Are there any new developments in hearing aids?" Torray asked innocently. "Not one," said the chairman. "The nerve is damaged. What can you do?"

Torray sold the stock, which soon after lost half its value.

Another time he bought Xerox, thinking that despite its low price the company had a bright future. Fortunately, it was only a small part of the portfolio. The stock had dropped from $64 to $20; earnings were projected at $1.90–$2 per share; the 80-cent dividend provided a hefty 4 percent yield.

Management's spin was that the deteriorating earnings outlook was the result of a sales force reorganization, weakness in the Brazilian operation, and a few other more-minor issues. The real problem, not disclosed then, was that competition, especially from Hewlett-Packard, was decimating Xerox's high-margin copier business. Although the stock rallied from $20 to $30 after we invested, it soon retreated to $20. Then, as more bad news came out, we sold the stock from $20 down to around $7.

In retrospect, it seems that management was not completely forthright about the depth of Xerox's problems, and may even have employed accounting gimmicks to mask them. There's usually no defense against that.

Compared with Buffett

Like Buffett (and Fisher), Torray buys growing companies, sometimes when they are a bit under a cloud. He concentrates. He rarely sells. He pays little attention to economic forecasts and ignores the stock market's short-term fluctuations. He's been light on technology: Recently his fund had only 6 percent of its assets in tech, less than a third of the S&P 500's 19 percent weighting.

And he boasts a splendid record: up 15.5 percent a year for 28 years, which is double the rise in the S&P 500.

Torray tries to evaluate management before he buys, avoiding people who don't seem shareholder friendly and who focus on short-term stock performance. How does he differ from Buffett? "He's got a lot more money!" replied Torray jovially.

Buffett is also willing to have a more concentrated portfolio. Torray explains: "Federal securities law and institutional client guidelines pretty much dictate that we're always going to hold at least 25 stocks." Today his fund has around 35.

Torray also would never buy anything but stocks—not even bonds. "The attraction of bonds escapes me," he said disdainfully. "Their pre-tax after-inflation return has been only 2 percent annually over the past 75 years or so. That's a tough record to like." Obviously, both he and Buffett are given to telling what's on their minds.

Charming, warm, outgoing, and voluble, Torray, 63, kept calling me by my first name during the interview, à la the gospel according to Dale Carnegie; he apologized profusely for brief interruptions; he never rushed me, even though it was a long interview. Would that all money managers were so gracious! He's also wonderfully quotable. Clear, colorful, interesting, unconventional.

Not a Value Investor

Morningstar classifies Torray's fund as "large, value." The fund's average stock, according to Morningstar, has a price-earnings ratio of 25.1, only about three-quarters that of the S&P 500, and historically the fund's p-e ratio has been only 83 percent of the S&P 500's. Its price-book ratio, another measure of value vs. growth, was recently 4.5, a little more than half the p-b ratio of the S&P 500.

But as recently as 1997 Torray's fund was classified as a blend fund, as it was in 1996 and 1995. And back then it was sometimes a mid-cap fund. Torray isn't biased in favor of larger companies. It's just that, he explained, larger companies have been so irresistible in recent years.

Surprisingly, he isn't happy being called a value manager, and has some unkind words about value investing in general.

> Superior companies, make the best long-term investments. Weak companies almost always prove disappointing, even if you buy them at a low price. Some, of course, work out for one reason or another, but in the long run there won't be many.
>
> Value investing is generally understood to mean buying stocks at below market price-earnings ratios, higher-than-market dividend yields, and—to a lesser extent—lower than market price to book value ratios. Unfortunately, most stocks falling into these categories are issues of companies having lackluster economic fundamentals. We avoid them. We're searching for sound, growing, well-managed businesses that are fairly priced.
>
> The problem is that the best companies are well known, and as a result their shares often sell at prices we are unwilling to pay. So we simply wait until something happens to change that.
>
> In today's world, regardless of the trigger, we try to assure ourselves as best we can that the problems will not over time result in a permanent impairment of our investment. We want sustainable growth over decades, not short-term gratification. From our perspective, anything measured in less than five years is largely meaningless. In the long run, if businesses perform, their stocks follow suit. If they don't, no amount of smoke and mirrors will have the slightest impact.
>
> We're on the lookout for the stocks of sound companies that have dropped to a level we're comfortable with. When we find one, we study the company reports and talk to Wall Street analysts. If these efforts are encouraging, we visit management. Then making decisions is easy.

We avoid managements that talk about their stock price instead of the business. Efforts to light a fire under poorly performing stocks all too often end in disaster for shareholders. In this regard, acquisitions have proven to be a particularly costly strategy. It all comes back to the fact that value evolves from the business, not the stock.

Solid businesses, even the best, inevitably face challenges, but most of the time they can be overcome. For weak ones, there is normally no cure. That's why it's so important to buy the best you can afford, at a price you can live with, and forget about everything else.

Is his strategy, then, "growth at a reasonable price"? GARP? "I just don't think about stuff like that," he replied. "We're just trying to buy good businesses."

The High Expenses People Pay

He warmed to the subject, sounding like no less than John Bogle (Saint Jack), founder of the Vanguard Group, in his unhappiness about the expenses that investors must pay to buy and own mutual funds.

Why people find it necessary to attach definitions like GARP (growth at a reasonable price) to the process escapes me. The only answer I come up with is that in so doing, armies of consultants and brokers, rating services, and the media position themselves to make a handsome living comparing one approach to another, record against record, and so on.

This charade is responsible for the wasteful churning of portfolios and the public's nonsensical jumping around from one mutual fund to another.

Last year trading amounted to 40 percent of the assets of more than 4,000 stock funds. I've been in business 40 years, and during that time there has not been an ounce of value added by the crowd that's been feeding on the relative-performance game.

The Securities and Exchange Commission reports that taxes cost mutual fund shareholders 2.5 percentage points of return annually over the past 10 years. The industry's expense ratio absorbed another 1.5 percentage points. On top of that, many investors pay 1 percent in fees to financial advisers to manage portfolios of funds for them. Together, these charges totaled 5 percentage points.

Corporate earnings grew only about 6 percent annually over the past 50 years. The irony will be lost on no one that investors have been hit by all three of those costs—taxes, fund expenses, advisers' fees—have transferred nearly the entire value of their owning stocks, their growth in earnings, to financial intermediaries and to the Internal Revenue Service.

Not Going by the Numbers

All mechanistic approaches make no sense, Torray believes. "I buy companies on a long-term basis. I might buy 8 percent growth at a p-e of 14, 15, or 16. That might be attractive. At 15 percent growth, it might be worth a p-e of 22. I don't analyze things that closely. But I wouldn't buy 30 percent growth at twice that. That's crazy." (The recent three-year growth rate of the average stock in his portfolio: 12.9 percent.)

Because a 30 percent rate isn't sustainable? "It won't last very long. Certainly not for decades. Look at Lucent now. Technology's growth is cyclical, and it's difficult to forecast the cycles. Often investors own the most at the peak of the cycle, when the prices are inflated. It's hard to identify high p-e, high growth companies for what we're attempting to do"—namely, buy long-term winners.

The Secret of His Success

How does he do it? He regularly looks for stocks hitting new lows. He talks with analysts. He reads. He visits managements. And then he puts everything together. "Making a decision is easy. It's like a sixth sense, an instinct."

The $1.9 billion Torray Fund has invested in 35 names. The top five recently accounted for about one-third of the portfolio, and the top ten for more than 50 percent. (Including pension funds and other institutional accounts, the Torray Companies manage around $6 billion.) "We normally invest 3 percent–5 percent in one company," he said. "Sometimes we've ended up with more than 10 percent in a few cases due to appreciation. But that's the limit. Heavier concentrations are fine for people dealing with their own money, but when you're looking after other people, it's inappropriate."

He buys mostly big companies with long histories. Recently in his portfolio: Abbott Laboratories, Disney, J.P. Morgan, Gillette, Bank of America, AT&T, Du Pont, Procter & Gamble, and Kimberly Clark.

"But at the time we buy them or we're considering them," he

explained, "there's some cloud over their long-term future. Investors are disaffected. We would want to bow out if we think the negative view has merit, of course. And often it does. But occasionally it's clear that the problem can be taken care of. It may take two or three years. The price may go even lower while we're waiting.

"Other times, we don't believe the popular view—and to our regret. We wind up taking a loss. But that hasn't happened very often. And when it has, adequate diversification has muted the impact."

One of his stocks, Abbott Labs, for example, sank in 1999 when there was bad news about expiring drug patents and a Food and Drug Administration investigation. In 2000 the stock shot up more than 50 percent.

Patience Is a Virtue

When Torray talks with his friends in the investment world about the long-term outlook for companies he buys into, many of them agree. The stock's a bargain, its long-term prospects are rosy. But the timing is wrong. They can't wait eighteen months, two years, or three years.

"Many mutual fund managers are under the gun," he said, a view that Edwin Walczak of Vontobel U.S. Value (Chapter 28) would wholeheartedly endorse. "Shareholders will vote with their feet, and the manager will soon be out of business. It's hard for an institutional investor to be long-term oriented. Problems can be painfully slow to work out. And the way the investment world works, few money managers can afford the luxury of waiting two or three years."

He himself has held onto stocks for as long as three or four years before they proved their mettle.

> The portfolio management business is intensely competitive, and investors tend to take flight if they're not keeping pace with the market's best-performing stocks or the hottest mutual funds. This tends to keep investment managers constantly in motion trying to land in just the right place at the right time. Generally, that translates into buying stocks with the greatest upward price momentum, no matter what their fundamentals or valuation levels happen to be.
>
> In that sort of game, the three- to five-year outlook for Abbott Laboratories, Johnson & Johnson, Gillette, or Procter & Gamble is irrelevant.

> As a result their shares may stagnate or fall temporarily, making them attractive to investors like us. These companies and others we own are big, safe, and generally well managed. As a group, their overall economic position is superior to that of the combined companies in the various market indexes. So we assume that if we hold them long term, we will do better than the market—which we have. It's really as simple as that.

Something else he thinks is important: "We are focused on making money and avoiding the risk of permanent loss—not focused on beating the market and beating other funds. We really don't care what others are doing or how they're doing it. We're looking out for our investors, which includes ourselves."

Did his own fund investors drop out in the year 2000, when his fund was down? "Actually, last year was a standoff in this regard," he replied. "I'm comfortable with the outcome. Our fund was down 3.4 percent, which we're not happy about, but it had returned 29 percent annually during the preceding five years. A slowdown was inevitable. The S&P 500 was off 10 percent, and the Nasdaq collapsed nearly 40 percent. We weren't swimming against the tide. That happens every three, five, eight, or nine years. Prices were ahead of fundamental values. And when that happens, even good stocks are highly unlikely to go up."

When to Sell

While Torray is disinclined ever to sell, his turnover rate is never zero. Usually it's between 20 percent and 30 percent. In 2000, in fact, it was unusually high—33 percent. "I made three or four mistakes," he admitted. Another reason he sells: when a new opportunity presents itself. "We've got to sell an old holding to buy a new one."

Does he bail out if a stock seems overpriced? "Some I'll hold onto. The big problem is, I may be wrong. The stock may not be overpriced. And if I sell it, I'll have to buy something else just as good—and that's not easy to do. Besides, value doesn't lie in the stock's price. It's in the business. That's something I learned from Buffett. Like him, I'm mainly interested in the business, not in the stock.

"Most investors just 'play' the market. Investors see a penny or a two drop in earnings, and there's a 20 percent decline in the stock. I pay no attention to short-term earnings. I just want to make sure that the growing power is still there."

Questions and Answers

Q. When you visit companies, what do you want to see in management?

R.T. Forthrightness. A focus on long-term developments.

I'm put off if they're stock conscious. If they talk about mergers and acquisitions, that's usually only a short-term benefit. I want them to focus on the business and forget the stock.

Also, sometimes management will say things that don't support our view of the business and where it's headed.

Q. Will you close your fund if it gets large enough?

R.T. With new money, you can buy new stocks. You can bolster some older stocks and adjust your portfolio weightings. Cash flowing out is terrible: You may have to sell stocks when you want to buy more.

Q. Why is it that some money managers with superb records are here one day, gone the next? Or that they seem to lose their golden touch?

R.T. You need to be independent and pretty well established for your investors to stay with you. People don't know what will pan out, so it helps to have a good long-term record. Our average client has been with us for 19 years—out of 28. And the institutions that hire us tend to have multiple money managers, 10 or maybe even 30. They'll never fire us—unless we were so bad that we stuck out.

Besides, we have a sensible philosophy and we can explain it. That gives people comfort. If you can't explain your strategy, and people can't read about you, you'll lose your investors and wind up working for Fidelity. [In other words, not running your own business.]

In general two classes of money managers have gotten into trouble of late.

- Hedge funds, like Long Term Capital Management. "Some of them have had stunning returns, but they had made large-scale investments, such as on the direction of interest rates and with enormous leverage. Sometimes they were right. But when they made investments that lost money, their bets couldn't be unwound." There were no buyers.
- Value investors, who "have been crushed in the last few years. We made 29 percent a year for the last five years, and I don't know a value investor who's done that. They were buying Old Economy

companies, Caterpillar Tractor, General Motors, the old International Paper. They all own the same stuff. Even I bought some. They used to go in during a down cycle and sell during an up cycle. In recent years, these stocks went from 54 to 15 or from 60 to 20 as everyone left and went into high tech and dot.coms.

Q. But Morningstar reports that Torray owns a ton of General Motors. How come?

R.T. [Annoyed] I've told them ten times that we don't own any General Motors and we never have. They still say we do. We own General Motors Hughes Electronics, a spin-off of General Motors, not General Motors. It's one of our best holdings. As for General Motors, one thing you can say about it is that for 40 years it's been the same price. Fifty dollars. Or around $50. That's all you need to know about General Motors.

Torray is skeptical of the Old Economy, of old industrial stocks in general, maintaining that their free cash flow has been drying up for the past 10 or 15 years. Every last cent they make now goes into new plants, research, and development, he claims. Just to pay their dividends, they must now issue new bonds.

Unconventional Opinions

Some of his other unconventional opinions sound distinctly reminiscent of that gentleman from Omaha:

- "Ignore what academia has to say, and ignore market strategists. Keep it simple. Buy and hold good companies and you'll be a winner."
- "Conventional thinking produces conventional results. And we're not interested in conventional results."
- "I've never known anyone whose fortunes were improved through diversification. [He modified that to:] Diversification is important up to a point, but too many investors overdo it."
- "Owning a half-dozen or more mutual funds makes absolutely no sense. The average fund holds nearly 150 stocks, so a multiple-fund portfolio could easily own 1,000. Stock turnover within funds runs nearly 100 percent a year, and advisers often switch funds in their clients' accounts. There is no chance that this hyperactivity will add value. In fact, the embedded costs and futile randomness of the process virtually guarantee investors a lousy result."

Basics

Minimum First Investment: $10,000 (same for an IRA)
Phone Number: (800) 443-3036
Web Address: www.torray.com

- "Asset allocation is total nonsense. All it does is keep a lot of people employed. The only thing worth owning is stock in growing companies. Never buy bonds, commodities, futures, derivatives, strips, and all that other nonsense."
- "Brokerage firms don't want salespeople who think too much, even if they think about the companies they recommend. They just want gregarious people who'll go out and sell."

His record speaks for itself, he said proudly. Up 15.5 percent a year for 28 years. Over five years, up more than 17 percent. Since the fund's inception, up more than 18 percent.

Even so, he added, he has regularly made mistakes—and he still does. "After 40 years in the business, it's still not too late to learn."

CHAPTER 28

Edwin D. Walczak of Vontobel U.S. Value

Edwin D. Walczak (Photo courtesy of Vontobel Funds).

Edwin D. Walczak was engaged in a session of intense self-scrutiny when I dropped in at his office on Park Avenue in New York City not long ago. Sometimes, he even seemed to contradict himself, as in dealing with the question of: Is exhaustive research the secret of investing?

After 10 years of managing Vontobel U.S. Value, he's beaten the S&P 500 by a hair—but fairly soundly if you don't include expenses. But why, he has been asking himself, hasn't he risen to the top? "They're not the kickass returns I would have liked. How do I do better?"

His numbers: 1.8 percent over the S&P 500 after 10 years, 2.25 percent over without expenses. Morningstar rates the fund "average" now, but usually it's rated "above average."

Walczak is open, articulate, engaging, wired.

In his company's conference room—a painting of Vontobel himself, the family founder, gazes down on us—Walczak, blue shirt, no tie, asks himself:

- Should he concentrate more? Buy 10 stocks he knows very well instead of 25 he can't know quite so well?
- Should he hold on and on, instead of trimming positions when stocks begin approaching and reaching their supposed intrinsic values?
- Is it just that value investing was so out of favor in recent years, and in more normal times he and other value investors will do far better? Before the tech bubble, he was 3 percent ahead of the S&P. "Don't change, they tell us," he says. "And I don't want to panic. But how do I do better?"
- Why haven't he and other Buffett Moonies, as he calls them, done as well as the Master himself? "Why have we trailed behind?"

It isn't that he's dumb. "If I were three times smarter, a great intellect," he said candidly, "it wouldn't solve the problem. There's only so much you can know. I'm no Einstein, I'm just a regular guy. But twice the brains wouldn't solve the problem."

His ego is not easily wounded, either; he can admit mistakes and analyze them. With a rueful smile he recalled that a former employer used to ask him, "What's on your alleged mind, Walczak?" And he told of visiting Mario Gabelli (a fellow graduate of Columbia Business School) to ask for a job in 1983 or 1984. He made an impassioned case for stocks like Chrysler and Ford. Gabelli listened, then told him bluntly, "If you want to work here, you'll have to pay *me*."

Walczak now knows that Gabelli was right about those dismal companies: "I didn't know shit." But he hopes that if he applied for a job today and talked up Markel Insurance, Mario might not "laugh me out of the room. Gabelli really knows his stories."

Maybe he's too conservative, Walczak grants. His own answer is a gardening metaphor: When you plant shrubs, you've got to get down deep, to your elbows. You must do more in-depth research. . . . But he already does a ton of research, he reminded himself. And "There's only so much you can know about Coke and Hewlett-Packard."

What about calling the CFOs more often? "Nnyah," he answers, making a face.

A quandary.

The Lower Depths

His mantra, Walczak revealed, is: "There is hardly anything that I know, and there is hardly anything that I can or should do." Modesty to the point of self-loathing, but that outlook should keep his turnover pretty low and his portfolio concentrated.

The nonvalue years were a nightmarish time. Walczak thought he might even get fired. Robert Sanborn at Oakmark did. Other value investors, like Denis LaPlaige at MainStay and David Schafer at Strong Schafer Value, formidable and admirable people, mysteriously disappeared. At one point, Vontobel U.S. Value had $600 million in assets. Assets plunged to $125 million.

So despondent was Walczak back in 1999 that he went to the Berkshire Hathaway annual meeting, hoping to get inspiration from the Master himself, like a priest assailed by self-doubts visiting the Vatican to see the pope.

He talked about "the imperfections of the business." You can't be an investor and a money manager at the same time. A money manager is at the mercy of his customers; and the average customer is a momentum investor and fickleness and emotionalism run in his or her veins. The average investor holds a tech stock for 40 days. So either run a closed-end fund, Walczak thinks, or just manage your own money, so you can forget about the sweet simplemindness of Irving and Irma Investor. "They're in at the highs and out at the lows."

Questions and Answers

Q. Well, what about your institutional clients—the pension funds, for example?

E.W. Institutional clients don't want their money managers to deviate much from their index, from the S&P 500. So you're hemmed in. And even they are apt to leave when the weather turns chilly. We have no long-term clients. Now, if the markets calm down and we had the right kind of investor. . . .

I've been here 12 years, and I've been reasonably free—freer than most. I can even be nondiversified [run a fund with concentrated industry weightings and relatively few stocks].

But there's no liferaft when value stocks fall into the pit and growth stocks climb to the skies. If you sell straw hats, there's no salvation when the snowflakes start to fall.

A few famous value funds didn't suffer so much, like Tweedy, Browne and Sequoia. "I'm envious. They've been around longer, and they're bigger," Walczak said. "We're small, and we have no distributors. In 1998, a good year for us, money was out the door. I'm lucky to have stayed in the business." In 1998, his fund rose 14.71 percent; in 1999, down 14.07 percent. The year 2000, though, was super: up 35.18 versus the S&P 500, down 10 percent. (See Figure 28.1.)

Even without momentum investors ready to skip without a moment's notice, running a value fund would be no picnic. Today, there are hardly any good companies out there that you can scoop up for a song. "It's a limited universe," Walczak said grumpily. "The potential is very, very narrow. There may be 150 companies good enough for us to buy. There used to be only 50 or 60, but now I'll even consider Intel and Microsoft and Ford—though I haven't pulled the trigger on any of them yet. Not even at their lows. They're not predictable enough."

FIGURE 28.1 Vontobel U.S. Value Fund's Performance, 1994–2001.
Source: StockCharts.com.

Supposedly all you have to do is choose a company that will prosper over the next 10 or 20 years, isn't that right? "It's hard to find great companies," he answered. "It's hard to make good forecast for even three years. Hardly any company continues to grow at 15 percent a year for ten years. There's competition, there's screwups." Gillette, Rubbermaid. "In tech, who will be the winners in three years? These companies have too many moving parts." In this business, "Certainty is very hard to come by. I'm kidding myself if I'm sure that a great franchise will still be a great franchise five years from now."

Other value investors have suffered blue periods, too. Richard H. Jenrette, former CEO of Equitable, noted in his book *The Contrarian Manager* (New York: McGraw-Hill, 1997) that "I'm not sure that the contrarian approach to investing is any longer applicable to the management of today's institutional capital. . . . The pressures for short-term investment performance are so great that a contrarian approach, which means going against the herd, becomes very risky to the personal well-being of the portfolio manager."

More Questions and Answers

Q. Have you ever thought of becoming a growth investor?

E.W. I'm chicken. I'm afraid of losing money. When a stock gets to be fairly valued, I'm nervous. I tend to trim. A discipline has to work, and it has to suit your personality. I like value investing, it makes sense, and it suits my used-Toyota personality.

All growth companies can be value buys—at the right price. You're trying to buy Michael Jordan for the price of a minor league ballplayer. You don't want to buy no-growth junk. We're not *deep* value. We don't want Chrysler or Ford. We want Interpublic, AIG, Automatic Data Processing—at our prices. We want a company that delivers the goods. It's not that complicated.

Q. How do you calculate a company's intrinsic value?

E.W. You need a strong stomach and a strict discipline. Analytical success accounts for only 25 percent. You had to buy banks in 1990, pharmaceuticals in 1993, growth stocks in 1997, and insurance companies and finance last year. You need enough confidence and enough knowledge—and you never get enough. Whoever knows the most wins.

Q. Aren't there any magic formulas?

E.W. There's no *magical* way to arrive at intrinsic value. Discounted cash flow. Garbage in, garbage out. The real question is, does the company have a sustainable competitive advantage? Hardly any do. ADP is on my list. But I've never owned it. Walgreen would be perfect. I've never owned it. What companies will do in five or ten or fifteen years isn't knowable. You've just got to mindlessly extrapolate.

Q. What about all the arithmetic?

E.W. That formula stuff isn't predictive.

If it were, you know what Buffett said: Librarians would be billionaires. It's not that inanely simple. Something is going on beyond those inane wooden numbers, beyond a decent return on equity. Math is 10 or 15 percent, and qualitative is 90 percent. What does a company do, how does it work, and does it have too many moving parts? You've just got to get your hands dirty.

I was never that good at math. I need help in figuring out tips to pay in restaurants. There are just three or four variables you have to know, as Marty Whitman has said. It's an evaluative process. You've got to study the pros and the cons.

Walczak doesn't rely much on analysts. He finds that reading five newspapers in the morning, along with financial magazines, is as good if not better than analysts' reports. He singles out Sanford Bernstein, a former employer, for praise, though. And he talks to analysts on the "buy" side—those who don't work for brokerage firms but for, say, mutual funds.

He mentioned that Charlie Munger said that he hadn't seen Buffett doing a whole lot of math. Buffett's response: He doesn't have to. A stupendous bargain isn't hard to spot. You don't have to measure Mount Everest to recognize that it's one big pile of rock.

Q. Why shouldn't the ordinary investor just buy Berkshire Hathaway B shares? Why a fund like Vontobel?

E.W. We're more flexible, more agile. We're not buying whales, we're buying minnows. We're so small, we can have a larger array of ideas.

Not that he isn't a great admirer of the Sage of Omaha. When he went to the Berkshire annual meeting, he drove by Buffett's house. "I like where he lives," he said. "A modest house in Omaha instead of in the Hamptons. And I like his intellectual honesty."

Basics

Minimum First Investment: $1,000 (there's a 2 percent redemption fee)
Phone: (800) 527-9500
Web address: www.vusa.com.

CHAPTER 29

James Gipson of the Clipper Fund

On the tenth anniversary of the Clipper Fund, in 1994, I asked James H. Gipson, the manager, why his fund—unlike so many other contrarian funds—had been so successful.

"We do a more diligent job of analyzing companies," he answered. "Also, other people say they're contrarians but they don't invest that way." This was before the ascension of Bill Miller, the Legg Mason money manager (Legg Mason Value Trust) who committed heresy by purchasing a variety of Internet stocks.

Questions and Answers

Q. Do you look for a catalyst that will revive a stock that's out of favor?

J.G. In some cases, you can find a catalyst. But that's too clever by half. Most of the time we don't try to be that clever. One of the hardest things to do is to know what stock will go up and when. You never know. Still, 75 percent to 80 percent of our stocks work out.

Q. What else do you do differently?

J.G. We concentrate to a greater degree. We have only 30-odd stocks. That's very unusual. If you're intellectually honest, you know that your top 10 best ideas will do better than your 40 to 50 best ideas. If you have the courage of your convictions, you feel that your best ideas will do best.

Gibson, Michael Sandler, and Bruce Veace, the managers of Clipper, were named Morningstar's stock fund managers of the year for 2000. As Morningstar noted, by sticking with seemingly cheap stocks, and retreating to bonds and cash when stocks just didn't look attractive, the fund trailed the Standard & Poor's 500 for four consecutive years. The year 1999 was the worst: As investors sought big tech stocks, the S&P 500, dominated by such stocks, rose 20 percent; Clipper fell by 2 percent. The year 2000 saw the righteous rewarded: Clipper rose 35 percent, the S&P 500 went down 10 percent. (See Figure 29.1.)

The three men look for stocks with powerful franchises, stocks that are selling for 30 percent less than their intrinsic value. Its stocks aren't "supersexy," said Sandler, "but they have fundamentally strong businesses and throw off a lot of excess cash." Among Clipper's big winners in 2000: Philip Morris, Freddie Mac, Fannie Mae. Sandler calls Philip Morris "a cash machine," apparently not being frightened away by its legal woes.

FIGURE 29.1 Clipper Fund's Performance, 1994–2001.
Source: StockCharts.com

Basics

Minimum First Investment: $2,500 (IRAs: $1,000)
Phone: 800-776-5033
Web Address: clipperfund.com.

A far more volatile version of Clipper is UAM Clipper Focus, without the cash or the bonds. Recently it had 35 stocks, but the top five made up 36.5 percent of the portfolio. It has not only more stocks than Clipper; it has two more managers: Douglas Grey and Peter Quinn. The minimum is $2,500. Phone: 877-826-5465. Web address: UAM.com. You can buy this fund through Waterhouse and Schwab.

Clipper is an unusually stable fund, with a beta of only 0.37. Its correlation with the S&P 500 is only 25 percent. But its turnover was surprisingly high for this kind of fund: 63 percent in 1999, 65 percent in 1998. Recently it held 31 stocks and was 28 percent in cash. Morningstar rated the fund "highest" both vis-à-vis other stock funds and vis-à-vis other large-value funds. With some exaggeration, Morningstar called Clipper "a good choice if you can hang on for 15 years."

CHAPTER 30

Michael Price of the Mutual Series Fund

Michael Price (Photo courtesy Mutual Series Fund).

In 1999 the Mutual Series family of funds held a press conference at the Yale Club in New York to mark the family's 50th anniversary. The very first fund in the family, Mutual Shares, was founded in 1949 by the late Max Heine and by Joseph Galdi.

I suspect that the conference was also held to point out that—despite the decision of the former manager, Michael Price, to play a lesser role—the funds haven't fallen off a cliff.

Many investors (including me) left when Price stepped down after he sold Mutual Series to the Franklin family, which levels sales charges. Franklin Mutual Series' assets shrank from $32 billion to $22 billion.

The conference was top notch. All the Franklin Mutual managers who spoke were interesting and shrewd—and funny.

Robert L. Friedman, then chief investment officer, recalled that Max Heine had said that if you were a true value investor, over a decade you would enjoy one fantastic year, suffer one horrible year, and have eight good years. The challenge, according to Heine, is to stick with value stocks even during the horrible year.

Heine, a lawyer who emigrated from Nazi Germany in 1933, "had a flair for bargain-hunting," Friedman said. He used a three-pronged investment approach that the fund family still employs, Friedman went on, buying:

- Undervalued common stocks
- Risk arbitrages (buying the acquired companies before mergers and selling the acquirer)
- Bankruptcies and distressed companies

What put the Mutual Series funds on the map, Friedman went on, was Heine's buying Penn Central bonds for 10 cents on the dollar after the railroad went bankrupt in 1976. "He figured that even if they just melted down all the track, they could repay the debt." That episode underscored the family's edge: "courage in the face of panic; patience; and hard-core research."

Price, who succeeded Heine, began putting pressure on companies to work to raise their stocks' prices, Friedman said. Today, he added, all of the family's senior people are ready to urge top managements of companies the funds have invested in to make their companies more efficient.

The fund managers have three choices: (1) to sell the stock, (2) to say something privately, and (3) to say something publicly. If No. 2 doesn't work, Friedman explained, they will try numbers 1 or 3.

Another speaker, Larry Sondike, then co-manager of Mutual Shares, said that the under-a-cloud stocks that the fund buys may have been in deals that fell through, in litigation, or "in pain." We don't mind pain, Sondike commented, "as long as it's not ours."

David Marcus, co-manager of Mutual Discovery, said that he travels abroad again and again to talk with a company's executives. (Discovery invests heavily abroad.) Even in Europe, the family's habit of buying unloved stocks startles people.

When Marcus was buying 3 percent of a French water company called Suez, "a French stockbroker told me that I was stupid." The stock tripled in a little more than three years. Suez officers were grateful that Discovery had buoyed up their stock, so when they came to this country later on, they hurried to New Jersey (the family is in Short Hills) to meet with their benefactors.

Traveling abroad really helps, Marcus went on, because you can learn what the truth really is. When foreign executives come to New York to meet with money managers, he said, "they talk about restructuring, about shareholder value, about buy-backs." They tell the analysts what the analysts want to hear.

"But it's just puffery," Marcus said contemptuously. "You can see it in their faces."

David Winters, the funds' young (39) and new chief investment officer, is an unabashed admirer of Warren Buffett and attends Berkshire's annual meetings.

The secret of Michael Price's strategy, I suggested to Winters, is something Price once said to me: "We really kick the tires." He and his analysts go in and find out what a company's book value really is.

Yes, he agreed, that's what he learned working for Price. "Do the work." That's what Mutual Series is all about: hard work.

Is he also an admirer of Ben Graham? "Graham wrote the Bible," he answered. "Buffett, Heine, Price, Carret, and all the others are commentators."

When he interviews job candidates, Winters said, one of the first questions he asks is: "Have you read Ben Graham?" Depending on the answer, "You're either in or out. On the train or off."

Highlights of an interview with Price before he stepped down from the Franklin Mutual Series funds:

- No, he's not burned out. "I come to the office every day. I still get up every day and read the newspaper. I care about this place, and I'll always pay it a lot of attention. And I'll always be a money manager. I'll always be interested in the market. But I'm not going to start a hedge fund." (A hedge fund, an adventuresome investment for very wealth investors, would probably make him more money.)
- If anyone wants to purchase a first Mutual Series fund, a good choice would be Mutual Beacon, Price suggests. It's 25 percent invested in Europe, the rest U.S., and it's conservative. "One fund gets you a good mix." (See Figure 30.1.)
- On the stockbrokers who now sell his funds, which used to be no-loads: "They'll keep you out of trouble. They'll steer you to the right funds."

FIGURE 30.1 Mutual Beacon Fund's Performance, 1994–2001.
Source: StockCharts.com

I had asked for an interview after seeing part of a PBS documentary about problems in the American economy, "Surviving the Bottom Line with Hedrick Smith."

Price "had a feeling" that the interviews on the program would be a "hatchet job," but "I thought it would be more balanced."

The program ends with Smith proclaiming that while people have been tragically losing their jobs "the winners ride off with their gains."

Then you see Michael Price, a polo player, riding off on a horse.

Welcome to tabloid television.

I had told Price's secretary, Irene Christa, that the program had been a hatchet job. She replied that others had told them the same thing.

Price and a few others are portrayed as nineteenth-century blackguards, guilty of forcing companies to lay off their loyal employees, meanwhile themselves becoming disgustingly rich. There's a lot of film of Price atop a horse and playing polo—polo, of course, being a sport for the rich and decadent.

Later on, Smith, a South African journalist, follows Price as he meets with some people in an office. The camera lingers on the label in Price's jacket: "Made for Michael F. Price."

On the program, Price's sin is that, as Chase Manhattan Bank's biggest shareholder, he pressured Chase to raise its share price. Eventually Chase agreed to merge with Chemical Bank, and—there being a lot of duplication—closed offices, throwing 12,000 people out of work.

Chase officers are quoted as saying that they had been trying to focus on the long term, but they were forced to make short-term decisions thanks to pressure from Price and other shareholders. So they laid off workers—the first layoffs in Chase's history.

The heroes of the program are, first, the executives at Chase Bank. Now, I happen to know that these guys wouldn't dream of playing so priggish a game as polo. Heck, come a Friday night you can find Chase guys bowling and happily swilling beer at Nick's Bowl-a-Rama on Eighth Avenue, just like you and me. Sometimes, you'll even catch them hanging out at the roller derby, recalling old times with old Tuffy Brasoon herself, who would be in the Roller Derby Hall of Fame (if there were one).

Custom-made clothes? Forget it. Chase guys always buy stuff off the rack at Filene's Basement.

I told Price about a shamefully forgotten Chase executive named Al Wiggin. While chairman of the Chase National Bank (a predecessor of Chase Manhattan), he sold short 42,506 shares of Chase in 1929, borrowing money from Chase to do so. (When you sell stock short, you bet on the price going down.) Al did it sneakily, in the name of his daughters. In no time at all, he romped away with $4,008,538.

Selling a stock short helps drive down the price—not exactly what Chase, in the year 1929, was paying Wiggin $275,000 a year for.

By the way, I know that Wiggin lived on Park Avenue and summered at his place in Greenwich, Connecticut, and that he belonged to the Metropolitan Club, the New York Yacht, The Links, and other exclusive clubs, but I have not been able to ascertain whether he was guilty of playing polo. Still, if you're really looking for true villains, Al is your man.

Price seemed, understandably, a little ticked off by the TV program. He began by talking about polo. He plays because he likes riding horses and he loves team sports. "My knees are shot, so I can't play other team sports. [He had played football in high school.] Polo is hard work. It's not glamorous. If you don't ride, you won't understand."

Besides, polo isn't that expensive. "I spend less, as a percentage of my income, on polo than the average American pays to buy reels and lines at Wal-Mart for bass fishing."

In any case, the money he uses to play polo he earned "making money for 25 years for the average American. We've provided terrific risk-adjusted returns, and at Wal-Mart prices." The Mutual Series funds do have superb records, though most new buyers must now pay sales charges.

As for his custom-made suits, he apologized: He weight-lifts, so his arms and shoulders are too big to fit into ordinary suits.

Obviously, he was being too defensive. If I myself were really well-to-do, I'd wear custom-made suits, too. Why try to become rich if you're not supposed to enjoy spending money? Should Bill Gates live in a one-room flat, drive an old jalopy, and dine at Wendy's? You expect me to be ashamed that I blew several thousand dollars visiting Italy last year?

In any case, Price wasn't born with a silver spoon in his mouth. When he graduated from the University of Oklahoma, "I had no money. Zilch." And, last I looked, the U. of O. wasn't in the Ivy League. The PBS program didn't mention that Price just gave $18 million to his alma mater.

On Chase Bank: The Mutual Series funds, Price said, have invested a lot of money to help banks and other institutions stay in business. "In just 1991 through 1993, we saved seven banks from going under." Other firms that the fund bailed out include Penn Central and "a lot of companies no one heard of."

The consolidation of banks was inevitable because there were too many, Price went on. "They've gone from 12,000 nationwide a few years ago to 5,000 now, on their way down to 2,000 eventually."

The TV program itself, Price pointed out, was sponsored by the Alfred P. Sloan Foundation, Sloan having been an executive at General Motors. Price couldn't sleep the other night, and began watching the film *Roger and Me* on TV, about the former bumbling chairman of GM, Roger Smith, and his refusal to confront the havoc GM caused in towns where it closed factories.

The Mutual Series funds began buying Chase at $33. "We thought it was worth $65." Company officers, he learned, had been promised a huge cash bonus if the price rose to $55 in two years.

"We told them that we had a plan, that Chase could sell this off and spin this out. Why don't they do it tomorrow? We felt a sense of urgency."

If Chase hadn't merged with Chemical, Price argued, Chase would have turned into a very "sick" company, and many more people would have been laid off.

"Companies need to be loyal to their workers," Price went on. "They owe allegiance to their employees. I believe that." But Chase wasn't doing well. "It was the worst bank in its peer group. It had the lowest return on equity. And shareholders call the shots."

I told Price, somewhat facetiously, that if he had not done his best to raise Chase's price, I—as a shareholder of Mutual Discovery—would have sued him. "What have I been paying you for?"

"You wouldn't have sued me," he said pleasantly, but yes, his job is to buy cheap stocks and help push up their prices.

At the end of my interview I apologized to Price for the schlockiness of some my fellow journalists—and thanked him for enabling me (and a lot of other middle-class Americans) to live comfortably and to retire comfortably.

A few years ago, the Mutual Series funds held a shareholder meeting at the Madison Hotel in Madison, and a crowd of ordinary people, most of them elderly, showed up. They showered Michael Price with affection—for having made them good money, year after year. Some even presented him with little gifts. It was a love-fest.

From another interview, while Price was managing the funds:

Questions and Answers

Q. Would you describe your strategy?

M.P. Well, we are kind of a long-term investment company. We're categorized as a growth and income fund, which we are. But we really are a special situation fund and a long-term investor. We are bottoms-up investors; we buy companies because of specific reasons. We don't buy stocks because of feelings about the market, or interest rates, or the election, or inflation; we only buy assets at a discount.

We couple that with two other things: bankruptcy investing, which is just a cheaper or more interesting way to buy assets at a discount, and trading stocks of companies involved in mergers, tender offers, liquidations, spinoffs. We do those things to get rates of return on our cash.

That's it; that's all. Those are components of the portfolio. We don't have a strategy—it's the wrong word; we have a kind of philosophy of buying assets at a discount, and our approach is by those three things: Graham and Dodd [value] investing, bankruptcies, and deals. That's all we do. We don't really look at other groups.

If the market doesn't reward the value investor, and it didn't in 1990 and 1991, we don't change what we're doing—because we believe in what we're doing.

Q. What do you do differently from other value investors?

M.P. I don't know, it's how you do the work, having an attitude that you've got to do your own work. You can't just take what others tell you a company or an asset is worth. You have to get several inputs to value assets. You've got to be somewhat disciplined to make sure you wait until the market hands you the stock at a cheap price—it's very hard to do. In other words, do good work on the valuation side and then wait for the market to give it to you cheaply.

I think we do very good work on the valuation and on the market side, but sometimes we pay too much on the market, and sometimes we buy things at the right price. We stick to this philosophy. It's great if you can do the homework and then wait for the market to give you things at a big discount from what they're worth. That's the best philosophy, you know; you don't have to pay attention to technical analysis, or the gibberish on Wall Street, or new product conventions.

Wall Street basically doesn't eat its own cooking. In the last five or 10 years—I don't know how long you've been watching Wall Street—but you've had the invention of zero coupon bonds, PIKs, options, futures. They really take what is a very simple mechanism, which is capital formation and capital investment, and make it much more complex than it needs to be, because Wall Street can earn big fees in commissions on the issuance and trading of these instruments. But all those things create a lot of noise, a lot of distractions, from what is a very simple business for an investor, which is to buy a stock based on what the business is worth at half of that price.

If they're not there, you don't buy them; if they're there, you buy them and you wait—because sooner or later they're going to trade for what they're worth. All this nonsense Wall Street creates—junk bonds, PIKs, zeroes, futures and options, or all the different strategies, all the things you read about in the [*Wall Street*] *Jour-*

nal—they tend to pull investors' attention away from the fundamental things you should pay attention to.

What we try to do at Mutual Shares is view the world simply; don't get distracted by all of the stuff Wall Street cooks up. Stick to the simple stuff. Buy oil at below $5 a barrel, and gas for 50 cents, and a dollar for 50 cents. You buy liquid assets as cheap as you can . . . because then you can't lose much money.

We are not stock players, and we're not trying to guess future earnings. We don't come in the morning and say, "Oh, the market is high, let's buy some S&P puts." We just would never do those things.

Q. What qualities unite successful investors?

M.P. There are lots of successful investors who do things other than what we do. I'm saying this is our philosophy. I think there are several very successful people who kind of take this view, who have been around a long time. People in Sequoia are wonderful and have a very simple direct approach. John Templeton is still great; he still has very long-term views on how to buy stocks.

So we are active in situations to create cheap securities because we have the energy and the knowledge to know how to do the work, to figure out a bankruptcy, to create a cheap stock. But at the end of the day, we want the cheap stock; we're not trading in the bankruptcy just to trade. We don't do that; our turnover rates are low, our fees are lower than most. We just want to perform well for our shareholders.

Q. Do you do a lot of in-house research?

M.P. We do all in-house research. We give orders to brokers, and we see their research and see what they're saying. But we do most of our own research. I have a dozen analysts who are terrific and we do all our own work.

Q. How important is good research?

M.P. It's all-important.

Q. Do you market-time at all? Would you go more into cash if you saw no opportunities?

M.P. That's how it works. Cash balance goes up if we don't find stocks. If we find stocks, cash comes down. We don't come in saying, "Let's raise cash." We come in saying, "Let's buy stocks."

Q. Is the hardest part deciding when to sell?

M.P. That's really hard because you never know what the buyers are thinking or know how high something may go. What we kind of do is start selling things when they are about 85 percent of what we think the company's value is, and we start selling it slowly each day, and if it goes higher, great, we get out of it and we don't look back.

Q. Do you have stop-loss orders?

M.P. No, but I sit at a trading desk and watch the market all day, so we're very set up to pay attention to the stock market. You know, if you're a doctor and you must be in surgery and the stock goes down, you don't want a big loss, so you'll have a stop order. But you can't be looking at Quotron machines when you're doing brain surgery, right? I sit here all day watching the market, so we don't need stop orders.

Q. What advice do you have for ordinary investors?

M.P. The most important thing, even though most people won't do it, is to read the prospectus. People are lazy. They work really hard to save the money that they have to invest, then all of a sudden they become very lazy. Most people don't want to take the time to call what is usually an 800 number to get what is more or less a pretty simple document. You read it, paying attention to the fees, the terms. The reason you must read it is that the mutual fund industry has found ways to put in both 12b-1 fees and redemption fees as well as loads on the front end, in ways you may not be aware. You might put money into a fund thinking it's a no-load fund, you see, and you may have missed the little asterisk which shows you there's a redemption fee and after the first four years you redeem, you will have a 4 percent discount. Well, that's terrible. So if you read the prospectus, you'll know it's there.

Q. Any other advice?

M.P. Do some of your own research, looking back over what the guy's track record was for five and ten years. Five and ten years gives you bull markets and bear markets, not just bear markets. A quarter or a one-year performance just isn't long enough. You need to look at a record for a minimum of three to five years, if not ten. You want to know whether it's been the same guy running it and then . . .

The next step is to take the time to look at the three, four, or five biggest holdings of the fund. That will give you a sense of what the guy buys. And read a few articles about these companies. And before you buy the fund, ask yourself, Do I want to own these companies? Because in effect you're owning those companies, you're paying a guy a hundred basis points to watch over it, right?

You know, one of the things we do here from time to time when the markets are a certain way is, we'll buy closed-end funds at 25 percent discounts. Well, the first thing you do is look at the four or five biggest holdings in the closed-end funds. I remember doing this back in 1984; there was a closed-end fund in London and it was trading at a 25 percent discount; they had 30 percent in cash, and the balance of the portfolio was made up in liquid U.S. oil and gas companies and Royal Dutch Petroleum. So, in effect, I was buying Royal Dutch Petroleum at a 25 percent discount. You couldn't miss—you could *not* miss, you know?

But likewise if I hadn't looked at the holdings, maybe it wouldn't have been Royal Dutch, which is the cheapest and the best company in the world. Maybe it would have been some phony Canadian exploration company that trades on the Vancouver Stock Exchange for $13 when it's only worth $2. That's why you have to look at what the fund owns. . . .

Q. What lessons have you learned?

M.P. Well, we make lots of mistakes. I mean, the lesson I learned is this is the way to invest, the value approach. You have to do your own homework. We learned to be diversified; we own a couple of hundred different things. It's very important from time to time to have plenty of cash; you don't have to be invested all the time. Being good all the time is better than being great one year every now and then. . . .

So, which portfolio manager did Michael Price tell me that he admired the most? William Ruane.

CHAPTER 31

A Variety of Other Value Investors

Charles Royce

Running a mutual fund isn't as easy as it looks. That's the dry comment of Charles "Chuck" M. Royce, who's been running small-company mutual funds for almost 30 years—and very skillfully.

Along with having a nice way with words, Royce is awesomely smart (he studied with David Dodd, who collaborated with the legendary Ben Graham at Columbia). He's easy to recognize, too, what with his ever-present bow ties. He reminds me a bit of Ralph Wanger, who runs the Acorn funds in Chicago. (They happen to be good friends, although Wanger is largely growth and Royce is mainly value.)

I visited Royce at his office on West 58th Street in Manhattan. Fifteen or so years ago, I had interviewed him for the first time, at the same place, and I still remember things he had said—he was that impressive. Most people's portfolios, he told me, have no rhyme or reason. They're a complete mess. (I also asked him what a "value" investor was. As I recall, he was momentarily shaken by my ignorance.)

Getting back to the woes of managing a fund: One pitfall is that the stocks you invest in may be out of favor—as value stocks were for several years before the year 2000. Another problem: Running value funds in particular is never a cakewalk.

"Investing in growth stocks is much more fun," Royce says candidly. "There are lively stories, the stocks are doing well. It's easy to get comfortable with the portfolio because they're important household names. You all but forget the price you pay. But the price can screw you up because it may be too high. Still, it's a reasonable way to make money.

"With value stocks, at least expectations are low. The price I pay does count. That way, negative surprises don't wipe you out. You'll lose less. Growth stocks can lose 50 percent or 60 percent of their value in one day."

Value investing not only requires more courage; it requires almost infinite patience, which sometimes goes unrewarded. Royce may buy unloved stocks and wait years for them to be recognized. Then the company's management, recognizing how cheap the stock is, steps in to buy the company—very cheaply. Royce's patience goes for naught. "It's a big problem," he says unhappily.

Then there are redemptions: Disgusted investors begin bailing out, as Edwin Walczak has complained. One thing about investors is absolutely certain: Whether it's stocks or bonds, precious metals or frozen pork bellies, they seem determined to buy high and sell low.

Royce's funds have suffered less than most other small-company value funds have, probably because his investors are smarter and they're familiar with his fine long-term record. Also, his funds—for small-caps—are surprisingly conservative: Their volatility is startlingly low.

Still, his oldest fund, Pennsylvania Mutual (which dates to 1973), has lost shareholders—something that happens with older funds as their investors age, move from stocks to bonds, and buy homes for their children.

Questions and Answers

Q. Just why did value funds do so poorly for years and years?

C.R. The whole world is cyclical, and growth and value take turns. It's the natural order of things.

Q. Why do value players decide to become value players in the first place?

C.R. After suffering some pain. Often they have lost a good amount of money. They develop a heavy dose of realism and become sensitive to risk.

Q. What kind of stock do you look for?

C.R. Stocks that just have the flu, not pneumonia. It could be a fine company whose growth is slowing—from 20 percent a year to 12 percent. And the market has, as usual, overreacted, dropping the stock's price-earnings ratio from 25 to 8. But a stock that earns 12 percent at 8 times [earnings] is great.

In general, what he does is buy stocks that have fallen, then sell them when they have bounced back. Will he sell a small company that becomes a mid-sized or big company? "That would be absurd," he replied, a bit surprised. "We're trying to make money, not clip the flowers when they begin blooming. We invest in accord with common sense."

At some level, he grants, choosing stocks calls for a little guessing. "At the end of the day," he confessed, "I ask myself: What will people think of this stock two years from now? Will people adjust to its new, lower level of growth? Will it be taken out of the penalty box?"

In any case, only 20 percent of his choices turn out to be big winners. Still, those winners "have a great deal of effect on the whole portfolio."

How does he avoid mistakes, choosing old mutts instead of healthy puppies? Studying their balance sheets, including the footnotes. Visiting companies and talking with management—and talking with suppliers and competitors. "Management gives you the party line; competitors tell you the truth."

His advice to investors: Recognize that a value fund may at any time be buying cheap stocks ("seeding") or selling formerly cheap stocks ("harvesting"). The better time to buy is when stocks in general are down and the fund is scooping up bargains. "A period of underperformance is really a time of opportunity."

Royce's funds are split between small companies and microcaps, diversified funds and concentrated funds. His two recommendations for investors who want small value funds: Royce Total Return, which enjoys a remarkable stability because it invests in dividend-paying small companies (yes, there are such things), and Royce Low Priced Stock Fund, which has done well in part because so many investors are suspicious of inexpensive stocks—so you can buy them cheap.

Yes, running a mutual fund may be tough. But Royce acknowledges that "this business is so much fun." And there are rewards. Investors expect very little from value funds—and expect the world from growth funds. Value players "are always getting boos from the stands." So, when they go on a bit of a spree, their investors are overjoyed. Whereas, "With the growth guys, everyone always cheers—but then they may strike out."

www.roycefunds.com

Jean-Marie Eveillard

Jean-Marie Eveillard, who was born in France and runs the First Eagle SoGen funds, was making an appearance on *Wall $treet Week*, arguing the case for the bears (this was some years ago). Logically, persuasively.

And then one of the panelists, a nasty glint in his eye, asked, "You say you're so pessimistic about this market now. But how come you have 30 percent of your investments in the stock market?" Then he sank back into his seat looking smug and self-satisfied.

Said Jean-Marie, evenly, "I may be wrong."

The panelists, every last one of them, were thunderstruck.

No one had ever, it seems, uttered those words on the program before. Utter quiet.

And then Jean-Marie added, "I've been wrong before."

I thought all the panelists would now faint dead away. Two consecutive statements that you would never expect a portfolio manager to utter. When the panelists regained their senses, they looked upon Jean-Marie with new-found respect.

Remembering Bernard Baruch

I've interviewed Eveillard several times over the years. The first time I interviewed him, he was not as well-known as he is now. And I heard that he was boasting to a relative of his, who worked at our magazine (*Sylvia Porter's Personal Finance Magazine*), that we had just interviewed him. An early taste of fame.

I keenly recall one conversation with him, right after the crash of 1987. His fund wasn't badly hurt. He's almost always pessimistic, and he had been keeping a low profile.

"When the market goes up," he said, "you always wish you had had more money in the market. When the market goes down, you always wish you had had less."

He added, "I always sell too soon."

Said I, brightly, "That's what Bernard Baruch said."

A pause. "Who is Bernard Baruch?"

Agreeing with Buffett

In 1998 or so, the SoGen funds were doing terribly.

As he pointed out during a speech in New Jersey, he invests not just in foreign stocks, which were out of favor, but in small-cap stocks, which were also out of favor, and in value stocks, which were also out of favor. (SoGen is short for Société Générale, the French bank that runs the funds.)

But Eveillard urged people attending the meeting not to assume that large U.S. growth stocks will continue their reign forever. Ten years ago, he mentioned, everyone thought the Japanese market was also invulnerable—before it began sinking beneath the waves. And now, with the stocks in the Standard & Poor's 500 Stock Index selling at 35 times earnings, he suggested, the U.S. market may be similarly overvalued.

Those earnings themselves, Eveillard went on, may be overstated: Some corporations are "playing around" with their accounting, he said, just to keep stock prices high. (That famous investor Warren Buffett, Eveillard mentioned, had said the same thing.) He and Buffett, in fact, share other views. At that meeting, he said, "There is no such thing as an efficient stock market."

Eveillard is a charming, cultured gentleman, and he still speaks with a French accent. One of his interests, I happen to know, is attending the Metropolitan Opera.

Five years ago, Eveillard told the investors' group, too much money was flowing into foreign funds, so he closed his own flagship fund, SoGen International, to new investors for a while. But in recent years too much money has been leaving. "The lesson that people should learn," he said, "is that you should be very careful not to extrapolate recent experiences." Whatever is fashionable now may not last long.

He urged investors to diversify their portfolios away from just U.S. large-company growth stocks. "The world is a dangerous place today," he said. "And not even [Alan] Greenspan [chairman of the Federal Reserve] walks on water.

"There is an enormous discrepancy between big growth stocks and small value stocks on the other hand," he went on. "Quite a few small value stocks are reasonably priced, nothing like S&P 500 stocks. Either the small caps will catch up, or the big growth stocks will come down. And in recent weeks, small value stocks seem to have been catching up."

What about just buying multinational companies, such as IBM, which do a lot of business abroad, and avoiding individual foreign stocks? His answer: "Why close yourself off from potential opportunities?" Europe is only in the early stages of corporate restructuring, he said, so stocks there may have a rosy future.

On the other hand, stocks in the larger European countries may be almost as overpriced as U.S. large companies, he warned. "Nestlé is about as expensive as U.S. multinationals." (Nestlé, the chocolate company, is based in Switzerland.) "But small companies in the United Kingdom are as cheap as they've been in 25 years. And there are better investment values outside the United States."

While accounting practices in emerging countries "are sometimes bizarre," he went on, "the United States is not perfect, either." Some European countries, in fact, "have an extremely conservative bias."

About Japan he was guardedly optimistic, saying it would take time for corporations there to make the "wrenching changes" required, like laying off unneeded workers. But he predicted that these things would eventually happen: "The Japanese will let the dice fall where they may."

Someone asked Eveillard whether Europe can thrive economically when workers in Germany take six-week vacations. Eveillard replied that a six-week vacation isn't harmful "if during the remaining 46 weeks they work with typical German discipline."

A few months ago, I had heard Eveillard say that he had sold all his shares of Johnson & Johnson—which bothered the heck out of me because I own some shares.

"Why?" I asked.

He had bought it when the two Clintons were making plans to change the health-care system, he explained, and the stock became cheap. But now that it's recovered, he said, it doesn't belong in a value-oriented portfolio. "But obviously I sold too soon," he said, referring to the stock's neat performance that year.

SoGen International is still rated four stars, for "above average," by Morningstar Mutual Funds, a leading newsletter. Writes Morningstar, "With Eveillard at the helm, this fund should remain a fine global asset-allocation vehicle." The SoGen Funds have 3.75 percent sales charges.

www.firsteaglefunds.com

William Lippman and Bruce Baughman

What stock might someone buy—and hold forever? A few years ago, the answer given by Bill Lippman and Bruce Baughman, value investors at the Franklin Funds, was: Automatic Data Processing, headquartered in Roseland, New Jersey.

Their reasoning: The stock has raised its dividend for umpteen consecutive years, the management is shareholder-oriented, and the payroll business should thrive far into the future.

Do they own it? Nope. "It's a little high-priced," Lippman said.

An interesting choice, but something you would expect from these two savvy guys. Lippman, 76, is president of Franklin Advisory Services, part of the huge Franklin Templeton group of funds in San Mateo, California, which now owns the Mutual Series funds in Short Hills, New Jersey.

Baughman, 52, a CPA, is senior vice president and runs the group's flagship fund, Franklin Balance Sheet, which has an unusual 1.5 percent sales charge. He also runs Franklin Microcap Value. Don Taylor, who came from Fidelity, runs Rising Dividend. (Most Franklin funds have 5.75 percent loads.)

Lippman has launched a new fund called Franklin Large Cap Value, which buys large-company stocks. Any real estate investment trusts? "Never," Lippman said. "They're too hard to figure out." And naturally, they don't own any pharmaceuticals—too high-priced for value investors. "I'd like to see them selling at 15 times, not 24," Lippman said, talking about their price-earnings ratios.

Lippman is a slender, wiry, quick-thinking fellow with a neat sense of humor. Among the stocks he has bought is TJ Maxx. "It's like a museum," Lippman said. "And the stuff is cheap. You can get a decent white shirt for $15. And the stock has a high return on equity."

He also claims to be a razzle-dazzle tennis player but for years has politely declined an invitation to play against me. (Very wisely, I might add.)

The two were in a good mood when we had lunch recently in Fort Lee, New Jersey, where they work. After several years during which growth stocks have annihilated value stocks, the sun had begun peeking through the clouds.

During all those lean years, I asked, had they stuck to their discipline and continued buying only cheap stocks? Weren't they tempted to buy Cisco, America Online, and such?

"We remained steadfast," Lippman said. And he expressed some skepticism about certain "value" mutual funds that bought stocks such as AOL and Cisco. (I think this is called "running with the foxes and hunting with the hounds.") He described two styles of "capitulation": (1) "Buying those ridiculous dot-coms that aren't making any money" and (2) "Just not buying good cheap stocks, like those selling at only six times earnings and below book (value)."

Baughman added that fund managers have a lot of latitude even if they're determined to remain in one corner of the Morningstar style box. (Managers want to be consistent because financial planners and pension managers want consistency.) They can just make sure that their median stock, the one in the middle, is value—if they want to be classified as value investors.

Lippman started as a mutual fund salesperson, then launched his own operation: the Pilgrim funds. There he started the first "rising dividend" fund, MagnaCap, buying stocks of companies in such good shape that they could boost their dividends regularly.

Franklin Balance Sheet was launched to buy closed-end funds; its strange sales charge, 1.5 percent, is the highest that a fund can legally charge if it buys other funds.

What advice would they give beginning investors? "Read Graham and Dodd," Lippman replied.

Also: Lippman quoted the late Max Heine, who started the Mutual Series funds, as saying, "Many roads lead to Jerusalem." Meaning: You can make money many different ways. (Lippman had organized a memorable panel discussion years ago featuring Heine, Philip Carret from Pilgrim, and Julian Lerner from the AIM funds. As I recall it, Heine had actually said, "All roads lead to Jerusalem." Not "many.")

Also: If you're a value investor, he advised, take a long-term view. "Buy good quality, low-debt companies. Things may go against you for a period of time, but if you get suckered out, you'll never make money."

Do they try to assess company management? Yes, and one way to gauge whether management really cares about shareholders is to scrutinize proxy statements. Lippman and Baughman check options awarded, options repriced when the stock didn't go up, insider sales, executive pay, whether the chairman's nephew is on the payroll. I mentioned that Charles Royce's complaint that he sometimes holds a cheap stock for years, only to have management greedily buy the company for a song and put him out in the cold.

"It happens and we hate it," Baughman said, clearly annoyed. But sometimes management is forced to raise the bids when outsiders get interested.

When management offers to buy the company, he added, it's usually a sign that the stock is dirt cheap and better times lie ahead.

They echoed Royce in agreeing that running open-end mutual funds is no cakewalk.

"You can't control the flow of money," Lippman said. If shareholders sell, you have to raise money. In recent years, with shareholders leaving, they've had to sell good stocks. "We shaved a little here and there," he said, hoping that by the end of a month, the portfolio will look exactly the same—but there will just be fewer shares of everything.

What do they think of index funds? "A self-fulfilling prophecy," Lippman said dismissively. In recent years, everyone has been buying them, so they went up. "The reverse may also be true." If the S&P goes down for a year or two, people may sell their index funds and buy something else, driving the S&P down even further. (A good reason to buy Vanguard Total Stock Market, I think, rather than the less-well-diversified S&P 500 index.)

Baughman shrewdly noted that the indexes are always adding hot stocks and dropping cold ones. "There's an element of momentum investing in this, and theoretically it can work in reverse, too," he pointed out. The hot stocks may turn cold.

Isn't their job boring? Just waiting for cold stocks to turn warm? No, says Baughman, with their portfolio, something is always happening. That's a good reason to own a variety of stocks: You don't ever have a chance to fall asleep.

How do their funds differ from their sister Mutual Series funds? Those funds buy more distressed merchandise than they themselves would.

Do they talk with other value managers at Mutual Series? Not at all. One reason: A fund is inhibited from owning more than 10 percent of a company. If a Mutual Series fund owns, say, 7 percent of the shares, Balance Sheet (say) might not be able to buy more than 3 percent—unless the funds keep walls between themselves. Then each can have up to 10 percent.

Lippman said, "Otherwise, I'd love to compare notes with the people at Mutual Series."

www.franklin-templeton.com

Colin C. Ferenbach

Asked about his investment strategy, Colin C. Ferenbach, co-manager of the Haven Fund in New York City, explains: "I'm scared a lot."

He likes to quote an old adage: "There are old portfolio managers and there are bold portfolio managers, but no old bold portfolio managers." (There is a Morningstar study showing that veteran money managers tend to be very conservative.)

As one might expect, the Haven Fund is mainly for conservative investors. Even so, it invests in mid-cap stocks—certainly not so safe as large companies. But compared with an index of mid-cap stocks, the Haven Fund is only 77 percent as volatile. Its Morningstar rating is usually 4 stars—"above average."

Although it's more than 15 years old, Haven remains a tiny fund, with only $90 million in assets. Still, the few hundred shareholders have an awful lot of confidence in the fund: They invest an average of $325,000 each.

Haven almost never appears at the top of the charts, although in some years it does very nicely indeed: up about 15.91 percent in 2000, a staggering 25.01 percentage points above the S&P 500.

Ferenbach, 67, has a sharp mind and a good sense of humor. Would he welcome more money and more shareholders into his fund? His answer: Would he accept a date with Michelle Pfeiffer? (He answers his own question: "Of course. But she hasn't asked me yet.")

In pursuit of safety, Ferenbach looks for companies that should do okay in a downturn. "Many funds are like riding a bike downhill. You can do brilliantly. But when they come to an uphill, they're no Lance Armstrong." (Bicyclist Armstrong won the Tour de France.)

In searching for stocks Ferenbach looks for such things as low price-earnings ratios, high estimated private market value (what someone might pay for the whole company), and low debt—and doesn't pay much attention to book value (assets per share outstanding) because he thinks it can be manipulated.

Dividends are also nice: "We like to cover our expenses."

And yes, as often as possible, he talks to the management of a company he owns or is interested in. In 1977 he attended a dinner in New Orleans given by the oil company that is now Total Fina Elf. Only three investors showed up. He was very impressed by the presentation. He then checked out the company with his friends in Paris, and bought in—very profitably.

What turns him off management? "Some people I don't like or trust."

He doesn't pay attention to market weightings and will sometimes load up on an out-of-favor sector. In 1998 he was overweighted in oils; in 1993, pharmaceuticals. "We have a strong contrarian streak."

When does he sell? "If I feel we've made a mistake, we part company, sooner rather than later. We're very tax conscious, and we have no hesitation in cutting losers." (Losers balance out the capital gains of winners he's sold.) He'll even double-up on a losing stock that he's confident about, and sell half the shares after 31 days, which gives him a deductible tax loss and the same investment position. ("Doubling up," it's called. Unless you wait 31 days before buying a stock again, you cannot deduct a loss.)

His recent portfolio consisted of only 46 stocks. Around 70 stocks is the maximum he thinks he could follow.

His worst mistake: buying Owens-Corning. It got creamed because of asbestos litigation. "It was a cheap stock," said Ferenbach ruefully, "and it got a lot cheaper."

For help, he relies on regional brokers who follow mid-cap stocks: "They're more objective" than analysts at the national wire-houses.

He himself reads a lot: "I'm always looking to spot good ideas." Haven buys and holds stocks—"keeping a stock three years is nothing," he says. The fund's turnover rate in 2000 was 80 percent, which is the equivalent of his selling fewer than four out of five stocks during the year. (The average turnover of a mid-cap blend fund: 104 percent.)

Ferenbach isn't a big fan of indexing: "It's beginning to unwind," he says skeptically. Momentum investing—where you stick with hot stocks—is going out of style, he believes, and that's what has helped the Standard & Poor's 500, which has been dominated by a few hot stocks. "Indexing fed on itself and justified itself."

Is the stock market going to continue going up 20 percent a year? "It can't," he says. "If it did, everyone could buy the island of Manhattan. It's been a great run, but it will end in either a bang or a whimper. I expect the 2000s will be a re-run of the 1970s, where stocks go up 3 or 4 percent a year, inflation-adjusted."

Haven had been a limited partnership set up by Goldman Sachs people, and it became an open-end fund in 1994.

Ferenbach graduated from Yale in 1955 with a B.A. in history, and served in the U.S. Air Force for two years before joining Goldman, Sachs. He has 43 years of investment experience.

Unlike some managers, who seem monomaniacal about investing, Ferenbach has outside interests. He even owns a vineyard in France, and loves to talk about the "intriguing mystery" of why some wines turn out to be superb but not others.

Okay, but what advice does he have for ordinary investors? He thinks a moment, then says, "Be patient."

www.havencapital.com/index2.htm

Mario Gabelli

I had asked Mario (the Great) Gabelli to explain his strategy in 25 words or less, and he came up with: "Graham and Dodd plus Warren Buffett."

Mario is bursting with energy, bursting with fresh ideas. The kind of guy who would come to a Barron's Round Table, during the tech bubble, carrying a bouquet of . . . tulips. (When someone tracked the stock tips made by the Round Table experts, only Mario acquitted himself with honor.)

He studied at the Columbia Business School under Roger Murray, who edited the second edition of Graham and Dodd's *Security Analysis.*

To find stocks to buy, Gabelli looks for companies with a "franchise," with dominant positions in their markets. Such companies will survive downturns, and perhaps emerge even stronger. He also looks at a company's free cash flow, then at its price, to determine whether he's buying it at 40 percent or 50 percent off.

Then he looks for a catalyst that will unlock the values. He calls it "surfacing the values." (He's good with words. He once called junk bonds "stocks in drag.")

A company might spin off an unprofitable division—appoint a dynamic new manager—or industry fundamentals just might improve.

The final test is the balance sheet. He looks for what might be wrong: unfunded pension liabilities, environmental problems, lawsuits.

But Super Mario's genius seems to lie in spotting powerful trends before others do—such as his seeing how profitable cable TV companies would become before almost everyone else did.

A second-generation Italian–American, Gabelli grew up in the Bronx, New York, and though his family was poor, they were fortunate in that they didn't know it. Long before he obtained his education, he says, he had a Ph.D.: He was poor, hungry, and driven. In hiring people, he looks for similar qualities: people who will "sacrifice for success."

He became interested in investing when he kept overhearing wealthy investors talk about stocks while he caddied at golf clubs in Westchester County. He bought his first stocks when he was 13; he helped finance his own education at graduate school by trading stocks from a phone booth on the Columbia campus.

What mistakes has he made? Sometimes his painstaking research—talking with management, with competitors, digesting financial reports—has him still on the runway when the stock takes off.

If you ask him whether he market-times or not, he gives a typical ironic Gabellian reply: "No, I'm not smart enough to market-time."

The first time I met him was right after the crash of 1987. I said to him, "Why does the stock market go up and down? Do you know?"

He replied, "I've been in this business a long time, and I still have no idea."

www.gabelli.com

Robert A. Olstein

No less than Marty Whitman has spoken highly of Robert Olstein, saying that he has a knack for buying good, cheap stocks very early.

Here are a few excerpts from a quarterly report of his:

- "Our simple definition of a value investor is one who attempts to buy stocks selling at a discount to the intrinsic value of the underlying business. Good minds may differ as to what that value may be, but any fund not paying attention to value (momentum funds or crowd psychology funds) is relying on the foolishness of other investors to make money. I prefer to call those funds 'overvalued funds.'"
- "Value funds aim to take advantage of misperceived crowd psychology, which causes investors to abandon and ignore valuable businesses as they seek short-term fortunes in current market fads. At other times, value is created by temporary problems surrounding a specific company, an industry, or the markets in general. Any negativity, which is usually highlighted prominently by the analytical community and the media, goes against the investment crowd's desire for instantaneous gratification, resulting in a mass exodus from those stocks."

• "The three most important factors we consider when purchasing stocks for our portfolio are price, price, and price."

• "Mispriced securities rarely turn around overnight, as crowd misperceptions are slow to change."

• "Momentum investors who trade in overvalued stocks based on crowd psychology are in essence engaging in a game equivalent to Russian roulette, hoping that the bullet is not fired at them."

• On why his fund has a 150 percent turnover: "When stocks reach prices in which our risk/reward equation tilts toward risk, we sell. The long-term holders of great companies such as Cisco, Microsoft, and Sun Microsystems, which eventually reached unrealistic prices, are currently wishing that their funds had more turnover."

• Can his fund become more tax-efficient? "Absolutely! We can purchase overvalued stocks, lose money, and reduce your tax bill to zero. On a serious note, we always review the tax implications of investment decisions, but will never allow tax decisions to take precedence over investment decisions."

• Should you wait for a catalyst before you buy a value stock? "Earlier this year [2001] the Fund owned Shaw Industries, a leading carpet company, which was purchased at about $13 a share. At the time . . . we believed the stock was worth $20 a share (based on future cash flows) with long-term appreciation expected from our calculation of private market value. Many analysts agreed with us about the $20 value but advised investors not to purchase Shaw Industries for about a year until the earnings turned around. Shaw was experiencing what we believed was a temporary earnings downturn. . . . Unfortunately for the analysts, an investor named Warren Buffett did not worry about the timing and had a time horizon which extended well into the future. He made a tender offer for the outstanding shares of Shaw Industries at $19.25 a share. Mr. Buffett took advantage of the current price. . . ."

www.olsteinfunds.com

John Gunn

The three Dodge & Cox Funds—Stock, Balanced, and Income—are very similar. Balanced buys the stocks and bonds the other two funds own. A veteran fund, Balanced first saw the light of day in 1931, and all the funds have rock-solid records.

I interviewed John Gunn, the chief investment officer, a few years ago.

Questions and Answers

Q. How are the Dodge & Cox funds different from other funds?"

J.G. Among mutual funds, we're a strange beast. One writer has even said that Dodge & Cox is not in the mutual fund business—which is why he likes us. What he meant was that we don't advertise or bend over backward to publicize ourselves; we're not in the distribution business.

It's true that we're different. We don't want to have phalanxes of people. . . . We don't even have any new funds on the horizon, beyond the three we have now.

We're in the investment business, concentrating on stocks and bonds to buy and trying to keep our costs low. . . .

Our stocks have done well, I think, because of our strong, extensive research and our determination to understand each investment as best we can. We're trying to buy bargains and be well-informed about those bargains. Then there's our long-term orientation. And our low turnover. Also, our employees are active investors in our company. We eat our own cooking. All of our pension and profit-sharing plans are invested in the three funds.

Our team approach is another advantage. Everyone here started out at or near the beginning of their business careers, and everyone shares the same general business philosophy. We're on the same wavelength, even though some of us have different camera angles. All of us are even on one floor, so we can meet quickly.

We try to avoid stocks that in three or four years will be known as value stocks and to buy stocks that we hope someday will be known as growth stocks—unpopular to not-very-popular stocks with low-to-average expectations of profits. We're not knee-jerk contrarians, but we're always going to be looking at stocks whose prices are dropping.

Of course, if a stock is selling at the low end of its historic valuation, it's not that everyone else sees worries and we see nothing but blue skies. The worries are there. But a lot of times they get overdone. And we also may see chances of good surprises. . . .

www.dodgeandcox.com

CHAPTER 32

Putting Everything Together

To invest like Warren Buffett, you have a variety of choices—and you can mix them up.

- Buy shares of Berkshire Hathaway.
- Buy individual stocks that Berkshire owns, possibly along with stocks that seem to fit Buffett's criteria, possibly along with stocks in Buffett-like funds, like Clipper, Legg Mason Focus, and Tweedy, Browne.
- Buy Buffett-like funds themselves.

Traits of Superior Investors

What do superior investors, like Warren Buffett, have in common? A poll I conducted a few years ago of 24 respected investors* found that these were the criteria that *value* investors considered most important:

- Sticking with your strategy
- Having better research
- Willingness to be contrarian
- Being logical and unemotional

- Following a sell discipline
- Experience
- Flexibility

Here are the criteria that *growth* investors emphasized:

- Sticking with your strategy
- Being logical and unemotional
- Having better research
- Following a sell discipline
- Experience
- Flexibility
- Pulling the trigger quickly and knowledgeably

Which of these criteria seem to apply most to Buffett? Being logical and unemotional. Sticking with your strategy—although his strategy did shift, from deep value (those cigars with a few puffs left in them) to value with a growth tinge. (That shift would fit under "flexibility.") A willingness—indeed, an eagerness—to be contrarian. Experience, certainly. Pulling the trigger quickly—certainly. Following a sell discipline? Berkshire has actually bought and sold with more alacrity than investors in general recognize. Buffett's favorite holding period may be forever, but not for any company he thinks has turned into a dog. How about his having better research? We don't have in-depth knowledge about his investigation into certain companies that he has bought, but we do know that he studies the numbers and he studies the people—and he will even go to such lengths as to visit a movie theater in Times Square to see a matinee of *Mary Poppins* just to gauge the appeal of Walt Disney stock. In fact, he parted company with Ben Graham because of his own eagerness to visit companies and interview the management, which is something that not all value investors care to do.

All in all, Buffett fits these criteria quite nicely—although there are other criteria as well.

*Among those participating in this poll were James Craig, then with Janus; Richard Fentin of Fidelity; Mario Gabelli; Warren Lammert of Janus; William Lippman and Bruce Baughman of Franklin funds; Thomas Marsico; Gary Pilgrim of PBHG; Michael Price of Mutual Series; Brian Rogers, formerly of T. Rowe Price; Richard Strong of the Strong Funds; and Donald Yacktman of the Yacktman Funds.

Buffett's Investment Strategy

In Russell Train's *Money Masters of Our Time* (HarperBusiness, 2000), he tried to summarize Buffett's investment strategy, and Buffett himself apparently read over the list with approval:

- You must be a fanatic—"fascinated by the investment process." But you cannot be excessively greedy, or not greedy enough.
- Have patience. If you buy a stock, you should not mind if the stock market closed for 10 years. (This is also an indication of how much confidence you have in that stock.)
- Be an independent thinker. Don't be swayed by what the vulgar mob thinks. Buffett quotes Benjamin Graham: "The fact that other people agree or disagree with you makes you neither right nor wrong. You will be right if your facts and reasoning are correct."
- You must have self-confidence. If you automatically sell when the stock market or your stocks retreat, out of nervousness, you're not behaving rationally. It's as if you bought a house for $1 million, and when someone offered you $800,000, you immediately agreed to sell it.
- You must accept the fact that you don't know something. (The significance of this seems to be: Either you can't know everything, and you should go ahead anyway—or, if you don't know something, it could be something vital. So be wary.)
- Buy any kind of business, but don't pay up. Don't pay too much and then count on finding a "bigger fool to take it off your hands."

Train added four more requirements that a good investor along the lines of Buffett should have:

1. Ten or fifteen years of study and experience.
2. "Be a genius of sorts." (Have a special talent for the game.)
3. Be intellectually honest. (Don't try to delude yourself into thinking that a mistake you made wasn't a mistake.)
4. "Avoid significant distractions." (This might mean: Focus on the basics—not on secondary or tertiary reasons to buy or not to buy a stock.)

Train went on to define the "wonderful businesses" that Buffett attempts to buy:

- They have a good return on capital, without "accounting gimmicks" and lots of debt.
- They are easy to understand.
- Their profits are measured in cash.
- They have strong franchises and some freedom to raise prices.
- They don't need a genius to run them.
- Their earnings are predictable because they're consistent.
- They are not regulated or targets of regulation.
- They have low inventories and high turnover. They don't need large and regular infusions of capital.
- The managers think of shareholders first.
- There's a high rate of return on inventories plus plant.
- The best businesses grow along with other businesses, with little need of their own capital. (Example: advertising)

Final Thoughts on Buffett

- He is determined to invest in almost-sure things. No gambling.
- He concentrates on areas he knows.
- He does his homework.
- He insists on working with people he trusts and admires.
- He's good at evaluating people.
- He ruthlessly studies his mistakes and tries to learn from them.
- He's no Nervous Nellie, ready to trade his securities for little or no reason at all.
- While he isn't Simon Legree, he does put his shareholders' interests before other people's interests—employees, for example.
- He doesn't make the foolish mistakes that ordinary investors make.
- He's uncannily knowledgeable about a wide variety of American companies.
- He has a splendid reputation, lots of charm, and lots of friends.
- He is modest and humble, but also self-confident—at the appropriate times.

- He's an unconventional, skeptical thinker. He distrusts popular opinion. "In my opinion," he has written, "investment success will not be produced by the price behavior of stocks and markets. Rather an investor will succeed by coupling good business judgment with an ability to translate his thoughts and behavior from the super-contagious emotions that swirl about the marketplace."

APPENDIX 1

Wanted: Cheap, Good Companies

When Berkshire Hathaway does things, it does them simply and sensibly. It wants to buy good businesses, preferring to become 100 percent owners to becoming partial owners just by purchasing stock. So Berkshire has promulgated an advertisement, printed below, seeking sellers.

Notable Is Berkshire's Interest in Companies

- with "[d]emonstrated consistent earning power." Pie in the here and now, not pie in the sky.
- "Businesses earning good returns on equity."
- ". . . employing little or no debt." Why not seek perfection?
- "Management in place." Changing horses in midstream is especially unwise when those horses have proved their merit.
- "Simple businesses . . ." The less you understand about a business, very likely the more nasty surprises lie in store.
- "An offering price. . . ." In bargaining, you might try to tie up your opposite number's time. The more of his or her time you waste, the more eager he or she may be to arrange some sort of deal, any deal. It's better to wind up being paid $5 an hour than nothing an hour. Berkshire doesn't want to fall into this trap and waste a single mo-

ment of its time. Once Berkshire has obtained an offering price, it can just walk away if the seller is asking for too much. If the price is reasonable, Berkshire can try to bargain the seller down.

In short, Berkshire's Help Wanted ad is representative of what Warren Buffett is seeking in any business he invests in: something as close to perfection as possible. Almost a sure thing.

Berkshire's Acquisition Criteria

We are eager to hear from principals or their representatives about businesses that meet all of the following criteria:

- Large purchases (at least $50 million of before-tax earnings)
- Demonstrated consistent earning power (future projections are of no interest to us, nor are "turnaround" situations)
- Businesses earning good returns on equity while employing little or no debt
- Management in place (we can't supply it)
- Simple businesses (if there's lots of technology, we won't understand it)
- An offering price (we don't want to waste our time or that of the seller by talking, even preliminarily, about a transaction when price is unknown)

The larger the company, the greater will be our interest. We would like to make an acquisition in the $5–$20 billion range. *We are not interested, however, in receiving suggestions about purchases we might make in the general stock market.*

We will not engage in unfriendly takeovers. We can promise complete confidentiality and a very fast answer—customarily within five minutes—as to whether we're interested. We prefer to buy for cash, but will consider issuing stock when we receive as much in intrinsic business value as we give.

Charlie [Munger, Buffett's partner] and I frequently get approached about acquisitions that don't come close to meeting our tests: We've found that if you advertise an interest in collies, a lot of people will call hoping to sell you their cocker spaniels. A line from a country song expresses our feelings about new ventures, turnarounds, or auction-like sales: "When the phone don't ring, you'll know it's me."

Berkshire Hathaway's Subsidiaries (2000)

Acme Building Brands
Ben Bridge Jeweler
Benjamin Moore & Co.
Berkshire Hathaway Group
Borsheim's Fine Jewelry
Buffalo *News*, Buffalo, N.Y.
Central States Indemnity Company
CORT Business Services
Dexter Shoe Company
Executive Jet
Fechheimer Brothers Company
FlightSafety
GEICO Direct Auto Insurance
General & Cologne Re Group
Helzberg Diamonds
H.H. Brown Shoe Company
International Dairy Queen, Inc.
Jordan's Furniture
Justin's Brands
Lowell Shoe Company
MidAmerican Energy Holdings Company
National Indemnity Company
Nebraska Furniture Mart
Precision Steel Warehouse, Inc.
RC Willey Home Furnishings
Scott Fetzer Companies
See's Candy Shops
Shaw Industries
Star Furniture
United States Liability Insurance

APPENDIX 3

Quotations from the Chairman

"I'm rational. Plenty of people have higher IQs and plenty of people work more hours, but I'm rational about things. You have to be able to control yourself; you can't let your emotions get in control of your mind."

"The most important quality for an investor is temperament, not intellect. You don't need tons of IQ in this business. You don't have to be able to play three-dimensional chess or duplicate bridge. You need a temperament that derives great pleasure neither from being with the crowd nor against the crowd. You know you're right, not because of the position of others but because your facts and your reasoning are right."

"I have never met a man who could forecast the market."

"Coke is exactly the kind of company I like. I like products I can understand. I don't know what a transistor is, but I appreciate the contents of a Coke can. Berkshire Hathaway's purchase of stock in

the Coca-Cola Company was the ultimate case of me putting my money where my mouth was."

(On Gillette) "It's pleasant to go to bed every night knowing there are 2.5 billion males in the world who will have to shave the next morning."

"We've done better by avoiding dragons than by slaying them."

"Look at stocks as businesses, look for businesses you understand, run by people you trust and are comfortable with, and leave them alone for a long time."

Notable conversation:

MARSHALL WEINBERG (a broker who had taken Graham's course): Why don't we go to a Japanese steakhouse today for lunch?

BUFFETT: Why don't we go to Reuben's? (An East Side deli)

WEINBERG: We ate there yesterday!

BUFFETT: Right. You know what you're getting.

WEINBERG: By that logic, we'd go there every day.

BUFFETT: Precisely. Why not eat there every day?

"Bull markets can obscure mathematical laws, but they cannot repeal them."

"Berkshire is selling at a price at which Charlie and I would not consider buying it." (When the stock split into A and B shares, in 1995.)

"In my early days as a manager I, too, dated a few toads. They were cheap dates—I've never been much of a sport—but my results matched those of acquirers who courted higher-priced toads. I kissed and they croaked."

"Charlie and I have found that making silk purses out of silk is the best that we can do; with sow's ears, we fail."

"All I want is one good idea every year. If you really push me, I will settle for one good idea every two years."

"Sound investing can make you very wealthy if you're not in too big a hurry."

"From [Fisher] I learned the value of the 'scuttlebutt' approach: Go out and talk to competitors, suppliers, customers to find out how an industry or a company really operates."

"Graham's premise was that there would periodically be times when you couldn't find good values, and it's a good idea to go to the beach."

"There seems to be some perverse human characteristic that likes to make easy things difficult."

"This is the cornerstone of our investment philosophy: Never count on making a good sale. Have the purchase price be so attractive that even a mediocre sale gives good results."

"With enough inside information and a million dollars, you can go broke in a year."

"[O]ccasional outbreaks of the two supercontagious diseases, fear and greed, will forever occur in the investment community."

"We don't get into things we don't understand. We buy very few things but we buy very big positions."

"Intelligent investing is not complex, though that is far from saying that it is easy. What an investor needs is the ability to correctly evaluate selected businesses. Note the word 'selected': You don't have to be an expert on every company, or even many. You only have to be able to evaluate companies within your circle of

competence. The size of the circle is not very important; knowing its boundaries, however, is vital."

"Your goal as an investor should simply be to purchase, at a rational price, a part interest in an easily-understandable business whose earnings are virtually certain to be materially high five, ten and twenty years from now. Over time, you will find only a few companies that meet these standards—so that when you see one that qualifies, you should buy a meaningful amount of stock. You must also resist the temptation to stray from these guidelines: If you aren't willing to own a stock for ten years, don't even think about owning it for ten minutes."

"I'd be a bum on the street with a tin cup if the market were always efficient."

"We like stocks that generate high returns on invested capital where there is a strong likelihood that it will continue to do so. For example, the last time we bought Coca-Cola, it was selling at about 23 times earnings. Using our purchase price and today's earnings, that makes it about 5 times earnings. It's really the interaction of capital employed, the return on that capital, and future capital generated versus the purchase price today."

"Anything is a buy at a price."

"If the business does well, the stock eventually follows."

"As long as we can make an annual 15 percent return on equity, I don't worry about one quarter's results."

"If [the true value of a company] doesn't just scream at you, it's too close."

"I probably have more friends in New York and California than here, but this [Omaha] is a good place to bring up children and a good place to live. You can think here. You can think better about

the market; you don't hear so many stories, and you can just sit and look at the stock on the desk in front of you. You can think about a lot of things."

"Would you believe that a few decades back they were growing shrimp at Coke and exploring for oil at Gillette? Loss of focus is what worries Charlie and me when we contemplate investing in businesses that in general look outstanding."

"I keep an internal scoreboard. If I do something that others don't like but I feel good about, I'm happy. If others praise something I've done, but I'm not satisfied, I feel unhappy."

"You don't have to make it back the way you lost it."

[His favorite companies are like] "wonderful castles, surrounded by deep, dangerous moats where the leader inside is an honest and decent person. Preferably, the castle gets its strength from the genius inside; the moat is permanent and acts as a powerful deterrent to those considering an attack; and inside, the leader makes gold but doesn't keep it all for himself. Roughly translated, we like great companies with dominant positions, whose franchise is hard to duplicate and has tremendous staying power or some permanence to it."

"You need a moat in business to protect you from the guy who is going to come along and offer it [your product] for a penny cheaper."

"In investments, there's no such thing as a called strike. You can stand there at the plate and the pitcher can throw a ball right down the middle, and if it's General Motors at 47 and you don't know enough to decide on General Motors at 47, you let it go right on by and no one's going to call a strike. The only way you can have a strike called is to swing and miss."

"I've never swung at a ball while it's still in the pitcher's glove."

[Graham] said you should look at stocks as small pieces of the business. Look at [market] fluctuations as your friend rather than your enemy."

"Read Ben Graham and Phil Fisher, read annual reports, but don't do equations with Greek letters in them."

"Of course some of you probably wonder why we are now buying Capital Cities at $172.50 per share given that this author, in a characteristic burst of brilliance, sold Berkshire's holdings in the same company at $43 a share in 1978–1980. Anticipating your question, I spent a lot of time working on a snappy answer that would reconcile these acts. A little more time, please."

"Diversification is a protection against ignorance. [It] makes very little sense for those who know what they are doing."

"A lot of great fortunes in the world have been made by owning a single wonderful business. If you understand the business, you don't need to own very many of them."

(On owning many stocks, quoting showman Billy Rose) "If you have a harem of 40 women, you don't get to know any of them very well."

"Ben Graham wanted everything to be a quantitative bargain. I want it to be a quantitative bargain in terms of future streams of cash. My guess is the last big time to do it Ben's way was in '73 or '74, when you could have done it quite easily."

"Great investment opportunities come around when excellent companies are surrounded by unusual circumstances that cause the stock to be misappraised."

"It's not risky to buy securities at a fraction of what they're worth."

"You have to think for yourself. It always amazes me how high IQ people mindlessly imitate. I never get good ideas talking to other people."

"To invest successfully, you need not understand beta, efficient markets, modern portfolio theory, option pricing or emerging markets. You may, in fact, be better off knowing nothing of these. That, of course, is not the prevailing view at most business schools, whose finance curriculum tends to be dominated by such subjects. In our view, though, investment students need only two well-taught courses—How to Value a Business, and How to Think about Market Prices.

"We try to price, rather than time, purchases. In our view, it is folly to forgo buying shares in an outstanding business whose long-term future is predictable, because of short-term worries about an economy or a stock market that we know to be unpredictable. Why scrap an informed decision because of an uninformed guess?

"We purchased National Indemnity in 1967, See's in 1972, Buffalo News in 1977, Nebraska Furniture Mart in 1983, and Scott Fetzer in 1986 because those are the years they became available and because we thought the prices they carried were acceptable. In each case, we pondered what the business was likely to do, not what the Dow, the Fed, or the economy might do.

"If we see this approach as making sense in the purchases of businesses in their entirety, why should we change tack when we are purchasing small pieces of wonderful businesses in the stock market?"

"We do not need more people gambling on the nonessential instruments identified with the stock market in the country. Nor brokers who encourage them to do so. What we need are investors and ad-

visers who look at the long-term prospects for an enterprise and invest accordingly. We need the intelligent commitment of capital, not leveraged market wagers. The propensity to operate in the intelligent, prosocial sectors of capital markets is deterred, not enhanced, by an active and exciting casino operating somewhere in the same arena, utilizing somewhat similar language, and serviced by the same workforce."

"The business is wonderful if it gives you more and more money every year without [your] putting up anything—or very little. And we have some businesses like that. A business is also wonderful if it takes money, but where the rate at which you reinvest the money is very satisfactory. The worst business of all is the one that grows a lot, where you're forced to grow just to stay in the game at all and where you're reinvesting the capital at a very low rate of return. And sometimes people are in those businesses without knowing it."

"If you own See's Candy, and you look in the mirror and say, "Mirror, mirror on the wall, how much do I charge for candy this fall?" and it says, 'More,' it's a good business."

"I don't think you can really be a good investor over a broad range without doing a massive amount of reading. You might think about picking out five or ten companies where you feel quite familiar with their products, but not necessarily so familiar with their financials. . . . Then get lots of annual reports and all of the articles that have been written on those companies for five or ten years . . . Just sort of immerse yourself. And when you get all through, ask yourself, 'What do I not know that I need to know?' Many years ago, I would go around and talk to competitors and employees . . . I just kept asking questions . . . It's an investigative process—a journalistic process. And in the end, you want to write the story. . . . Some companies are easy to write stories about and other companies are much tougher to write stories about. We try to look for the ones that are easy."

"The most common cause of low prices is pessimism—sometimes pervasive, sometimes specific to a company or industry. We want to do business in such an environment, not because we

like pessimism but because we like the prices it produces. It's optimism that is the enemy of the rational buyer.

"None of this means, however, that a business or stock is an intelligent purchase simply because it is unpopular; a contrarian approach is just as foolish as a follow-the-crowd strategy. What's required is thinking rather than polling. Unfortunately, Bertrand Russell's observation about life in general applies with unusual force in the financial world: "Most men would rather die than think. Many do.'"

"Everyone has the same objective—to end up with more dough than they start with [with] a minimum of risk."

APPENDIX 4

"65 Years on Wall Street"*

I had a friend who was a therapist at a mental hospital, and he asked me if I would talk to his patients about investments. And I said okay, and he introduced me, and so I started to talk about investments. And after a few minutes a big fellow in the front of the audience got up and said, "Shut up you idiot and sit down!" I looked at my friend and I said, "What do I do?" He said, "Sit down. That's the most intelligent thing that fellow's said in months."

Well, I want to talk about Ben Graham because he was very helpful to me and I think it might be interesting to you to know how he started. Well, we know about his background at Columbia, but he got the job and became a manager of money because he was very intelligent about his investments, and in the 1920s he had a deal where he took 50 percent of the profits but he also took 50 percent of the losses. And that worked great until 1929 when the market went down and obviously his stocks were affected, too, and he was not only affected by that, but many of these people pulled out because they needed money for their own purposes, or they had lost a lot of money in other places.

*Remarks by Walter Schloss, founder, Walter & Edwin Schloss Associates, before Grant's Interest Rate Observer investment conference, November 1998.

So he figured out how he could possibly never have this happen to him again. He was very upset about losing money. A lot of us are. So he worked on a number of ways of doing this, and one of them was buying companies [selling for] below working capital, and in the 1930s there were a lot of companies that developed that way. And then in 1936 he formed a company called Graham–Newman, which was, I'd say, an open- and closed-end company in that he was able to open it up to his stockbrokers and he'd sell stock with the rights to buy new stock below asset value. That is, if you didn't exercise your option, you were able to sell the rights for money.

At the beginning of 1946, I was out of the army and Graham hired me to work for him as a security analyst, and Graham–Newman was then ten years old and had a nice record. One of the reasons they had a nice record was that they had bought these secondary stocks which had big book values but not particularly good earnings. When the war came along he was able to profit from this because the excess-profits taxes really hurt the companies with small book values. But the big book-value stocks were in the war, and so they made a lot of money based upon the fact that they didn't have to pay these excess-profits taxes. And those stocks went up and he did very well. Ben realized that most of them had gone to prices that were no longer cheap, and so he sold a great many of them.

So, when I came to work for Ben, he had 37 stocks in his common stock portfolio. That was a really big investment company. They had $4,100,000, of which $1.1 million was in common stocks. I looked at the portfolio and I saw that of their 37 stocks that were in the portfolio as of January 31, 1946, only two of them are still around. All the others were taken over, merged, disappeared. And the only two—one was Tricontinental Corporation and the other was McGraw-Hill. He had very small amounts of these stocks, and you figure $1,100,000 with 37 stocks, it wasn't very much.

They weren't all industrials. He had investment company stocks and he had some American Surety, and other insurance company stocks. Basically, the rest of his portfolio was made up of bankrupt bonds, against which he sold "when-issued" securities, some convertible preferred stocks where he shorted the common stocks against them. In those days, if the stock went up you took a long-term gain on the profit side for the preferred, and you took a short-term loss on the short side, which was a pretty good deal for them—and, of course, that isn't true anymore.

Anyhow, at that time my job was to find stocks which were undervalued. And we looked at stocks selling below working capital, which were not very many. Among them, for example, was a stock like East Washing Machine A. The B stock was all owned by the management or owners. You might know that back in the 1940s a lot of companies were family controlled. There was a play about ten years ago called *Other People's Money*. It played off-Broadway, and it was about a little company in New England that struggled along, the family controlled it, and they weren't making any money but they didn't want to put any more money in it because it was a marginal business. And what happened is a fellow from New York comes up and he offers them a pretty good price to buy the company, but the president doesn't want to sell. There was a lot of double-crosses, and it ends up that the family sells out to this guy from New York, who then liquidates the company, throws people out of work. But the family made money out of it.

I was reminded of that by some of the things that have happened over the years since then. In the case of Warren Buffett, who everybody knows or has heard of if they don't know him, Warren told me a story I thought was kind of interesting. He owned a lot of Berkshire Hathaway. He probably paid $8 to $10 a share for it. He went up to the management and spoke to the president about his selling a block of stock back to the company. (The company had previously repurchased stock.) The president agreed to buy it back from Warren at $11.50 a share.

Well, Warren got that tender offer. It came in at 11^{3}/_{8}$—and Warren was sore. So he bought control of the company. So sometimes if you miss something at an eighth of a point, you might think about that.

One of the experiences I had when I worked for Ben was that he had very strict rules. He wasn't going to deviate. I had a fellow come to me from Adams & Peck. . . . A nice guy, he said, "The Battelle Institute has done a study for the Haloid Company," a company in Rochester that had paid a dividend through the depression, a small company that made photographic paper for, I think, Eastman Kodak. Haloid had the rights to a new process and he wanted us to buy the stock. Haloid sold at between $13 and $17 a share during the depression, and it was selling at $21. This was probably about 1947, 1948 or something like that. I thought it was kind of interesting. You're paying $4 for this possibility of a copying machine which could do this. Battelle thought it was OK. I went into Graham and said, "You know, you were only paying a $4 premium for a company that has a possibility of a good gain." And he said, "No, Walter, it's not our kind of stock."

And, of course, it was Xerox.

So, you can see, he was pretty set.

The only consolation I had on that one was that I was almost sure that if they had bought this stock at $21 and it had gone to $50, they would have sold it because they did not project what the thing could do. And one of the things about these undervalued stocks is that you can't really project their earnings. There are stocks where there's growth, and you project what's going to happen next year or in five years. Freddie Mac or one of these big growth companies, you can project what they're going to do. But when you get to secondary companies, they don't seem to have that ability. You can't really say, Well, next year they're going to do well because this year they did poorly, and they're secondary stocks.

And one of the things we then try to do is to buy a secondary stock that's depressed. And today, because of the high level of the stock market, almost everything's been picked over. You've got some analysts, 34,000 Chartered Financial Analysts, you have a tough time finding something to buy.

I'll give you one, which you probably won't like, which would be typical of an undervalued stock. It's been mentioned before by others and it's a stock that was at one time in the Dow Jones Average. It's come upon evil days and struggle, and nobody likes the industry, and so forth. But the stock sells at about $21 a share, and it has a book value of about $40 a share. It got down to maybe $17 when the market broke a few months ago. It's a copper company called Asarco, which just cut its dividend in half.

Now, that stock has got a lot of assets in Peru. They have some big copper mines there. And nobody likes it because it doesn't have growth. But I think Asarco is cheap. We own some, and so I don't want you to think I'm pushing it just because I own it. But I thought you might be interested in the kind of stock I'm talking about.

We bought a lot of these stocks for Ben Graham. We would buy a lot of those undervalued stocks, and they'd work out, and then we'd sell them.

The great example, as you probably know, was one company that sold at $45 a share with a book value of $20, and then [Graham] would use the example of a company selling at $20 with a book value of $40, and of course it was the same company, Boeing Airplane. And Boeing Airplane, before World War II, sold at a big premium over its assets because it had a great future. But in 1946 nobody wanted Boeing Airplane because they didn't think it had much of a future.

We would have liked to buy Boeing when it was selling at $20 with a book of $40, but not the other way around. And I don't know many people here who tend to buy companies which are having problems. One of the reasons is that if you buy a company that's having a problem and you have customers, they don't like that. They want to own companies that are doing well. You're going against human nature when you buy companies which are having problems, and one of the things we do in our field is buy stocks on the way down. If we buy a stock at $30 and it goes to $25, we'll buy more.

A lot of people don't like it if you buy a stock at $30 for a customer, and they see it at $25. You want to buy more of it at $25. The guy doesn't like that and you don't like to remind him of it.

So one of the reasons I think that you have to educate your customers or yourself, really, is that you have to have a strong stomach and be willing to [sit with] an unrealized loss. Don't sell it, but be willing to buy more when it goes down—which is contrary to what people do in this business.

Ben was really a contrarian, but he didn't use those terms because he was really buying value. And when I went to work for him, there were many people doing this kind of thing, buying stocks on the way down. . . .

I tried to follow Ben Graham's ideas of doing it that way. And, of course, it's much more difficult now because you don't have that group of companies selling below working capital. You find a company selling below book value, that's very unusual, and usually the ones that do have a lot of problems—and people don't like to buy problems.

The big thing in the way we invest is to buy against price, and Graham said, in *The Intelligent Investor*, you buy stocks the way you buy groceries, not the way you buy perfume. Now, that doesn't seem so good today because the Gillettes and the Coca-Colas are the perfume stocks. But basically we like to buy stocks which we feel are undervalued, and then we have the guts to buy more when they go down. And that's really the history of Ben Graham.

Questions and Answers

Q. Now, it is often said that the market sometimes knows more than the investors. So when a stock goes down, could that mean that you've got the analysis wrong? You're supposed to get out?

W.S. Well, that could happen. You have to use your judgment and have the guts to follow through. And the fact that the market doesn't like it doesn't mean you're wrong. But, again, everybody has to make their own judgments on this. That's what makes the stock market very interesting—because they don't tell you what's going to happen till later.

Q. There were a group of you that all learned under Ben Graham, and you all seem to be incredibly successful investors. What do you think is the common thread amongst all of you?

W.S. I think, Number One, none of us smoked. . . . I think if I had to say it, I think we were all rational. I don't think that we got emotional when things went against us, and of course Warren is the extreme example of that.

I think we were all nice guys, and I think we were honest. I don't think we had—you know, there are people who've made a lot of money who I wouldn't want to invest with because they just aren't trustworthy, and you probably know who they are. And some of those stocks sell at low prices because other people feel the same way. And I would say that this was a good group of people, and Warren was very nice about inviting us [to a reunion] every two years, we'd have a meeting somewhere. . . .

Q. Japan today has a lot of cheap stocks, but there seems to be little corporate governance. Would you bother?

W.S. My problem with foreign companies is that I do not trust the politics. I don't know enough about the background of the companies. I must tell you, I think the SEC does a very good job, and I feel more comfortable holding an American company. . . .

Q. People like to try to find comparisons between today's market and markets in the past. Do you see any repetition in history, any year that this year's evaluations remind you of?

W.S. Well, I'll tell you, at the end of last year I refused to accept money for our partnership because I felt I had no idea what the market was going to do. I couldn't find anything to buy. My son couldn't find anything to buy. So he said, "If we can't find anything to buy, why should we take our clients' money?" So we didn't. And to that extent, I thought last year the market was overvalued. . . .

Each market is different, you know? The first stock I bought back in 1955 when we started the partnership [was Fownes Brothers Gloves] at $2\frac{1}{2}$. Tweedy, Browne bought it for me, and it went up to $23 and I sold it. I had a lot of it and we sold it. And then I couldn't buy it back. It didn't go down as far and it dried up. So it finally did sell out around $32 a number of years later. Sometimes you have to take advantage of the opportunity to sell and then say, OK, it'll go higher. Since we sell on a scale, most of the stocks we sell go up above what we sold them at. You know, you never get the high and you never get the low.

Q. What is your sell discipline, and how has it changed?

W.S. Selling is tough. It's the worst, the most difficult thing of all. . . . We owned Southdown. It's a cement company. We bought a lot of it at 2½. Oh, this was great. And we doubled our money, and we sold it at something like $28 or $30 a share, and that was pretty good in two years. When next I looked, it was $70 a share. So you get very humbled by some of your mistakes. But we just felt that at that level it was not cheap.

Q. Has your approach changed significantly?

W.S. Yes, it's changed because the market's changed. I can't buy any working capital stocks anymore so instead of saying, Well, I can't buy 'em, I'm not going to play the game, you have to decide what you want to do. And so we've decided that we want to buy stocks if we can that are depressed and have some book value and are selling near to their lows instead of their highs and nobody likes them. Well, why don't they like them? And then you might say there may be reasons why. It may simply be they don't have any earnings and people love earnings. I mean that's, you know, the next quarter that's the big thing and, of course, we don't think the next quarter is so important.

Q. Tweedy, Browne is very quantitative, and Buffett's more qualitative. Where are you in that spectrum?

W.S. I'm more in the Tweedy, Browne side. Warren is brilliant, there's nobody ever been like him, and there never will be anybody like him. But we cannot be like him. You've got to satisfy yourself on what you want to do. Now, there are people that are clones of Warren Buffett. They'll buy whatever Warren Buffett has. Fine. I don't know, I don't feel comfortable doing that and the other thing is this. We happen to run a partnership and each year we buy stocks and they go up, we sell them, and then we try to buy something cheaper.

Now, if we buy a stock, I mean had only Warren Buffett stocks, and the stock was Freddie Mac and it goes from $10 to $50. Boy, that's a great deal. We sell it. But if you don't sell it and then the market changes and Freddie Mac goes down from $50 to $25, my partners they lost 50 percent—that year we lost 30 percent of our money on our securities. They'd all pull out because you can't lose 30 percent. And Charlie Munger actually lost 30 percent of his money two years in a row when he was managing his own money.

So that you have to be a little aware of the emotions of the people who have invested with you. And they trust you, but they don't like to lose 30 percent of their money. And we won't lose 30 percent of our money. And if you buy these high-grade companies which have a growth factor, they can take a beating and our investors are not sophisticated and therefore we try to protect them because we get a percentage of the profits, but we take a percentage of the losses. But they don't really, they aren't really happy if they lose that kind of money. So I don't feel comfortable with them.

But there are people that have made a great deal of money with them. So, again, you have to invest the way that's comfortable for you. And the way that's comfortable for us is to buy stocks where we have a limited risk and we buy a lot of stocks. Well, Warren, or somebody, said, Owning a group of stocks is a defense against ignorance, which I actually think that's to some extent true because we don't go around visiting companies all over the country and Peter Lynch did. He was killing himself. He was seeing 300 companies a year and he was running from one company to another and what's that going to do?

We're not set up that way. And Graham wasn't. And Graham's argument was that the directors of these companies are responsible for their success. If the company isn't doing well, change the management, do things that make the company do a better job. And it takes longer that way. No company wants to lose money continually. They're going to do something, but you do get changes in the way companies are operated. . . . They'll either merge or they'll change the management. So we do not spend a great deal of time talking to management or talking to our partners—we don't want to talk to our partners at all.

Emotionally, I find the stock market can be very unpleasant and I don't want to listen to people's cries. If they're unhappy—you may not be in that position to do that, but we are and I just don't want to listen to them. If they don't want it, out. But we do the best we can for what we are doing, and I feel that you have to understand where we're coming from and basically trust us because we've been doing this now for 40, about 43 years. So they just have to stay with us, hopefully.

Q. How much turnover have you had?

W.S. I guess 20 percent or 25 percent a year. About every four years we turn over. We want to get long-term capital gains, and when you buy a depressed company, it's not going to go up right after you buy it, believe me. It'll go down. And therefore you have to wait a while for that thing to go around, and it seems about, four years seems to be about the amount of time it takes. Some take longer. We have one stock, peculiarly enough, I bought from Warren Buffett. He owed me a favor and he had a group of stocks—very small amounts of each one—and he came to me back in 1963 and he said, "Walter, would you like to buy these companies?" I forget their names. Genesee & Wyoming Railroad I remember was one of them.

And I said, "Well, Warren, what price are you carrying them for?" And he told me. He said "I'll sell 'em to you at the price I'm carrying them for." I said, "Okay, Warren, I'll buy it." That doesn't sound like a lot, but in those days it was, you know, $65,000. It wasn't a lot of money for those five companies, and we sold everything over the years. They all worked out beautifully, and we have one left and it's called Merchants National Properties and they just had a tender offer. I paid $14 for the stock. They want to buy this at $553 a share. So you can see in these little companies there was a great chance to make money. But that's almost 35 years ago.

Q. Buffett keeps talking about a handful of thick bets. It sounds like you don't do that.

W.S. Oh, no, we can't. Psychologically I can't, and Warren, as I say, is a brilliant, he's not only a good analyst, but he's a very good judge of businesses and he knows. I mean, my gosh, he buys a company and the guy's killing himself working for Warren. I would have thought he'd retire. But Warren is a very good judge of people and he's a very good judge of businesses. And what Warren does is fine. It's just that we just really can't do it that way. [He finds] five businesses that he understands, and most of them are financial businesses, and he's very good at it. But you've got to know your limitations.

Q. Are you involved with commodities at all and if so—do you see silver as undervalued?

W.S. You know, I have no opinion about any commodity or where it's going to go, and Asarco is a commodity company in copper. I have no idea if copper can keep going lower. But I just think that the stock is cheap based upon its price, not necessarily because I know what's going to happen to the price of copper any more than silver. I have no opinion on any of those things. It saves me a lot of time.

Q. Do you sell short?

W.S. We did it a couple of times and we're always very upset after we do it. So I'd say not anymore.

APPENDIX 5

Martin Whitman on Value Versus Growth*

There is no dichotomy between value and growth. Indeed, most of the common stocks in which Third Avenue Value Fund invests are growth stocks.

There is a huge dichotomy, however, between value and *generally recognized growth.* When people speak of growth, they really mean *generally recognized growth.* That means buying what is popular when it is most popular.

I've been asked frequently, Has value come back? That is the wrong question. Rather the question should be, Have the gross speculative excesses that characterized the period from 1995 through the first quarter of 2000 gone away?

Let's look at how the garden variety of growth stock analysts analyze, and contrast that with what value analysts do.

Basically, growth stock analysts are outlook conscious and price unconscious. Or, in any event, they assign more weight to forecasts than they do to current prices.

*From a talk in January 2001 before the American Association of Individual Investors, Northern New Jersey Chapter.

Their outlook focuses on forecasting only future flows, whether revenues, cash, or earnings. The balance sheet is ignored as "what is."

They make bets on market forecasts—basically, top down. They try to buy at bottoms and sell at tops.

They make market judgments rather than investment judgments. They try to predict future prices.

Many are strictly market players. They try to predict the near-term market, with a lot of focus on actual earnings versus consensus forecasts.

This leads up to the growth stock trap. If you are wrong in any of your forecasts—the economy, market, industry, company earnings—market losses are huge and swift.

Indeed, very few growth stock analysts are really long-term conscious. They are interested only in short-term market movements. The long-term outlook changes every day as the price of the Nasdaq Composite changes.

If you want to be a growth stock investor to take advantage of the public's interest in grossly overpaying for mostly garbage, the way to do it is to be a promoter—a first-stage venture capitalist. Seed private companies with capital, with intent to take them public via IPOs.

What is right about growth-stock investing?

- It's the only way to get near-term stock performance. Buy what is popular when it is most popular.
- There is tremendous institutional pressure to keep the growth market buoyant.
- They create corporate value by cheap access to the capital markets.

Value analysts are price conscious. They take a balanced approach. To them, price is at least as important as what is forecast. They analyze businesses the way private businesses do, the way takeover people do. The goal is to create corporate wealth over time. There are many ways to create wealth: unrealized appreciation, asset redeployment, refinancings, having operating earnings. (Though operating earnings is the least desirable way of creating wealth because it is tax disadvantaged.)

There are four elements of how Third Avenue Value invests in stocks—cheaply and safely.

1. The companies have overwhelming financial strength as measured, first, by an absence of debt (whether on the balance sheet, in financial-statement footnotes, or elsewhere); and

second, by the existence of attractive assets, such as surplus cash.

2. The companies are reasonably well managed. This is usually the most difficult element for us to analyze. We conduct our evaluation of a company from the point of view of passive, outside minority investors—investors with little or no hope of having any influence over the way the company is run.
3. The company must have an understandable business. For us, this means, at a minimum, that the company meets all SEC disclosure requirements and has issued audited financial statements. We think that these documents constitute not necessarily the truth, but rather reliable and objective benchmarks.
4. The company's common stock must be selling at a price no greater than 50 percent of what we think it would be worth if the business were a private company or a takeover candidate.

APPENDIX 6

A Weekend with the Wizard of Omaha: April 2001

A man from Oklahoma asked: "What's going to happen when newspapers run the headline 'Buffett Kicks Bucket'?"

The question elicited gasps from the audience, but Warren E. Buffett himself, age 70, chairman of Berkshire Hathaway and by common consent the world's greatest investor, wasn't fazed. "I think it will be worded a little more elegantly," he said dryly, but he thought the question was legitimate.

He himself regularly asks the people who run the companies owned by Berkshire Hathaway (like Benjamin Moore paint): If you died today, what letter do you wish you had written for me to receive tomorrow?

His answer to the question about his own demise: The company ran nicely without him for a while when he left to become temporary chairman of Salomon Brothers in the early 1990s, and he's provided for succession via both an investment manager and an administrator.

It was the annual meeting of Berkshire Hathaway in Omaha on Saturday, by far the best-attended (12,000 shareholders) and longest-running annual meeting (six hours) in the history of civilization, and it was pure pleasure. Morning and afternoon you could listen to two super-smart guys (Charlie Munger, 77, is vice chairman) talk about almost everything under the sun, talk enlivened by their quick and perfectly delicious senses of humor.

An 11-year-old girl, a shareholder: "My father wants to know: Do you have a grandson near my age?" (Laughter.)

Buffett: "How many shares do you own?"

A young man, a shareholder, stood up and said: "Last year, Mr. Buffett, someone asked you to 'juice up' Berkshire Hathaway's returns by buying technology stocks." (Pause.)

"Well, I'd like to thank you for paying no attention to him." (General applause.)

Buffett, as is his habit, turned out to be right: Technology stocks weren't exactly a good buy in the year 2000. Munger, like Buffett, has a keen, no-nonsense mind and a dry, sly sense of humor. He tossed off at least one memorable line: "If you become rich quickly while you're young, thanks to passively investing in paper documents, and that's all you accomplish in life, you're a failure."

The two men have a high regard for each other, even though Buffett kids Munger a lot. (At one point, Buffett said that Munger would have a few words from Benjamin Franklin to quote, and Munger seemed ticked off. Buffett sensed that, and said something apologetic.)

Munger is laconic and sparing with compliments, but at one point he said that Berkshire had benefited from Warren's uncanny ability to invest money shrewdly—and Buffett looked as pleased as a child receiving a pat on the head from his teacher.

Some scenes from that weekend:

- Omaha isn't bad at all. Wide streets, plenty of parking lots, only rare traffic jams. All-day parking at the nearby airport costs $4. A lovely artificial stream is smack in the center of the city. A lot of new construction, but also a lot of old dark-brick buildings, some with quaint, early-twentieth-century ads printed on them. Example: A particular medication will clean out "your liver, kidneys and bowels."
- Buffett lives in a big, impressive house, but no better than other houses in the area. A young blond security guard peers at me as a cab drops me off. "Can I take pictures?" "From the sidewalk." The cab driver assures me that only during the annual meeting is there a security guard at Buffett's house. The offices of Berkshire Hathaway are in a modern office building a few minutes' drive away, and there's no sign outside that says Berkshire Hathaway.
- Big disappointment. I wanted someone to take a photo of me

standing next to Buffett. Then the newspaper I work for would run the photo with this caption: "Celebrated financial writer Warren Boroson with unidentified Berkshire Hathaway shareholder." No luck.

• The Yellow BRK'ers are the leading Berkshire Hathaway fan club; members have a message center on America Online. One of the founders is a New Jersey fellow: John Gartmann, 67, of Delran in Burlington County. The color yellow in their logos, he told me, is for the Yellow Brick Road, which you must take to visit the Wizard of Oz. (The stock symbol is BRK.)

Why did he invest in Berkshire? "I'm not the sharpest tool in the shed, and when I see someone brilliant, like Buffett, I hang on to him. He's the master. He can do no wrong."

Sherrie Gregory, who's from Nebraska: "We love his philosophy and his morals—his honesty, his fairness. We're an old-fashioned group."

I asked Mohnish Pabrai, a money manager from Long Grove, Illinois, whether owners of the expensive A shares are higher in the pecking order than people like me, who own the cheaper B shares. "The A share owners probably think they are," he answered dryly. Why was he wearing an especially gigantic yellow hat that said "Yellow BRK'ers"? Buffett gives you that hat, he answered, if you amass 100 A shares (worth $7,000,000). For a second I believed him.

The doors in the huge civic auditorium opened at 7 A.M. When I arrived at 7:20, I got a seat maybe 75 yards away from the stage—like the uppermost seats, the family circle, at the Metropolitan Opera. A woman sitting next to me was delighted at how "close" her seat was. I stared at her. Shareholders came from all over the country and even outside the United States. Some were New Yorker types, elegant and spiffy; others were just ordinary folks. Entire families were there—sisters, cousins, aunts. Almost everyone was friendly and willing to chat. A slim, elegant blonde, an older woman, inquired of a gentleman sitting near me whether an unoccupied seat was taken. Yes, it was, she was told. She swore. I giggled.

Someone walked around dressed as a brick (Berkshire owns a brick company, Acme); someone else walked around as a Dairy Queen cone. (Berkshire owns that, too.)

Buffett's health is a big concern among shareholders. When Buffett mentioned that he visited his physician once every five years, an elderly but remarkably well-preserved woman behind me, lunching on healthy fruits and vegetables, said that that was "indefensible."

Still, Buffett added that he was under no stress, and "I don't smoke or drink. And I'll end it right there."

A few young people asked for advice on investing, and at one point Buffett said, "Stay away from credit cards. Read financial publications. And save a few dollars."

Which are the best business schools? Columbia, which has a course on valuing securities, was mentioned, along with the University of Florida and Stanford. (Buffett and Munger are disdainful of business schools that play up the Efficient Market Hypothesis, the absurd notion that stocks are always reasonably priced.) "Financial teaching, in general," said Buffett, "is pathetic." And later, "If anyone ever starts talking to you about 'beta,' zip up your pocketbook." ("Beta" is a measure of risk used by the Efficient Market people.)

Why does Buffett drive such an old car? His has two air bags, he answered, and if there were a safer car, he would drive it. But there isn't, he insisted, and he doesn't want to spend time searching for a new car and becoming familiar with it. Why did Berkshire drop Fannie Mae and Freddie Mac? Because, the two men answered, the companies are taking on extra risk. How often do they get great ideas? Once every two years. "And," said Buffett, "there should be a few more before we're done." On companies that lose their edge: Kellogg's raised its prices too high; Campbell soup suffered because people's tastes changed. On selling short (betting on stocks going down): "It's ruined a lot of people," Buffett said. "Losses can be unlimited. But we see many more overvalued stocks than undervalued stocks."

Shareholders had a weekend of activities laid out for them, including watching Warren himself throw out the first pitch at a minor league baseball game, then bat against former big league pitcher Bob Gibson. Buffett hit a miserable, pitiful, feeble little roller to the mound. His charming secretary, Debbie Bosanek, later said she was amazed that he accomplished that much. (And still later, she rebuked me for having written what I did because, she explained, it lowered the chances that *Sports Illustrated* would cover next year's baseball game.)

Shareholders idolize Warren and Charlie, not just because Berkshire Hathaway boasts such a splendid record, but because they're obviously such wise and honorable gentlemen.

At a press conference on Sunday, guess who got to ask the first question? "Three well-known mutual funds," I said, "invest similarly to Berkshire: Sequoia, Clipper, and Tweedy, Browne. Which seems to adhere the most closely to your strategy?"

All are similar, Buffett replied, but all have certain differences, too. And the late Phil Carret, who ran the Pioneer Fund, Buffett continued, also invested in stocks the way Buffett has learned to. (See Appendix 7.)

An amusing film preceded the shareholders' meeting. Buffett gave a golf lesson to Tiger Woods, telling him that his right arm was too much in play. Woods apparently heeded his advice and hit a wicked shot; said Buffett, impressed by Woods' stroke, "You learn fast."

Woods did some juggling tricks with his golf club and golf balls; throughout the remainder of the film, Buffett tried to do the same—eventually succeeding, thanks in no small part to trick photography.

Judge Judy adjudicated a dispute between Buffett and Bill Gates over who had won a bridge game and who owed whom money. She mispronounced Buffett's name, but decided that he had won and Gates had lost. "Pay him the two dollars and make something of yourself," she told Gates severely.

Ben Graham Productions presented a short film on "Citizen Buffett," reviewing his life.

Buffett and some very rich Omaha friends appeared on "Who Wants to Be a Millionaire?" with Regis Philbin. When Philbin asked, "Who wants to be a millionaire?" the three multimillionaires walked off in disgust.

After returning, Buffett won a lot of money and announced that he would give each of his kids $300 (he's notoriously cheap), and buy a second suit and a comb.

Back to the meeting: Why had Buffett regretted not buying pharmaceuticals years ago, but still avoided technology? Munger's answer: It was much more obvious that pharmaceuticals in general would do well.

What mistakes had they made? Mainly errors of omission—not buying good stocks. "We've blown billions and billions of dollars," said Buffett. "And we're getting better at it."

Might some of Berkshire's holdings, like Dairy Queen and Coca-Cola, get into trouble for not being thought healthy? Buffett was reassuring: He has been living on such foods for 70 years.

David Winters of Mountain Lakes, New Jersey, inquired about Berkshire's advantages, and Buffett talked about the company's not being under any pressure to do anything. On the other hand, he added, the company's huge size was a handicap: Berkshire, with all its cash, must take huge positions. Winters, it turned out, is chief investment officer for the Mutual Series Fund in Short Hills, New Jersey.

In an elevator later on, I heard a young woman say to her husband, "The two of them are so cute!"

APPENDIX 7

"If You Own a Good Stock, Sit on It" —Phil Carret

When I asked Warren Buffett (at a recent press conference in Omaha) which mutual funds employed investment styles similar to his, he replied that the three funds that I myself had named—Sequoia, Clipper, and Tweedy, Browne—were similar . . . and dissimilar.

He then mentioned that when he was in his 20s he had been impressed by Phil Carret, who had started the Pioneer Fund in 1928, and had met him and learned a good deal from him. By coincidence, I interviewed Carret a few years before he died, in 1998, at age 101. He was an easygoing, unpretentious gentleman with a logical, nononsense mind.

I had first run into him around 1990, when he and two other giants of the investment world, Max Heine of the Mutual Series Fund and Julian Lerner of the AIM funds, took part in a memorable discussion. The panel had been set up by Bill Lippmann, who now runs a few Franklin funds. What impressed everyone about that discussion was how much all three money managers loved investing—Carret in particular. And how differently the three men invested—yet with similar, most excellent results. As Max Heine, an urbane, witty gentleman, said at the conference's conclusion, "All roads lead to Jerusalem."

Carret had an unusual hobby: viewing eclipses from around the world. As I recall, he had seen around 50. He was also one of the few investors who had lost money in both 1929 and 1987.

Here are excerpts from my 1994 interview with Carret at his office in New York City:

Questions and Answers

Q. Is it true that you influenced Warren Buffett?

P.C. I don't influence Warren. He influences me. I sent him a telegram the other day when his stock hit $20,000. I wrote: $20,000 WOW CONGRATULATIONS. [The stock is now around $70,000 a share.]

Q. Are you worried about how popular mutual funds have become?

P.C. No, I think mutual funds are ideal for the average citizen who doesn't want to bother to or doesn't have the necessary equipment to make judgments on his own. But they should understand that they will not make a lot of money out of it. Ten dollars will grow to $12 or $15, not to $150.

Q. Did you foresee the amazing popularity of mutual funds?

P.C. (laughs) No. I can remember thinking that if the Pioneer Fund ever got to $25 million I really would have arrived. Now, with $25 million you couldn't possibly cover even the overhead.

Q. How do you feel about investing abroad?

P.C. There are great companies abroad, but they keep books differently—or they used to. I had a good friend, and I told him I didn't understand foreign bookkeeping. Why do they keep three sets of books? He said that one was for the stockbrokers, one for management, and one for the real insiders. But I think things have changed, and now they keep the books in an up-to-date fashion. We get questions all the time, why not 5 percent abroad? But if we buy Coca-Cola, at least 60 percent of its revenue comes from abroad. We don't buy it. I don't like the drink.

Q. Don't let Warren hear you say that.

P.C. But I own some Berkshire Hathaway, so indirectly I own some Coca-Cola. For the small investor, I might recommend maybe 10 percent in foreign stocks. But if one is an American, brought up here, you understand the way things are done—it's much simpler to invest here instead of trying to figure out the mental processes of Amsterdam or Zurich. Our clients feel more comfortable with American companies rather than if you go fishing around the world.

Q. Like Buffett, you buy and hold, don't you? Your strategy is similar to Buffett's?

Pioneer Executive: Maybe Buffett's strategy is similar to Phil's.

P.C. Warren is obviously much smarter than I am. I've known Warren for probably 40 years, and if I phoned, he would take the call. But I don't bother him.

Q. How often are you right about the direction of the stock market?

P.C. Ten percent. Unfortunately, the contrary opinion school has a great deal of validity. When everyone is bullish, why, you should be very concerned. I was in Rome in 1987 when the market fell out of bed and lost 500 points in one day, and I still don't know why it happened. I hadn't foreseen anything. But I didn't owe anyone any money—I never do.

Q. Buffett has commented that you went through both the crash of 1929 and the crash of 1987. Were they similar?

P.C. [The crash of] 1929 was much worse. If it had stopped by January 1930, it would not have been so bad. But it was kind of exciting, you know. Those on margin in a big way were of course devastated.

Q. Do you market-time at all?

P.C. No. If you're doing the right things, a bear market is not going to kill you. And you should be philosophical. If the market is down 50 percent and your account goes down only 40 percent, why, that's a great triumph.

Q. Do you favor investing gradually in a stock—dollar-cost averaging?

P.C. If you find something attractive, buy it.

Q. In evaluating a company, how important is management?

P.C. Management is the important factor in a company. Anyone who gets to be chairman or president of a company is a fairly smooth operator, and talks a good fight, you know. You have to look at his record—how much of his own money is in the stock (my yardstick is a year's salary)—and is he wildly optimistic or cautious? If he says things are pretty good and the results were very good, that's great. If he says things are fine and there's a lousy quarter, I don't want his stock.

Q. When do you sell?

P.C. I never sell anything, by and large, unless somebody takes it away from me. If you have a good stock, sit on it. Unless you find something that's obviously much better, cheaper.

Q. I understand that you believe that doctors are terrible investors, and you have turned down doctors as clients.

P.C. If a doctor doesn't believe his diagnosis and his prescription, he shouldn't be in the profession. He has to believe that he's almost God. And many of them carry this over and tell you how to invest.

Q. Have you heard the worrisome talk that Social Security may run out of money soon? It might have to be eliminated, or a means test set up.

P.C. I'll be gone. I'll let you worry about it.

Q. You knew Dean Witter? You knew Clarence Barron, who owned the *Wall Street Journal*?

P.C. Dean Witter was very sharp. Barron weighed 300 pounds, and was handsome from here up, with his white beard. They said that he hadn't seen his feet for 40 years.

Q. How many stocks do you need, as a minimum, to be diversified?

P.C. For an individual, 25, I think.

Q. How many securities can one person follow?

P.C. I knew a brilliant man named Fred, and he was asked whether his fund should really own hundreds of different securities. "I own 400 or 500," Fred said, "and I can't watch them all. But if you buy them cheap enough, they watch themselves."

Q. Who is that on your coffee cup?

P.C. Ludwig van Mises, the greatest economist of the twentieth century, in my judgment. He was a founder of the Austrian economics movement, which has never taken off—compared with Lord Keynes, and I regard Keynes as disastrous for all concerned. Van Mises was in favor of free enterprise—and so am I. There's nothing like competition.

Q. Have you ever read Peter Lynch's books?

P.C. I've glanced through them.

Q. Lynch visited Buffett once, and Buffett said of him, "A very clever young man." I figured that what that meant was "I could have him for breakfast." (general laughter)

Q. What are the worst mistakes investors make?

P.C. The stupid thing we all do is to get more and more bullish as the market goes up—and be frightened out of our wits when it goes down.

Q. How do you stay in such great health?

P.C. I carefully avoid exercise. I eat what I like. And I enjoy my work. But the greatest success of my life was my wife. I enjoyed 63 years of perfection. I used to tell her that she was 99.99 percent perfect. But I really thought she was 100 percent.

Glossary

Actively managed mutual fund A mutual fund whose managers buy securities intending to do better than the average, represented by an index of that market. Opposite of a passively managed index fund.

Annuity A tax-deferred investment offered by an insurance company. When you receive an annuity, you receive payments in equal installments for a specified period of time.

Arbitrage Selling one security in one market and buying it in another market, or vice versa, to take advantage of price disparity.

Asset allocation How your money is spread across different types of investments, like stocks, bonds, and cash equivalents.

Balance sheet A statement of a company's assets and liabilities at a certain time.

Bear market A period when securities have become relatively low-priced. With stocks, a decline of 20% or more is considered a bear market. A decline of 10% to 20%, a correction.

Beta A measure of volatility that compares a security's volatility with the volatility of an index of the same securities. The market, or an index of the market, is assigned a beta of 1.00; a stock or a fund with a beta of 1.25 might be 25% more volatile.

Bond A fixed-income investment that typically pays the lender regular interest, and promises to repay the lender the principal after a specified period of time ("maturity").

Book value A company's total assets minus liabilities minus stock issues that are ahead of common stock (like preferred stock) in case the company is liquidated and shareholders are compensated. Book value can be more, or less, than market value—the price of the stock times the number of shares outstanding.

Bull market A period when security prices have soared.

Capital gains (losses) Profits or losses on an investment.

Capitalization The total value of all the securities—stocks, bonds—issued by a corporation.

Capitalization weighted Said of an index like the Standard & Poor's Index, where the power given to individual stocks depends on their capitalization.

Cash flow A company's income, after taxes, plus expenses that have to be paid—depreciation expenses, amortization expenses, and so forth.

Closed-end investment company A mutual fund whose shares are bought and sold on an exchange or over-the-counter by investors trading among themselves. Only a limited number of shares are issued. Managers of closed-end funds need not sell; shareholders buy and sell among themselves.

Common stock A unit of ownership of a company. Owners of preferred stock have first dibs in getting their money back in case of bankruptcy.

Contrarian An investor who bucks the majority opinion, perhaps buying stocks or a stock when most people are selling, for example, or selling when most people are buying. Contrarians are a species of value investor.

Current asset Cash, or whatever can be converted into cash, within one year.

Current ratio A company's assets divided by its liabilities. A measure of how readily a corporation can pay its debts from its assets.

Data mining Checking information to find patterns.

Discount When a security sells for less than its face value.

Diversification Investing in a variety of different securities and assets, to guard against one's entire portfolio bottoming at one time.

Dividend A distribution of earnings to shareholders.

Dollar cost averaging Investing a set amount into securities at a set period of time, not all at once. Purpose: to buy more shares when prices are low, fewer when prices are high.

Dow Jones Industrial Average A popular measure of stock market performance.

Efficient Market Theory The notion that market prices reflect the full knowledge and expectations of all investors, so that it is impossible for investors to outperform the market unless they take more risk. (See Nutty Investment Theory.)

Float Someone's ability to use money for a time before having to give it to someone else.

GARP Growth at a reasonable price. A strategy of growth investors, attempting to buy growing companies but not overpaying.

Goodwill Valuable and important attributes of a company, but hard to measure, such as its brand-name recognition, its reputation for integrity, the excellence of its personnel, its penetration of its markets. It's the difference between the value of the assets a company owns (buildings) and what a reasonable buyer might pay for the entire company. Also called "intangibles."

Growth strategy Investing in healthy companies, with relatively high price-earnings ratios and high price-book ratios. Growth stocks tend to do well at different periods of times from value stocks. Certain industries, like health care and technology, tend to be composed of growth stocks. Growth portfolios tend to have higher turnovers than value portfolios. Growth stocks are sometimes called "glamour stocks." A growth strategy may be "momentum" or "GARP."

Holding company A corporation that owns stock and manages other corporations.

Index Selected stocks or bonds that are meant to mirror an entire investment market.

Index fund A fund whose performance is tied to a specific market index, such as the Standard & Poor's 500 Stock Index.

Initial public offering (IPO) The first sale of a new stock or bond.

Intrinsic value The essential value of a stock. If you package 10 stocks together in one unit, like a closed-end fund, and sell that unit, and someone buys it for less than the individual stocks are worth, the unit is selling at a discount to its intrinsic value. The intrinsic value of a stock is difficult to measure, but clues are its potential to continue to produce profits and what reasonable buyers have paid for similar companies.

Leverage Buying stocks or other securities by borrowing money.

Liquidity The ease with which an asset can be turned into cash without loss.

Margin of safety In security analysis, buying a security for significantly less than its intrinsic value, just to protect the buyer in case of unexpected problems.

Market value The price that an investment instrument can fetch on the open financial markets.

Momentum investing Buying stocks whose prices have recently been climbing.

Multiple Price-earnings ratio.

Nifty Fifty Fifty or so stocks that during the early 1970s were considered sure winners; "one-decision" stocks. They crashed in 1973–1974.

Nutty Investor Theory The notion that market prices reflect neurotic human emotions, particularly the tendency to overvalue stocks when their prices have climbed and to undervalue stocks when their prices have declined.

Operating earnings The difference between a corporation's revenues, and its expenses.

Passively managed mutual fund A mutual fund that mirrors an index.

Preferred stock A class of stock that gives the owner a higher claim to dividends and to assets in the event of the company's liquidation.

Present value The value today of a future dollar amount after it has been discounted for interest that you did not receive.

Price to book ratio The share price of a stock divided by its net worth (book value) per share. An indicator of whether a stock is expensive or not.

Price to earnings ratio The amount that investors are willing to pay for $1 of earnings per share. Commonly, the earnings are for the past year. The higher the p-e ratio, by and large, the more optimistic investors are about a stock's growth—except that the p-e ratios of stocks whose earnings have fallen recently may remain high.

Qualitative analysis Assessing a stock by focusing on nonmeasurable factors, such as the quality of management, excellence of the product or service, resistance to competition, brand-name recognition.

Quantitative analysis A way to evaluate a company's stock using numbers; contrasted with qualitative analysis.

Quick ratio Cash, receivables, and marketable securities divided by liabilities; a measure of liquidity.

R-squared How much the changes in one factor (variable) are explained by the changes in another factor. Called coefficient of determination. It ranges from 1 (percent congruence) to 0 (no connection).

Return on equity Amount earned on a corporation's common stock investments over a certain time period. The percentage indicates how well shareholders' money is being used.

Risk The chances of losing value, or not gaining value. Different kinds of risks include market risk, economic risk, and inflation risk.

Security A stock, bond, or other investment instrument.

Security and Exchange Commission The federal agency that administers the laws regulating the securities industry.

Selling short Selling securities that you may have borrowed, intending to pay for them when (you hope) their prices have gone down. A way to make money on securities whose prices seem poised to decline.

Standard & Poor's 500 Stock Price Index An index of 500 stocks, mostly large-company stocks traded on the New York Stock Exchange.

Standard deviation The volatility of an investment, measured by comparing its average price with the degree of its ups and downs over three years.

Tangible book value Book value that does not consider good will, which is difficult to evaluate.

10K A report that the Securities and Exchange Commission requires of most companies. It is more detailed than the annual report.

Total return The interest from bonds, dividends from stocks, and capital gains and losses that a security receives in a specific period of time.

Turnover Trading activity—the frequency with which new securities are bought and old ones sold.

Value strategy Buying stocks that seem to be cheap, based on their price-earnings ratios and price-book ratios. Value stocks may be those of companies in trouble, or companies that don't promise to growth rapidly, such as utilities. Value stocks tend to excel or decline at different periods from growth stocks. Value stocks tend to have higher dividends than growth stocks, and value stock portfolios tend to have lower turnovers.

Volatility The degree to which a security's price bobs up and down.

Working capital The amount that current assets exceed current liabilities.

Yield The income that a security pays out in a year, as a percentage of the security's price.

Index